Draw Swords! In The Horse Artillery

by

George Manville Fenn

Draw Swords! In The Horse Artillery
by George Manville Fenn

ISBN: 978-93-68095-07-1

Published by

DOUBLE 9 BOOKS

2/13-B, Ansari Road
Daryaganj, New Delhi – 110002
info@double9books.com
www.double9books.com
Tel. 011-40042856

ABOUT THE AUTHOR

George Manville Fenn was a very productive author of novels, a writer, an editor, and an educator from England. He was born on January 3, 1831, in Pimlico, London. He mostly learned on his own; he taught himself Italian, French, and German. During the years 1851–1854, he went to Battersea Training College for Teachers and then became the head of a state school in Alford, Lincolnshire. In the early 1850s, Fenn started to write short stories and pieces for newspapers and magazines. The Old Forest Ranger, his first book, came out in 1856. Afterward, he wrote more than 100 books, many of them for teenagers and young adults. He was one of the most famous writers of his time, and his books were well-liked and read by many people. He also worked as a reporter and writer for Fenn. Among the newspapers and magazines, he worked for was The Boy's Own Paper, which he ran from 1866 to 1874. He worked hard to make children's books better and was a strong supporter of education and reading. The Englishman Fenn passed away on August 26, 1909, in Isleworth

CONTENTS

Chapter I
A Feather in his Cap

"Oh, I say, what a jolly shame!"

"Get out; it's all gammon. Likely."

"I believe it's true. Dick Darrell's a regular pet of Sir George Hemsworth."

"Yes; the old story—kissing goes by favour."

"I shall cut the service. It's rank favouritism."

"I shall write home and tell my father to get the thing shown up in the House of Commons."

"Why, he's only been out here a year."

Richard Darrell, a well-grown boy of seventeen, pretty well tanned by the sun of India, stood flashed with annoyance, looking sharply from one speaker to another as he stood in the broad veranda of the officers' quarters in the Roumwallah Cantonments in the northern portion of the Bengal Presidency, the headquarters of the artillery belonging to the Honourable the East India Company, commonly personified as "John Company of Leadenhall Street." It was over sixty years ago, in the days when, after a careful training at the Company's college near Croydon, young men, or, to be more correct, boys who had made their marks, received their commission, and were sent out to join the batteries of artillery, by whose means more than anything else the Company had by slow degrees conquered and held the greater part of the vast country now fully added to the empire and ruled over by the Queen.

It was a common affair then for a lad who had been a schoolboy of sixteen, going on with his studies one day, to find himself the next, as it were, a commissioned officer, ready to start for the East, to take his position in a regiment and lead stalwart men, either in the artillery or one of the native regiments; though, of course, a great deal of the college training had been of a military stamp.

This was Richard Darrell's position one fine autumn morning a year previous to the opening of this narrative. He had bidden farewell to father, mother, and Old England, promised to do his duty like a man, and sailed for Calcutta, joined his battery, served steadily in it for a year, and now stood in his quiet artillery undress uniform in that veranda, looking like a strange dog being bayed at by an angry pack.

The pack consisted of young officers of his own age and under. There was not a bit of whisker to be seen; and as to moustache, not a lad could show half as much as Dick, while his wouldn't have made a respectable eyebrow for a little girl of four.

Dick was flushed with pleasurable excitement, doubly flushed with anger; but he kept his temper down, and let his companions bully and hector and fume till they were tired.

Then he gave an important-looking blue letter he held a bit of a wave, and said, "It's no use to be jealous."

"Pooh! Who's jealous—and of you?" said the smallest boy present, one who had very high heels to his boots. "That's too good."

"For, as to being a favourite with the general, he has never taken the slightest notice of me since I joined."

"There, that'll do," said one of the party; "a man can't help feeling disappointment. Every one is sure to feel so except the one who gets the stroke of luck. I say, 'Hurrah for Dick Darrell!'"

The others joined in congratulations now.

"I say, old chap, though," said one, "what a swell you'll be!"

"Yes; won't he? We shall run against him capering about on his spirited Arab, while we poor fellows are trudging along in the hot sand behind the heavy guns."

"Don't cut us, Dick, old chap," said another.

"He won't; he's not that sort," cried yet another. "I say, we must give him a good send-off."

"When are you going?"

"The despatch says as soon as possible."

"But what troop are you to join?"

"The Sixth."

"The Sixth! I know; at Vallumbagh. Why, that's the crack battery, where the fellows polish the guns and never go any slower than a racing gallop. I say, you are in luck. Well, I am glad!"

The next minute every one present was ready to declare the same thing, and for the rest of that day the young officer to whom the good stroke of fortune had come hardly knew whether he stood upon his head or heels.

The next morning he was summoned to the general's quarters, the quiet, grave-looking officer telling him that, as an encouragement for his steady application to master his profession, he had been selected to fill a vacancy; that the general hoped his progress in the horse brigade would be as marked as it had been hitherto; and advising him to see at once about his fresh uniform and accoutrements, which could follow him afterwards, for he was to be prepared to accompany the general on his march to Vallumbagh, which would be commenced the very next day.

Dick was not profuse in thanks or promises, but listened quietly, and, when expected to speak, he merely said that he would do his best.

"That is all that is expected of you, Mr Darrell," said the general, giving him a friendly nod. "Then, as you have many preparations to make, and I have also, I will not detain you."

Dick saluted, and was leaving, when a sharp "Stop!" arrested him.

"You will want a horse. I have been thinking about it, and you had better wait till you get to Vallumbagh, where, no doubt, the officers of the troop will help you to make a choice. They will do this, for they have had plenty of experience, and are careful to keep up the prestige of the troop for perfection of drill and speed."

"No one would think he had been an old school-fellow of my father," said Dick to himself as he went out; "he takes no more notice of me than of any other fellow."

But the general was not a demonstrative man.

The preparations were soon made, the most important to Richard Darrell being his visit to the tailor who supplied most of the officers with their uniforms. The little amount of packing was soon done, and, after the farewell dinner had been given to those leaving the town, the time came when the young subaltern took his place in the general's train, to follow the detachment of foot artillery which had marched with their guns and baggage-train for Vallumbagh, where the general was taking charge, and preparations in the way of collecting troops were supposed to be going on.

Travelling was slow and deliberate in those days before railways, and the conveniences and comforts, such as they were, had to be carried by the travellers themselves; but in this case the young officer found his journey novel and pleasant. For it was the cool season; the dust was not quite so horrible as it might have been, and the tent arrangements were carried out so that a little camp was formed every evening; and this was made the more pleasant for the general's staff by the fact that there were plenty of native servants, and one of the most important of these was the general's cook.

But still the journey grew monotonous, over far-stretching plains, across sluggish rivers; and it was with a feeling of thankfulness, after many days' journey, always north and west, that Richard Darrell learned that they would reach their destination the next morning before the heat of the day set in.

That morning about ten o'clock they were met a few miles short of the town, which they could see through a haze of dust, with its temples and minarets, by a party of officers who had ridden out to welcome the general, and who announced that the detachment of artillery had marched in during the night with the heavy guns, elephants, and bullock-wagons. In the evening, after meeting the officers of his troop at the mess-table and not being very favourably impressed, Richard Darrell took possession of his quarters in the barracks overlooking the broad parade-ground, and, utterly tired out, lay down to sleep once more under a roof, feeling dreary, despondent, and utterly miserable.

"India's a wretched, desolate place," he thought as he lay listening to the hum of insects, and the night felt breathless and hot. He wished himself back among his old companions at Roumwallah, for everything now was depressing and strange.

A couple of hours later he was wishing himself back at the old military college in England, and when midnight arrived without a wink of sleep he began to think of his old country home, and how different a soldier's life was, with its dreary routine, to the brilliant pictures he had conjured up as a boy; for everything so far in his twelvemonth's career had been horribly uneventful and tame.

At last, when he had arrived at the most despondent state possible to a lad of his years—when his skin felt hot and feverish, and his pillow and the one sheet which covered him seemed to be composed of some irritating material which grew hotter and hotter—a pleasant moisture broke out all over him, bringing with it a sudden sense of confusion from which he slipped into nothingness and slept restfully till the morning bugle rang out, when he started from his bed wondering where he was.

Then it all came back, and he was bathing and dressing long before he needed to leave his couch, but the desire for sleep was gone. He had to nerve himself to master as manfully as he could the horribly depressing feeling of strangeness; for the officers he had for companions in the journey were with their own company, quite away from his quarters, and his new companions were men who would look down upon him for being such a boy; and at last he found himself wishing that he had been able to keep as he was, for the honour and glory of belonging to the dashing troop of horse artillery seemed to be nothing better than an empty dream.

The next three days were days of desolation to the lad, for he was left, as he expressed it, horribly alone. There was a good deal of business going on in the settling of the new-comers in the barracks, and his new brother-officers were away with the troop. He knew nobody; nobody seemed to know him, or to want to know him. There was the native town to see, but it did not attract him; and there were moments when he longed to go to the general, his father's friend, and beg that he might be sent back to his old company. But then there were moments when he came to his senses again and felt that this was folly; but he could not get rid of a strange longing to be back home once more.

Then he grew better all at once; the troop of horse artillery filed into the barrack-yard, and he hurried out to look at the men, horses, and guns, whose aspect chilled him, for they were in undress and covered with perspiration and dust. There was nothing attractive or glorious about them, and he went back to his quarters with his heart sinking once more.

Then it rose again with a jump, for his native servant met him at the door, showing his white teeth in a broad smile, to inform the sahib that the cases had come; and there they were, with each bearing his name branded thereon: "Lieutenant Richard Darrell, Bengal Horse Artillery."

"Hah!"

It was a loud expiration of the breath, and the lad felt better already. Those cases had come from the regimental tailor's, a long journey across the plains, and looked very ordinary, and cumbered the room; but then there were the contents—medicine to the disconsolate lad at a time like that—a tonic which completely carried the depression away.

Chapter II
Fine Feathers make Fine Birds

Richard Darrell was not a vain or conceited lad, but the time had arrived when he could not help feeling like a young peacock. He had gone on for a long time in his ordinary dowdy plumage, till one fine spring day the dull feathers began to drop out, and there was a flash here and a gleam there—a bit of blue, a bit of gold, a bit of purple and violet, and golden green and ruddy bronze—and he was strutting along in the sunshine in the full panoply of his gorgeous feathers, from the tuft on his head to the grand argus-eyed train which slants from the back, and is carried so gingerly that the tips may not be sullied by the dirt; all which makes him feel that he is a bird right glorious to behold.

And the day had come when, in the secrecy of his own room, Dick was about to moult from the simple uniform of the foot and preparatory days into the splendid full dress of the Bengal Horse Artillery, a commission in which was a distinction, a feather in any young soldier's cap.

Call it vanity what you will; but it was a glorious sensation, that which came over Dick, and he would have been a strangely unnatural lad if he had not felt excited.

No wonder that he shut himself up for the first full enjoyment of the sensation alone, though perhaps there was a feeling of dread that he might be laughed at by any one who saw him for the first time, since he was painfully conscious of being very young and slight and smooth-faced, although there was a suggestion of something coming up on the narrow space just beneath his nose.

Those things did not come from the military tailor's in common brown-paper parcels, but in special japanned tin cases, with his name in white letters and "R.H.A."

How everything smelt of newness! The boxes even had their odour. It was not a scent, nor was it unpleasant—it was, as the classic term goes, *sui generis*; and what a rustle there was in the silver tissue-paper which wrapped the garments!

But he did not turn to them first, for his natural instinct led him to open the long case containing his new sabre, which was taken out, glittering in its polish, and glorious with the golden knot so neatly arranged about the hilt.

It felt heavy—too heavy, for it was a full-grown sabre; and when he drew it glistening from its sheath, he felt that there was not muscle enough in his arm for its proper management.

"But that will come," he said to himself as he drew it slowly till the point was nearly bare, and then slowly thrust it back, when, pulling himself together, he flashed it out with a rasping sound, to hold it up to attention.

Yes, it was heavy and long, but not too long for a mounted man, and the hilt well balanced its length. Nothing could have been better, and, after restoring it to its scabbard, he attached it to the slings of the handsome belt and laid it aside upon the bed.

The cartouche-box and cross-belt followed, and were examined with the most intense interest. He had seen them before as worn by officers, but this one looked brighter, newer, and more beautiful, for it was his very own, and it went slowly and reluctantly to take its place beside the sword upon the bed. For there was the sabretache to examine and admire, with its ornate embossings and glittering embroidery.

"Pity it all costs so much," said Dick to himself as he thought of his father, the quiet doctor, at home; "but then one won't want anything of this kind new again for years to come, and aunt has paid for this."

But soon he forgot all about the cost; there was no room in his mind for such a thing, with all that military panoply before his eyes. He had to buckle on the belt, too, and walk to and fro with the sabretache flapping against his leg, while he felt strange and awkward; but that was of no consequence, for a side-peep in the looking-glass showed that it appeared magnificent.

He was about to unbuckle the belt and take it off, but hesitated, feeling that it would not be in his way. But the boy was strong-minded; he had made up his mind to try everything separately, and he determined to keep to his plan. So the belt was taken off, sabretache and all, and the case opened to draw out *that* jacket.

Yes, that jacket with its gorgeous cross-braiding of gold forming quite a cuirass over the padded breast, and running in cords and lines and scrolls over the seams at the back and about the collar and cuffs. It was heavy, and was certain to be very hot to wear, especially in the tremendous heat of India and the violent effort of riding at a furious gallop. But what of that? Who would mind heat in a uniform so brilliant?

The jacket was laid down with a sigh of satisfaction, and the breeches taken up.

There is not much to be admired in a pair of breeches, be they ever so well cut; but still they were satisfactory, for, in their perfect whiteness, they threw up the beauty of the jacket and made a most effective contrast with the high, black jack-boots—the uniform of the Bengal Horse Artillery-man of those days being a compromise between that of our own corps and a Life Guardsman.

The temptation was strong to try the white garments, and then draw on the high, black boots in their pristine glossiness; but that was deferred till a more convenient season, for there was the capital of the human column to examine—that glistening, gorgeous helmet of gilded metal, with its protecting Roman pattern comb, surmounted by a plume of scarlet horsehair, to stream right back and wave and spread over the burnished metal, to cool and shade from the torrid beams of the sun, while the front bore its decoration of leopard-skin, emblematic of the fierce swiftness of the animal's attack and the dash and power of the Flying Artillery, that arm of the service which had done so much in the subjugation of the warlike potentates of India and their savage armies.

It was almost idol-worship, and Dick's cheeks wore a heightened colour as he examined his casque inside and out, gave it a wave in the air to make the plume swish, tapped it with his knuckles, and held it at arm's-length as proudly as any young knight of old donning his helmet for the first time.

At last he put it on, adjusted the scaled chin-strap, gave his head a shake to see if it fitted on tightly, and then turned to the glass and wished, "Oh, if they could only see me now!"

But *they* were far away in the little Devon town, where Dr Darrell went quietly on with his daily tasks as a general practitioner, and Mrs Darrell sighed as she performed her domestic duties and counted the days that must elapse before the next mail came in, wondering whether it would bring a letter from her boy in far-away Bengal, and feeling many a motherly shiver of dread about fevers and cholera and wounds, and accidents with horses, or cannons which might go off when her boy was in front.

And the boy made all this fuss about a suit of clothes and the accoutrements just brought to his quarters from the military tailor's.

Does any lad who reads this mentally exclaim, with an accompanying look of contempt, "What a vain, weak, conceited ass Dick Darrell must have been! Why, if under such circumstances I had received the uniform I should have behaved very differently, and treated it all as a mere matter of course."

At seventeen? Hum! ha! perhaps so. It would be rude for me, the writer, to say, "I don't believe you, my lad," but one cannot help thinking something of the kind, for we all have a touch of vanity in our composition; and as for the uniform of the Bengal Horse Artillery, there was not a man who did not wear it with a feeling of pride.

Dick fell proud enough as he gazed in the glass to see a good-looking, sun-browned face surmounted by that magnificent helmet; but the lad's head was screwed on the right way, and he was not one of those who were turned out when fools were being made. For, as he gazed at himself and admired his noble helmet and plume, his proud delight was dashed with disappointment.

"I've got such a little face," he said to himself, "and it's so smooth and boyish. I seem so young and thin. I wish I hadn't tried so hard to get appointed to the horse brigade. I shall look ridiculous beside all those great, finely-built men. I wonder whether they'll laugh. Well, it's too late now. I wish I could go back home for two years to do nothing but grow."

Dick had gone through everything, even to the gloves, and was having a fight with the desire to try everything on at once, when there was a sharp rap at his door, the handle was turned, and a manly voice shouted:

"May I come in?"

Chapter III
Chums!

Before an answer could be given the door was thrown open, and a brother-officer strode into the room in the shape of Lieutenant Wyatt, a tall, broad-chested fellow of seven or eight and twenty, a man whom nature had endowed with a tremendous moustache, all that was allowed to grow of a prolific beard.

Dick turned scarlet as he faced his visitor, who looked sharply round and burst into a hearty fit of laughter.

"Hullo, shrimp!" he cried. "What! have I caught you?"

"I don't know what you mean," said Dick sulkily.

"Of course you don't. Get out, you wicked young fibster. You have not been inspecting your new plumage—not you! Trying on, and having a good look in the glass, have you?"

"Well, if I have, what then?" said Dick fiercely.

"Cock-a-doodle-doo!" cried the visitor, after giving a very fair imitation of the challenge of a game-fowl. "Hark at him! Oh, the fierceness of the newly-fledged officer! Don't call me out, Dick, and shoot me. There, I apologise."

"I suppose it was quite natural that I should look at the things and see if everything was there."

"Quite, dear boy, quite. Well, has the snip sent in everything right?"

"I don't know. I suppose so."

"Don't be cross, Dicky. Don't sing out of tune. Well, do they fit?"

"I don't know," said the lad coldly.

"Haven't you tried them on?"

"No."

"Bless us! what self-denial! Well, I'm glad I dropped in at the nick of time. We'll have 'em all out again."

"That we won't," cried Dick shortly.

"That we will, my boy. I'm precious proud of our troop, and I'm not going to have my junior turn out a regular guy to make the men grin."

Dick ground his teeth at the very thought of it. Grinned at—for a guy!

"Our uniform takes some putting on, my lad, and we can't afford to let the ignorant sneer. We're the picked corps, and why such a shrimp as you should have been allowed to join passes my comprehension."

"Look here, Mr Wyatt, if you've come here on purpose to insult me, have the goodness to leave my room!" cried Dick fiercely, and feeling hot all over.

"Bravo! Well done, little un," cried Wyatt, patting him on the back; "I like that."

"Keep your hands off me, sir, if you please!" cried Dick furiously.

"Better still, shrimp."

"And look here," cried Dick, who was now bubbling over with anger, "if you dare to call me shrimp again I'll—I'll—Look here, sir, your conduct is most ungentlemanly, and I shall—I shall—"

"Kick me, and make me call you out; and we shall meet, exchange shots, shake hands, and be sworn friends ever after—eh, shrimp, lad? No; we'll do it without all that. Yes, precious ungentlemanly of me, and it's not nice to be laughed at and called names," said Dick's visitor. "Only my way, my lad. But I say, you know," continued the young officer, taking a chair by the back, turning it round, and then mounting it as if he already had his left foot in a stirrup, raising his right leg very high so as to clear an imaginary cantle and valise, throwing it slowly over, and then dropping down astride, "I like that, but you are little and thin, you know."

"I suppose I shall grow," retorted Dick hotly, and the words were on his lips to say, "as big and rude and ugly as you are," but he refrained.

"Grow? Like a weed, my lad. You're just the big-boned fellow for it. We'll soon make you put on muscle."

"Thank you!" cried Dick scornfully.

"Bless us! what a young fire-eater it is! You'll do, Dicky; that you will. From what I saw of you last night, I fancied you'd be a nice, quiet, mamma's boy, and I was sorry that they had not kept you at home."

"Indeed!" said Dick.

"Cool down, my lad; cool down now. You've shown that you've got plenty of stuff in you. There, shake hands, Darrell. Don't be upset about a bit of chaff, boy. I am a bit of a ruffian, I know; but you and I have got to be friends. More than that—brothers. We fellows out here have to do a lot of fighting. Before long, perhaps, I shall have to be saving your life, or you saving mine."

"That sounds pleasant," said Dick, resigning his hand to the firm grip which closed upon it, and responding heartily, for there was something taking in the young man's bluff way.

"Well, hardly," said the latter, his face lighting up with a frank smile. "But never mind that; I only wanted to tell you that we're a sprinkle of Englishmen among hundreds of thousands of fierce, fighting bullies, and we've got to set up our chins and swagger, and let every one see that we're the masters. We don't want milksops in the Flying Artillery."

"And you think that's what I am," said Dick contemptuously.

"That I just don't, shrimp. No, Dicky, I think quite t'other way on, and I'm a bit of a judge. I shall go back to Hulton and tell him you'll do."

"Thanks. But who's Hulton? Stop, I know—the captain I met last night at the mess."

"'Who's Hulton?' Hark at the young heathen!" cried the visitor. "He's your captain, my lad—captain of our troop, the finest troop of the grandest corps in the world. Now you know Hulton and the character of your troop. Don't you feel proud?"

"Not a bit," said Dick.

The young man reached forward and gave Dick a sounding slap on the shoulder.

"That settles it!" he cried. "I was right before. Yes, you'll do. So now, then, let's set to work."

"To work? Now?"

"Yes; Hulton told me to come and look you up. 'Go and see the young cub, and try and lick him into shape,' he said."

"One moment!" said Dick sharply. "Are you the bear of the corps?"

"The bear of the corps?" said the visitor, staring. "Oh, I see—a joke! The bear, to lick the cub into shape. Ha, ha! Yes, you'll do, boy—you'll do. But, to be serious. He said that we must make the best of you."

"But, what nonsense!" said Dick. "I've gone through all my drilling at Addiscombe, and I've gone through a lot more with the foot regiment."

"Oh, yes; but that's as good as nothing to what you've got to do with us. You've been used to crawl, my lad; now you have to fly. I've got to help you use your wings, and it will make it easier for you with the drilling. What about the riding-school? Ever been on a horse?"

"Yes."

"You learned to ride?"

"Yes."

"That's a pity, because you'll have to unlearn that. But we shall make something of you. Here, put on your helmet."

"Pooh! I have tried that on, and it fits."

"You do as I tell you. What you call a fit perhaps won't suit me. Bring it here."

Dick obeyed unwillingly, and his brother-officer turned the headpiece upside-down and looked inside.

"Just as I expected," he said, pointing: "not laced up. Look at this leather lining all cut into gores or points. What's that for?"

"For ventilation, I suppose."

"Venti—grandmother, boy! Nonsense! Look here; a lace runs through all those points. You draw it tight, tie it so, and it turns the lining into a leather skullcap, doesn't it?"

"Oh yes, I see."

"But you didn't before, because you didn't know. Helmets are heavy things, and you haven't got to walk in them, but to ride, and ride roughly, too. Consequently your helmet must be kept in its place. Now, try it on."

Dick slipped it over his head, and passed the chin-strap beneath.

"How is it? Humph! you look like a candle with the extinguisher on."

"Can't help that," said Dick shortly. "It fits close and firm."

"Of course it does. Seems to rest all over your head instead of being held on like a band round your brows. There, I've taught you something. Better let me see to your straps and slings. These tailors never have the slightest notion of how a man's accoutrements are to be worn."

The lieutenant examined straps and slings, altering the sword and sabretache buckles, and when these were to his satisfaction he turned to the jack-boots.

"Tried those on?" he said.

"Not yet."

"Jump into 'em."

"Oh, but not now."

"Yes, now. If a man has a good-fitting pair of boots he's half-dressed."

"Rather a small half, isn't it?" said Dick dryly.

"Bah! you're talking about clothes; I'm talking about a horseman's accoutrements. A man can ride twice as well if he has good boots. On with them."

Once more Dick obeyed.

"Humph! seem to go on pretty easy. Hurt you?"

"No. A little tight perhaps."

"They'll soon give. Humph! Yes, those will do. You can manage about your clothes yourself. You did try 'em on for the tailor?"

"Yes."

"Then they will not be so very full of wrinkles, I suppose. Let's see; there was something else. Oh, yes, I remember. What about a horse?"

"I've done nothing about that yet."

"I suppose not. You must have a good one, you know; but anything could carry you—you're light as a feather—not like me. But there's Morrison's horse to be sold."

"Morrison's? Who was Morrison?"

"One of ours, he was killed, poor chap! and his effects were sold—all but his horses. There's the one he used to ride in the troop, and it would make it easier for you, Hulton said, if you bought him; but—"

"But what?"

"He's rather an awkward horse to ride unless you know him."

"Well, I could get to know him," said Dick.

"Humph! yes—in time; but he has bad habits."

"I should have to break him off them."

"Of course."

"What does he do?"

"Likes playing tricks—biting his companions' necks; and when he can't get at them he tries men's legs."

"Pleasant!"

"Oh, very! Then, if he has some one on his back that he doesn't like he's fond of going on two legs."

"Which two?" said Dick, laughing.

"Oh, he isn't particular. Sometimes he chooses the forelegs, sometimes the hind. Then he dances a regular *pas seul*. Splendid horse to go when he has a strong hand at the rein and a big curb about the jaw."

"I say,"—said Dick, and he stopped.

"Yes! What?"

"The horse did not kill his master, did he?"

"Morrison? Poor old chap! No; a bullet from one of those miserable old matchlocks finished him. He was too good a rider for any horse to kill. There, tuck your new toggery away. It looks nice and bright now, but it soon gets tarnished and dull—worse luck. Mind your man takes care of it, so as to make it last as long as it will. We're obliged to keep up our character. Come out then, and let's go and see Hulton, to get his opinion about a horse for you. By the way, what is your father?"

"A country doctor."

"Very rich?"

"Oh, no; he's comfortably off."

"Ah, well, then you mustn't be coming down too hard upon him for a horse. You've run up a pretty good bill for him already over your new outfit."

"Oh, no," said Dick quickly; "my Aunt Kate put five hundred pounds for me to draw upon to pay for my outfit."

"What!" cried Wyatt, "you've an Aunt Kate with plenty of money who has done that?"

"Yes."

"Give me her address, my dear boy; she must be everything that's good."

"She is," said Dick warmly. "But why do you want her address?"

"To write and propose for her at once, sir," said Wyatt, drawing himself up; "such a good woman ought not to remain single. She is single, of course?"

"Oh, yes," said Dick, smiling.

"That's right. I don't suppose I shall get back to England for a dozen years, but I shall still be young. Let's see; twenty-eight and twelve make forty, and that isn't old, is it?"

"Oh, no—middle-aged."

"You don't think she'd mind waiting, do you, till then?"

"I can't say," said Dick merrily. "But, let's see; sixty and twelve are seventy-two—would you mind waiting?"

"Ahem!" said Wyatt, clearing his throat; "five hundred pounds for you to draw upon. You can easily afford a good horse out of that."

"Of course; it was meant for the purpose."

"Then let's go and see Hulton at once, and hear what he says."

The uniform was quickly put away, Dick's native servant being summoned; and then the two officers crossed the parade-ground to Captain Hulton's quarters, where that quiet, thoughtful-looking personage gave Dick a friendly nod, and proceeded to chat over the subject in a very decisive manner after Wyatt had opened it and had not omitted to allude to Aunt Kate's money.

"What do you say about Morrison's Arab?" he said after a while.

"What! for our young friend here?"

"Yes."

"Decidedly no!—There is no hurry, Darrell, and you need not be too eager about spending your money. Let it rest till a good, quiet, fast mount turns up—one that would suit you. Poor Morrison's Arab is only fit for a rough-rider. We'll find you something for the present—something that will not want much riding."

"Very well, sir," said Dick quietly; "you know best."

"Well, I think so, Darrell," said Captain Hulton, smiling. "When you have been out here ten years with the troop you will have had my experience. You do ride a little?"

"Yes, sir."

"But not our way, of course. Done a little hunting at home, I suppose?"

"Yes, a little; but my father never encouraged me in it."

"Of course not. Well, I'm glad you have joined, Darrell, and we will do our best to make you like the troop; but I'm afraid you will find our drill a bit rough, for we stand first as smart troop, and we have to work hard to keep our position.—I'm busy, Wyatt; so you must take Darrell round and show him the men, horses, and guns."

"Right," said Wyatt.—"Come along, Dick, my lad."

"I wish he wasn't so fond of Dicking me," thought the boy; "but I suppose it's his way."

Chapter IV
Such a Boy!

Wyatt performed his task thoroughly,

"You shall see the guns first," he said: and he marched his new brother-officer across to the gun-shed, where a smart, six-foot gunner in undress uniform drew himself up to salute as they passed to where the light six-pounders stood in an exact line, with their limbers and ammunition-boxes, rammers, sponges, and trails—the very perfection of neatness, and everything that would bear a polish shining like a gem.

On the walls were rockets in racks, and stands for their discharge were close at hand; while spare wheels and tackle of every kind possible to be wanted, and beautifully clean, took Dick's attention, showing, as they did, the perfect management over all.

"Now for the stables," said Wyatt. "Better be on your guard, for some of the horses are rather playful with their heels."

Dick nodded, and followed his conductor into the plainest and cleanest stable he had ever seen. Here they came upon several syces or grooms, whose task it was to give the horses' coats the satin-like gloss they displayed; for the drivers and gunners of the Honourable Company's corps were far too great men to run down their own horses, or do much more than superintend the cleaning of their own accoutrements.

"It's different to being at home," said Wyatt laughingly; "and we want the men to fight, not for grooms and servants. They're a bit spoiled, but the niggers are plentiful, and we let them do the work."

Dick had seen the stables at a cavalry barracks once, and admired the horses; but these were nothing to the beautiful, sleek creatures he saw here. Wild-looking, large-eyed, abundant of mane and tail, perfect beauties without exception, but certainly playful as the lieutenant had said, the entrance of the visitors seeming to be the signal for the long line to begin tossing their heads, rattling their halters, and turning their beautiful arched necks to gaze at the new-comers before snorting, squealing, and making ineffectual attempts to bite at their fellows—ineffectual, for they could not reach them.

"What do you think of them?" said Wyatt, smiling at his companion's display of excited appreciation. "Will they do?"

"Do!" cried Dick enthusiastically; "why, there isn't one that would not make a magnificent charger."

"Bating temper, you're quite right. Arab stallions, every one. But you've seen them before."

"Only once, at a distance, and then they were going fast."

"Yes, we do go pretty fast," said Wyatt quietly; "the men on the limbers have to sit pretty tight in their leather slings. Seen enough?"

"No," cried Dick; "one could never see enough of such horses as these."

"That's right, young one," said Wyatt approvingly. "Well, you'll see enough of them now. We'll walk down to the other end, and go out of the other door."

Dick followed his companion unwillingly, for the desire was on him to go and pat and handle several of the beautiful creatures.

"No, no," said Wyatt, stopping him; "it's rather too risky; some of them are likely to be nasty with strangers. You see, so long as a horse is a good one we don't study much about his character."

"Nor yet about the characters of the men," said Dick dryly.

"That's so. We want men—perfect men—sound in wind and limb; and as to the men's characters, well, they're obliged to behave well. They know that, and they do. Come and see them."

This was the most crucial part of the business to Dick. The horses, as they turned their beautiful eyes upon him and shook their manes, seemed one and all to be gazing at him with a kind of sovereign contempt. But then they were horses—dumb animals, and did not matter; but the men—what would they think?

He felt younger, slighter, and more boyish than ever as he crossed the parade-ground towards the barracks, and involuntarily drew himself up, frowned, and strode more heavily, unconscious of the fact that his conductor was looking slyly down at him from the corner of his left eye, enjoying the boy's effort to look more manly. Then his face turned grave, and he laid his hand upon the lad's arm.

"Don't do that, Dick," he said.

"Don't do what?" cried the boy flushing guiltily.

"Don't be a sham. It will make a bad impression on the men."

Dick stopped short, and looked half angrily at his brother-officer.

"I'm speaking seriously, lad," said Wyatt, "to my brother-officer. You see, Dick, you are only a boy yet, and there's nothing to be ashamed of in that. Be proud of being a boy till nature turns you into a man, and then be a man."

"I don't quite understand you, sir," said Dick.

"Yes, you do; and now you're being a sham with me while I'm trying to keep you from being a sham with the men, who would see it directly, and laugh at it as soon as our backs are turned. I say, young un, don't you know that a good boy is far better than a bad man?"

"A good boy!" said Dick, with his lip curling. "You speak to me as if I were a child. You'll be calling me a naughty boy next."

"What a young fire-eater you are!" said Wyatt good-humouredly. "I didn't mean a good boy, the opposite of a naughty boy. You know well enough what I mean—a boy who is a boy, a frank brick of a boy who acts up to what he really is—not one of your affected imitation men, young apes, puppies who are ashamed of being boys—young idiots. Look here, young un; I took to you last night because you were frank and straightforward, and behaved as if you knew that you were only a boy."

"Well, I do know it, of course; but I don't want people to be always throwing it in my teeth."

"Nobody will, my lad, unless you make them. It's in your own hands. Whenever a lad gets that it's because he has been making a monkey of himself by trying to imitate what he is not."

"Well, but I was not just now."

"What!" cried Wyatt.

"Well, I suppose I was—a little," said Dick, turning more red in the face.

"A little? Awfully, old fellow. Drop it. I wouldn't have taken you through the men's quarters like that for your own sake. Believe me, my lad, when I tell you that I'm going to take you through our troop of picked men—men we're all proud of. They're keen, clever fellows, who can read one like a book. You'll have to help lead them some day, and you've got to win their respect by your manliness and pluck. Then they'll follow you anywhere."

"Manliness!" cried Dick reproachfully; "and you ridicule me for trying to be so."

"For shamming it, my lad. A boy can be naturally manly without acting."

"All right; I'll try—to be a boy," said Dick, rather glumly.

"There, now, you're facing about in the wrong direction, my lad. Don't try—don't act. Be a natural British lad. Look honestly, enviously if you like, at the men. You are a boy yet, nothing but a boy—one of the youngest officers we've had; and if you're frank and natural with it, and the men see that you've got the pluck to learn our ways, with plenty of go, they'll make it ten times as easy for you as it would be, and make a regular pet of you."

"But I don't want to be the men's pet," said Dick sharply.

"Of course not. I only mean they'll be proud of you, and like you for being young. They'll put will into everything they do when you give your orders; and when," said Wyatt, with a grim laugh—"when you're beginning, and hot and excited, and give the wrong orders and would wheel the troop in the wrong direction, they'll go right."

"Thank you, Mr Wyatt," said Dick quietly.

The lieutenant looked at him sharply.

"I was going to say, 'Mean it?'" he said, "but I see you do. Why, Dick, lad, I often wish I was a boy again, as often perhaps as I used to wish that I was a man, and longed for a moustache."

He gave Dick a comical look and laughed.

"It's all right," he said; "it's coming up, and I don't say it will beat mine some day, for I've got about the biggest in the artillery, and a great nuisance it is when I'm eating soup.—Ah, here's some one for you to know."

For a fine, stalwart-looking, slightly-grizzled, deeply-bronzed man in the undress uniform of a sergeant-major suddenly came out from a doorway, and saluted both as he drew himself up like a statue.

"Ah, Sergeant," said Wyatt, stopping short. "This is my friend, Mr Darrell, our new subaltern."

"Glad to meet you, sir," said the old non-commissioned officer stiffly.

"I'm taking him round. We're just going to look at the men."

"Yes, sir. Like me to show you round?"

"Yes, you may as well. By the way, Mr Darrell is very anxious to get into our ways as soon as he can. You'll help him all you can?"

"Yes, sir," said the sergeant grimly, and Dick found it hard work to look natural; "but I'm afraid he'll find us a little rougher than they are in the foot."

"Oh, he won't mind that.—Will you, Darrell?"

"Well, I don't know," said Dick in a frank, outspoken way, giving the sergeant a good, earnest, straightforward look as he spoke. "I expect I shall find it very rough, and mind it a good deal at first; but I suppose I shall soon get used to it if I try."

The sergeant's grim visage relaxed as Dick spoke.

"I think you'll do, sir," he said. "That's half the fight—try."

"Do? Oh, yes, he'll do. Captain Hulton says you are to take him in hand."

"Proud to do my best, sir," said the sergeant bluffly. "Mr Darrell knows, of course, that he has a deal more to learn here than he had in the foot brigade, for we have to be wonderfully smart."

"Oh, yes, he knows all that, Stubbs."

"Then it sha'n't be my fault, sir, if I don't make you as smart an officer as Mr Wyatt here, if he'll pardon me for saying so."

"That's right, Sergeant.—He broke me in, Darrell, and you'll find him a splendid teacher. Ah, here we are! Now you're going to see some of the sergeant's pupils."

Dick walked with his companion into the barrack-room, where some forty or fifty men were lounging about in the easiest of costumes—*négligé* would be too smart a term for it; but all started to their feet as the officers entered, and looked sharply and searchingly at the new subaltern. But, as it happened, the lad did not feel the slightest nervous shrinking; for, as he went through the barrack-room, followed by the sergeant, the deep feeling of interest he felt in the aspect of the place, with the men's trappings and weapons in place and in the most perfect order, the neatness of all but the men's costume—and, above all, the aspect of the fine body of picked soldiers whom he was some day to lead—thrilled the young officer with a feeling of pride, and gave such a look of animation to his countenance that unwittingly he made as good an impression as the most exacting of friends could have wished.

The ordeal was soon passed; for, as Wyatt said, "One doesn't like to be interfering with the men in their easy times. But what do you think of our lads, Darrell?"

"Splendid!" cried the boy enthusiastically. "You're right; they are picked men."

"Yes, they are," said Wyatt.—"Eh, Sergeant?"

"Yes, sir. I often wish we could ride into Hyde Park with them on a review day. I think we could make the Londoners give us a cheer. Beg pardon, sir, but some of 'em seemed to like the look of Mr Darrell here."

"Think so?"

"Yes, sir; set some of 'em thinking, as it did me!"

"Set you thinking?" said Wyatt.

"Yes, sir; about when we were young as he is, sir. Hah! it's a good many years since, though.—When will you be ready to begin, sir?" he added quickly, for he detected a look of annoyance at the turn the conversation was taking.

"To-morrow morning?" said Dick sharply. "Will that do?"

"Yes, sir; the sooner the better. Riding-school half-an-hour after *reveille*, please. Like to see the riding-school, sir?"

"No, no!" cried Wyatt; "he'll see enough of that for many days to come. We've done enough for to-day."

The sergeant saluted, and the two officers marched away in silence for a few moments before Wyatt said sharply:

"Capital, Dick. Couldn't have been better. You were just the natural lad who was taking an eager interest in the men and their place. They saw it, and the sergeant was correct. All right, my lad; I'm glad you've joined us. You'll do."

"Think so?" said Dick, blushing.

"Yes; and so will Hulton when he knows you better."

"Then he didn't think so at first?" said Dick sharply.

"No; he was a bit savage about the authorities appointing such a boy."

Dick winced.

"But he knew nothing about what sort of stuff you were made of."

"Bah! don't flatter," said Dick angrily.

"Not going to. Sooner knock your head off. But look here, my lad; you have your work cut out, and we're going to show Hulton that he has got the right lad to grow up into our ways and fill poor Morrison's place."

"*We* are going?" said Dick wonderingly.

"Of course; I'm going to help."

Chapter V
A Test of Pluck

Dick wanted no morning trumpet to call him; he was awake before daylight, to lie thinking, his brain excited by the novelty of his position and the thoughts of all he had to go through.

To put it plainly, he felt new and nervous; but he recalled the fact that it was his own doing—it had been his ambition to get appointed to the Flying Artillery. "And to-day," he said to himself, "I have to begin to learn how to fly, and that means having some falls. Well, if I do I won't holloa. I don't mean to show I'm hurt."

This was while he was having his apology for a tub, but it was most enjoyable after a hot night, though awkward, and consisted in squatting down in a shallow tin and pouring earthen jars of cold water over his head, to run down his back.

"'Tis freshening," he muttered; "makes one feel ready for everything."

He was hard at work towelling when a trumpet sounded so peculiarly that he laughed.

"What's the matter with the fellow?" he said. "That can't be the *reveille*. Some one blowing for fun. How absurd!"

He hurried to the window as he realised what it was, and saw, looming up in the dim light, the figure of a gigantic elephant slowly following a man whose only garment was a strip of cotton cloth about his loins; while directly after three more of the great animals passed by.

"Gun-elephants, I suppose," he said to himself.

The trumpet had not sounded when he finished dressing, so he hurried down to have a breath of the fresh morning air, making his native servant start up from where he was lying asleep, to stare at his sahib who had left his couch so soon.

It was pleasantly cool out in the parade-ground, and Dick was hesitating as to which direction he should take, when the sound of voices from beyond the low range of stabling to his right, followed by a repetition of the elephants trumpeting and the splashing of water, took his attention.

"Taking them to drink," he muttered; and he made for an opening at the end of the shed just as the morning bugle rang out loud and clear, echoing from the different buildings near and rousing the sleepers throughout the barracks.

"I have half-an-hour, though," thought Dick; and he went on through the opening, to find himself in a paved courtyard, where the four elephants were standing, and about a dozen nearly nude Hindus were slowly drawing water from a well.

Just then the man who was in charge of the largest elephant marched up to it, bearing a pail, uttered a few sharp orders in Hindustani, and the huge beast slowly and ponderously went down on its knees and then laid itself over on its side, grunting softly as it settled its head on the pavement, stretched out its writhing trunk, and then lay blinking its little, piggish eye, and gently flapping the big ear at liberty.

Another man came up with a bucket, and Dick became aware that he was to be present at the morning toilet of the huge beast. This commenced at once by the men throwing the water all over the great heaving flank; and then, each armed with what looked like a piece of pumice-stone, the bare-footed pair walked on to it, and, squatting down, began work, as a maid at home would begin hearth-stoning a flight of steps.

The whole performance was most ludicrous—the elephant lying there grunting as if with pleasure, lifting ear or leg at a word, and grunting and uttering little, squealing and soft, whining noises, indicating satisfaction, while showing that, in spite of the thickness of its skin, it was sensitive here and there and ticklish to a degree.

One of the most absurd parts of the performance was the perfectly cool way in which the men paddled about all over it, their feet seeming to hold on well to the grey, indiarubber-like surface, and the elephant evidently approving of the whole business.

Dick stood watching the scrubbing, deluging with water, and re-scrubbing and showering till one side was done, and then stood as close up as he could without getting wet, when the order was given for the great brute to change sides, which it did by rolling itself over, the others following suit, and patiently waiting for the other flank to be done.

"Morning, sir," said a voice behind, and Dick started round to see the sergeant had followed him.

"Morning. It's not time yet, is it?"

"Wants about ten minutes, sir. I was on my way, but I saw you through the gateway."

"I didn't know this was done. Are these gun-elephants?"

"Yes, sir. Oh, yes, it's done regularly: keeps them beautifully clean."

"They seem to like it."

"Oh, yes, sir; they grant and enjoy it like pigs being scratched. You see, they're a deal worried by flies and things which lay their eggs in their tender parts behind the ears and under their arms."

"Their arms?"

"Well, legs, sir. But look at 'em; they're more like arms, and their hindlegs are more like ours. You look when they lie down. See that, sir?"

The sergeant drew the young officer's attention to the big elephant lifting up its foreleg for the stone to scour beneath, grunting the while softly.

"He itches just there, sir."

"Seems like it," said Dick. "But what an enormous brute it is!"

"Yes, sir: 'bout one of the biggest I've seen. The Rajah of Soojeepur up north yonder has some thumpers, but nothing bigger than this one."

"I didn't know you had elephants here," said Dick.

"We don't as a rule, sir, but these four have come up with a couple of heavy guns. There's something up, I suppose."

"What—fighting?" said Dick eagerly.

The sergeant shook his head.

"Don't know, sir. We never know till the last minute, when the order comes to move. May be to a bit of a scrimmage—perhaps only to hold some place. But time's pretty well up, sir, and the men will be there with the horse."

"I'm ready," said Dick, and he turned to go, but altered his mind, and made so that he could walk round the elephants, going so close to the first that he had been watching so long that, as he paused for a moment close to its head and spoke to the great, blundering creature, it responded by suddenly stretching out its trunk and taking a turn round the lad's ankle, holding him fast.

"Hurrah walla pala larna fa," or something like it, cried the man, jumping up from where he had squatted scouring what answered to the elephant's armpit.

"Phoonk! phoonk!" came in reply, the elephant seeming to be quite content with its capture.

"Tell him to let go," cried the sergeant: and the man began to jump and dance and stamp upon the elephant's ribs, yelling and calling it all the ill-names he could in his own tongue, and threatening what he would do with the goad the next time he was mounted behind the creature's ears.

But the great brute lay quite still, flapping its free ear up and down, rumbling like a young thunderstorm, and blinking at Dick, with the serpent-like coil about his leg.

"Oh, son of a wicked, squinting mother, am I to come and pull thy ugly, great tusks out by the roots?" shrieked the Hindu.

"Woomble! woomble!" went the elephant; and the sergeant stepped forward to give Dick his support.

"Woomph!" roared the animal angrily, and the sergeant started back.

"I don't think he wants to hurt me," said Dick; "it only feels tight."

"I don't know, sir," said the sergeant. "I don't know what to make of these brutes. They're not like horses."

"Not a bit," said Dick, with rather a forced smile, for his position was awkward, and he began to think of what might happen if the elephant held on and suddenly rose to its feet.

"Why don't you make him leave go?" cried the sergeant angrily.

"Thy servant is trying, sahib," whimpered the man, who jumped on the elephant again, but only brought forth a grunt.

"Shout at him; he understands you."

"Yes, sahib; but he is in one of his bad tempers this morning."

The man stepped forward and stamped with one foot on the beast's neck, and then kicked at his ear.

"That does no good. Where's your spiked hook?"

"It is not here, O sahib," whimpered the man, who then burst out with a furious tirade of vituperation; but the offending beast only twitched its contemptible little tail and winked good-humouredly at Dick.

"Oh, vile, pig-headed brother of a mugger!" shrieked the man, while all his fellows stopped short and watched the encounter; "am I to curse thee till thou dost shrivel up into a chicken maggot? Am I to cease cleaning thy dirty hide, and leave thee to be eaten up by wicked flies?"

The elephant "chuntered," as a north-country man might say, and its meaning seemed to be, "Oh, yes, if you like."

"Will you let go of the young sahib's leg, oh first cousin of ten thousand demons?" shrieked the man.

"Will you let go of the young sahib's leg, oh first cousin of ten thousand demons?" shrieked the man.

"Poomph!" growled the elephant; and the Hindu started on another tack, while a couple of his fellows, bearing buckets of water, came nearer.

"Oh, sweet son of a beautiful little mother, beloved eater of cane and sugar-grass, handsome pet of the ivory teeth! unclasp the young sahib's leg, and thy mahout will paint thee in red and blue stripes with vermilion and indigo. He will gild thy tusks with gold, and put a velvet cloth with silken ropes on thy soft, mountain-like back, so that the elephants of the Rajah of Soojeepur shall be jealous, and run away maddened to the jungle when thou goest thy way."

"Pooroon! pooroon!" grumbled the great beast.

"What! Not when thy beloved mahout promises thee that?" cried the mahout, sliding off the flesh-mountain to bend down and lift up the great flap of an ear and whisper gently, "Sweet gums shall be thine, and bananas, great melons and cucumbers."

"Whoo—oomph!"

There was a kind of flesh-quake, the Hindu was thrown sideways, the trunk had been uncoiled, and the monster heaved up its huge bulk and stood over Dick, who had not moved, swaying its great head from side to side, and bringing its splendid great tusks within an inch or two every time it swept them by.

"Let the young sahib run before the evil-born beast with a miserable tail slays him by putting him under his foot!" cried the man.

"He won't hurt me," said Dick gently. "Will you, old chap? There, I haven't got anything for you."

Dick raised his hand and rubbed the monster's corrugated trunk, moving gently out of its way as it came forward to where the men who looked on had set down their buckets of water, and now fled hastily.

"Why, he's thirsty," said Dick.

So it proved, for the elephant reached out its trunk, which looked like a gigantic leech, curved its end down into the nearest pail, sucked up a third of the contents, withdrew it, turned it under into its mouth, shot the water down its throat, and went on repeating the process till both the pails were empty, when it raised its trunk in the air, blew a wild, weird blast, and then turned to Dick again, touched him softly with its trunk, and then stood gravely swaying its head from side to side.

"Hah!" ejaculated the sergeant; and Dick turned sharply from watching the elephant, for his companion's exclamation seemed to be echoed.

"Good-morning," said Dick. "I didn't know you were there, Mr Wyatt."

"I didn't dare to stir," replied that gentleman. "Why, Darrell, my lad, I've been standing there ever so long, with my heart in my mouth."

"Oh, I don't think there was anything to mind."

"I don't know. These beasts can be very awkward sometimes, and kill their mahouts. I say, didn't you feel frightened?"

"N-o, I don't think so; only a bit helpless. It was so curious."

"They have such power," said Wyatt.

"So I suppose," said Dick quietly: "but it was so curious to watch and listen to that mahout, sometimes scolding and sometimes petting the great elephant to let go. I hadn't time to feel frightened. But it was awkward."

"Yes," said Wyatt dryly, "very awkward. Been worse, though, if he had dragged you closer and set one of his feet upon you."

"Yes," replied Dick thoughtfully; "an animal like that must be very heavy."

Wyatt looked at the sergeant, and the sergeant raised his shaggy eyebrows a little as he returned the meaning look; and by that time they had reached the big entrance-door of the long, light building used as a riding-school.

Chapter VI
Putting through the Paces

However Richard Darrell might have felt when held by the elephant, he certainly was conscious of being uncomfortable now, for it was long since he had mounted a beast of any kind; and he was to take his seat upon a big, highly-trained trooper, in the presence of a man who was without doubt a magnificent horseman, as well as under the eye of one who acted as riding-master of the troop.

The place looked gloomy in the early morning—quite in accordance with the lad's feelings—while as soon as he passed through the doorway, which had been made high enough to allow for the passage of mounted men, he was conscious of being in the presence of his mount—a big, restive-looking horse, gifted with the bad habit of showing the whites of its eyes and tossing up its head in what seemed to be a vicious way.

"Hullo!" cried Wyatt, as the native groom began caressing the animal on seeing them enter, with the result of making the horse more restive; "why, you've got Old Bones."

"Yes, sir," said the sergeant; "he knows his business so well that I thought he would be best."

"But he's such a rough, hard-mouthed brute, Stubbs."

"Yes, sir; but he answers to the word of command better than any horse in the troop."

"Humph!" ejaculated Wyatt. "You must nip him well with your knees, Darrell."

Dick nodded, and stood looking at the horse, which was led up at a sign made by the sergeant.

"Been accustomed to horses, sir?" he said to his pupil.

"Yes, a little," said Dick.

"Then you won't be nervous, sir; and the ground bark is quite soft to fall on."

"Yes," said Wyatt; "and if you do come off you needn't mind, for you'll have no stirrups, and the horse will stop short."

At the words "no stirrups" Dick winced a little, but he set his teeth a bit harder.

The horse bore a regular high-peaked and pommelled saddle of the military type, and the sergeant took the reins while the syce went, as the lad supposed, to take off or cross the stirrups over the horse's back; but, rather to Dick's dismay, he rapidly unbuckled the girths and drew the saddle off, carrying it to a great peg near the door, and then hurrying back to take the reins from the sergeant's hand.

"Ready, sir?" said the latter.

Dick nodded.

"Then I'll give you a leg up. Take the reins. No, no; that's not our way, sir. Only pass your little finger between them this fashion, and let them both run through your hand, passing them together between your thumb and first finger. See; this way. Gives you a firmer pull in reining up short."

Dick nodded, after watching the sergeant, who then dropped the reins on the horse's neck.

"Now then, take up your reins."

Dick obeyed, holding them exactly as the sergeant had done the moment before.

"Wrong!" shouted his master. "Try again."

Dick dropped the rein, and turned an inquiring look at his tutor.

"You took up the wrong rein, sir. Civilians ride on the snaffle; soldiers ride on the curb."

Dick nodded, and took up the curb-rein this time.

"Good. Now give me your left leg, and when I say 'Mount,' put a little spring into it as I give you a lift, raise your right leg high as you throw it over to clear your saddle and traps, and open your crutch wide as you let yourself drop on to the horse's back. Of course there is no saddle, but you must mount as if there was. Ready!—Mount."

The sergeant raised the lad's leg, and seemed to be trying to throw him over to the other side of the horse, which kept on tossing its head about, but stood like a statue.

In an instant Dick was in his place.

"Off again!" cried the sergeant; and the lad threw himself off quickly. "Now, your leg. See if you can do that again."

The orders were given, and the lad dropped once more easily into his place, Wyatt giving a satisfied smile, and the sergeant nodding.

"Attention!" he cried. "Now take up the snaffle-rein to hold loosely in your hand. That's right. Get well down in your seat; sit perfectly upright, elbows more in, grip with your knees, and keep your toes pointed forward and your heels well down. Mind, you have to ride on the balance. That's right. You will advance now at a walk."

As he uttered the last word the syce darted back, and the horse went off at a quick walk down the side of the riding-school, along the end, right down the other side and bottom, and back to where the three were standing.

"Not bad, sir," said the sergeant. "Feel pretty safe?" Dick nodded.

"Keep those elbows in and your toes well up. Straighter, straighter. That's right. Once more—forward at a walk."

The horse started again, and as soon as the rider was out of hearing Wyatt spoke.

"Promises well, Sergeant."

"Yes, sir; not the first time he has been on a horse.—Trot!" he shouted, and the horse broke into a long, swinging stride, throwing his rider up so high that Dick felt how well his mount merited the term rough; but the lad kept his place pretty well, and as they reached the sergeant again a sharp "Halt!" rang out, the horse stopped short, and Dick went right forward upon the neck.

"I said 'Halt!'" cried the sergeant grimly. "Get back in your place, sir, and keep there. We ride on a horse's back, an elephant's neck, and the ears keep you from going any forwarder."

"The old joke, Stubbs," said Wyatt softly.

"Yes, sir; I have used it a good many times with recruits," said the sergeant grimly. Then to his pupil, "Now, sir, keep in your place this time."

"Yes. That was bad," said Dick.

"Silence! Advance at a walk."

The horse moved off again.

"Trot!"

Away he went, snorting and tossing his head, throwing his rider up at every stride of his long-legs right round the school, and Dick nipped the animal's sides with his knees, doing his best to keep his seat when the word "Halt!" should ring out; but, to his surprise, the horse went on past the group and passed again for another round.

Then came the order; the horse stopped short.

"Sit easy!" shouted the sergeant. "Make much of your horse. Sit easy!" he cried again, for Dick had not moved. "Pat your horse, sir; pat your horse."

Dick obeyed now, and the sergeant went on giving him instructions about his seat, and opening his crutch, getting his elbows in, and heels down.

"Sit well upright, sir, but not stiff as a ramrod. A good rider ought to be like a part of his horse."

And so on, and so on, for a few minutes, while the lieutenant looked on sternly without uttering a word, frowning severely the while.

"Attention!" shouted the sergeant again, as if he were addressing a squad of recruits; and once more the walking and trotting were gone through. There was another rest, some repetition of instructions, all of which Dick, a soldier by training, listened to in silence, and fixed as well as he could upon his memory.

But an hour had nearly gone by, and he was growing tired, while sundry internal hints suggested that breakfast would be acceptable. The lesson was not at an end, though. "Attention" was called, and the horse started again at a walk.

"Going to try him at the gallop?" said Wyatt softly.

"Yes, sir," replied the sergeant; "he can ride."

"Won't come off, will he?"

The sergeant shook his head.

"Trot!"

Away went the horse with his long, swinging stride, which without a saddle was rather a painful mode of progression for his rider.

"This is the finish," thought Dick.

"Gallop!" was roared, and in an instant the horse bounded off, swinging round the long building, while, delighted with the change, his rider settled down to the easy pace with a profound feeling of satisfaction.

But as he passed the sergeant there was a roar at him to sit up, and he had to recall his instructions and ride according to them.

"Better!" shouted the sergeant as they dashed by, scattering the soft covering of the ring, while the horse covered the ground as if this were the natural pace to which he was accustomed. And the third time round the young rider was on his guard—he expected the word "Halt!"—and when it came, and the horse stopped short, he kept his place.

"Dismount!" cried the sergeant, and Dick threw himself off, hot and panting.

"That will do for this morning, sir. You've been on a horse before."

"Yes," said Dick quietly; "I used to ride about with my father when I was at home."

The syce clapped the saddle on the horse again, and walked it away to the stables; and, after a word or two from the sergeant, the two officers marched back to quarters.

"Feel stiff, Darrell?" said Wyatt.

"Yes, and sore about the knees. I'm not used to riding without a saddle."

"Capital practice. Keep it up; the sergeant's a splendid teacher."

"Rather a rough one," said Dick.

"Ah, you're tired. Come and have breakfast. You'll feel better then. Go to your room and have a wash and brush; I'll wait for you. You'll just have time. Hulton likes us to be punctual. Here—No, I'll go straight on; join me there."

"Yes," said Dick quietly, and he went to his room, while Wyatt went on and found his brother-officer ready and the servants waiting to bring in the breakfast.

"Been to the riding-school?"

"Yes; just come away."

"Well, what's he like with a horse?"

"Tip-top," replied Wyatt—"for a beginner."

"Then you think we shall make something of him?"

"Not a doubt about it."

"They are going to bring out Burnouse this morning, so that I may come to some decision about whether it shall be sold. Will you buy it?"

"Can't afford another, my dear boy. Why don't you?"

"I'm in the same position. The horse is quite impossible for that boy?"

"Oh, yes; it would be murder to put him on it."

"Then the horse must go and be sold. It's a pity, too, for he's a splendid creature."

Chapter VII
A Beast of a Temper

Wyatt was quite right, for the breakfast partaken of with his two brother-officers set the lad thinking in a very different way. Before the meal he felt weary and rather despondent; after, he was only a trifle stiff and sore, and would have been ready for another lesson.

"You'll take it easy to-day, Darrell," said the captain. "We're going to have a march out, but as you have no horse yet you can only see us off, unless you would like to try one of mine. Think you could manage it?"

"I'll try, sir," said Dick.

"Hum—ha—yes," said the captain thoughtfully; "but perhaps you had better not. My two chargers are rather spirited beasts.—What do you think, Wyatt?"

"Better stop at home," said Wyatt bluntly. "It's too soon yet. Have a dozen of old Stubbs's drillings first, and by then I dare say we shall have helped you to choose a mount. We have plenty always being offered. Here, you will be able to see poor Morrison's Arab, Burnouse, this morning."

"Why wouldn't it do for me?" said the lad sharply. "It is used to the drill, and would keep in its place."

"Yes," said Wyatt, laughing; "but that isn't all. It's you that would have to keep in yours."

"You think it would be too much for me?"

"Yes, yes," said the captain. "Captain Morrison was a magnificent horseman, and about the only man who could ride the beast. It's quite out of the question."

"Very well," said Dick quietly; "I'll wait."

"Yes," said Captain Hulton dryly, "you had better wait.—By the way, Wyatt, you may as well come across to Sir George with me. I think you ought to be there."

"Very well. But what does he want?"

"It's about that Hanson."

"Oh, hang the fellow!" cried Wyatt.

"No we will not go so far as that this time, but I expect he will have to be flogged."

Dick started, and looked sharply from one to the other, for the last word jarred upon him, knowing what he did of military punishments. But the two officers paid no heed to him, and it was evident to the young man that he was not wanted; so he strolled out, to look about and make himself better acquainted with the cantonments, where, in addition to his own corps, there were in barracks a couple of native regiments and a company of foot artillery, who, he rightly conjectured, had charge of the heavy guns.

It was all wonderfully interesting, and he was tempted to wander off into the town, and stroll through the bazaars, on his way to the grand old temple by the side of the river which flowed through the place; but he wanted to see the march out of his troop, and hurried back, finding that the time had slipped imperceptibly away, and that he was barely soon enough.

To his great satisfaction, though, he reached the parade-ground just as the men were forming up. They were only in fatigue uniform, but their appearance was wonderfully striking and businesslike, while the guns were drawn up in line with the most perfect precision.

But it was the line of horses and teams of the guns which took the young man's attention most, and, recalling on the instant the lesson he had that morning gone through, a strange feeling of emulation filled his breast—a desire to work on as hard as he could till he was passed as fit for service—fit to ride one of the magnificent, spirited animals facing where he stood.

"I must have a horse soon," he said to himself; and the thought had hardly crossed his brain when, from the gateway leading to the stable enclosure, a couple of white-clothed syces came out, one leading a rather small, beautifully-formed Arabian horse of a peculiar, creamy, dun colour, with flowing, lighter-tinted mane and tail. The horse came ambling and showing itself off, and apparently resented the pull upon its bit, but was prevented from dragging thereon by the presence of the second native groom, who walked on its other side and raised a hand from time to time as if to soothe it, smoothing down its great mane when a lock was tossed over to the wrong side, as the horse lowered its proud head and then threw it up. The noble-looking animal was fully caparisoned, and looked the artillery officer's charger to perfection, sending a thrill of envy through the lad, seeming, as it did, the most beautiful and spirited creature he had ever seen—and just, too, at the moment when he was suffering from an intense longing for a mount.

"It must be the charger they spoke of," he thought—"Captain Morrison's. What did they call it—Burnouse? Why, I could ride that."

The stiffness caused by want of practice seemed to die out, and the soreness about his knees to pass away, in the presence of that intense longing; and his eyes ran from the magnificent head—with its slightly-curved muzzle and distended nostrils, which quivered as the animal snuffed the air, snorted, and threw specks of white foam from its well-champed bit—to the arched neck, hollowed back, and beautifully-rounded haunches, while through the glistening, thin, satin skin a perfect network of veins stood out. It seemed, too, so light and springy as it ambled along, its wide hoofs hardly touching the ground; and, though full of action and play, there was no trace of vice.

"Why, he could go like the wind," thought Dick; and, as if drawn by a magnet, the lad advanced to meet the white-clothed grooms, who seemed to be taking up their charge's full attention, till all at once it stopped short, tossed its great mane and forelock, drew up its head, and lashed its long, flowing tail as it assumed a beautifully wild-looking pose, and sent forth a loud, shrill, challenging neigh to the group of horses drawn up on its right front.

The challenge was replied to instantly, running along the line, and there was an uneasy movement and, good deal of reining in and spurring before the line was restored to its former evenness.

Meanwhile the beautiful, creamy Arab neighed again, rose upon its hindlegs, and struck out, pawing the air with each hoof alternately, looking grand in its wild, fierce attitude as it dragged at the rein.

"Oh, you beauty!" cried Dick involuntarily.

"Oh, you beast!" said a voice behind him, and he turned his head sharply, to find that Wyatt had come up unobserved.

"It's only spirit," said Dick resentfully. "He's fresh for want of work."

"Fresh? Why, look at him. He's spoiling for a fight. The brute's upsetting the whole troop."

"Is that Burnouse?" said Dick eagerly.

"Yes, my lad, that's Burnouse; and you seem quite wrapped up in him."

"Captain Morrison used to ride him?"

"Oh, yes; he used to ride him, but he could ride anything. We used to call him 'Mazeppa,' for Burnouse is a regular wild horse. Look at that; they can hardly hold him. Oh, here's Hulton.—Well, what do you think of him now?"

"I think it's a pity, for he's a splendid beast. I should like to see him have a final trial, though, with the troop before we decide."

"Well, ride him, then, to-day."

This was said just as two chargers were led out by their syces, and brought towards where the officers were standing.

"No, thanks," said the captain, smiling; "when I come to my end, I should like it to be by shot or sword. You're a better horseman than I am, and ought to be able to manage him. Try him."

Wyatt gave a peculiar writhe, and screwed up his face.

"My back isn't quite right yet from the fall he gave me. Once bit, twice shy. He took a piece out of my sleeve another time, and meant it to be flesh. Here, you keep that brute back."

This to the two syces, who were both now hanging on to the Arab's reins, the fierce animal having made a sudden dash to get at the two chargers being brought up.

The Arab was checked in time, and its attention diverted while the two officers mounted.

"Look here, Wyatt," said the captain, "let's give the brute a chance. I hate him to go out of the corps."

"Let me try him," said Dick eagerly.

"You?" cried the captain, turning upon him in wonder. Then, with a mocking smile, which made the lad wince, "You don't know what you are talking about, Darrell, my lad.—Here, Wyatt, ride across and ask for a volunteer. The men know what he is as well as we do."

Wyatt nodded, and rode across to the drawn-up troop, Dick, with every nerve on the quiver, watching him anxiously in the hope that every man would refuse; but, to his disgust, a man responded to the invitation, received the order to rein back, and came round to the front, riding towards the two syces behind the lieutenant, dismounted, handed his reins to Captain Hulton's groom, and stood waiting.

"Think you can ride him?" said Hulton.

"Oh, yes, I can ride him, sir. Captain Morrison always could."

"Mind, I do not order you to mount. You volunteer."

"Yes, sir; I'll take the risk," said the man, setting his teeth.

"Up with you, then; but mind, don't use the curb—he will not stand it; and keep your spurs out of his flanks, or he'll throw you."

Palpitating with the excitement from which he suffered, Dick saw the man stride up to the horse, who rolled his eyes back, watching him, but standing fairly quiet, while, with the two *syces* at the head, the gunner took hold of the rein, placed his foot in the stirrup, and, quick as thought, was in the saddle. As soon as he thrust his right foot in the stirrup the two syces sprang away, leaving a beautiful group in the middle of the parade-ground, statuesque in the absence of movement.

It was only for a few moments, though; for, with a shrill cry of rage, the horse gathered itself together and sprang into the air, came down, reared up, plunged, flung up its heels, and then, as the rider sat perfectly firm and unmoved, tried to wrench itself round and bite—an evolution which the strong hands at the rein stopped.

"Bravo! Well done!" cried both officers in a breath.

There was another shrill neigh, and a fresh effort was made—one of the most trying for a horseman. The Arab suddenly lowered its head with a sharp snatch at the reins, arched up its back, and began a series of tremendous, buck-like leaps, coming down each time with all four legs together, ready for the next spring.

"There, it's all over," said Hulton. "He'll throw him."

"Sure as a gun," said Wyatt, while Dick bit his lip, and felt vexed with himself for feeling pleased at the prospect of the accident which seemed certain to befall the gunner.

He was a capital rider, one of the best in the troop, and had ridden many a dangerous horse, but somehow Burnouse was too much for him. At about the sixth bound his seat was shaken; at the next he was mastered; and the next sent him sliding sideways, to fall heavily on his back and roll over and over.

The two syces, who had kept close by, dashed forward, active as cats, to seize the reins, in the expectation of the horse bounding off; but, with a wild squeal, it turned and ran, open-mouthed, at its late rider, and would have seized him but for a sudden check at the reins, when it threw up its head and neighed as if proud of its triumph.

"Ugh, the beast!" muttered Captain Hulton, pressing forward with Wyatt, and closely followed by Dick, who was trembling and flushed with excitement.

"Are you hurt, Smith?" cried the captain to the man, who was brushing the dust from his uniform.

"Bit shook, sir," said the man gruffly; "nothing broke. Why," he cried fiercely, "you might just as well try to ride a ball of quicksilver!"

At that moment Sergeant Stubbs came riding up, and heard the man's last words as he bent down to knock off some dust with his gloved hand.

"I'm glad you're not hurt, Smith," said the captain. "You did very well. The brute will have to go."

"There's none of us could ride him, sir."

"You hadn't a chance, riding him like that!" cried Dick angrily, and every one turned upon him in wonder.

Then Captain Hulton made the lad flush with annoyance.

"Let's see," he said sarcastically; "I believe you learned to ride this morning, sir, did you not?"

"No," said Dick sharply. "I had my first lesson in military riding, sir, but my father taught me years ago, and there was not a finer horseman with the hounds."

"But we are not fox-hunters, Darrell," said the captain sternly.

"No, sir; but, as my father said, soldiers ride in that stiff, balanced way, and have no grip of the saddle,[1] and if a regiment was put at a stiff fence and ditch, no end would come off."

[1] This has been greatly altered now. Our cavalry ride with shorter stirrups and in better style.

"You had better give Sergeant Stubbs some lessons, Mr Darrell," said the captain haughtily, "and if they turn out satisfactory we might exchange. But I think we can ride a little out here."

"I do not profess to teach any one, sir," said Dick angrily; "but I could ride that beautiful Arab, and it would be a shame to send it away."

"You don't know what you are talking about," said Wyatt in a low voice. "Hold your tongue."

"I beg your pardon, sir," said Dick proudly; "I've ridden restive horses before now. The gunner here took him on the curb, and he has a tremendous bit in his mouth; look how he champs. I'll ride him if you'll give me leave, Captain Hulton."

"Mount, then, and show us," said the captain haughtily.

Dick started forward at once towards the horse, while the sergeant looked frowningly from one to the other, as if he could not believe his ears.

"No, no," said Wyatt warmly; "he'll break the poor lad's neck."

"No; he will only fall lightly. It will take some of the conceit out of the young puppy. It's intolerable."

"But he was hot and excited. He's only a boy. Stop it."

"I will not," said the captain angrily. "A mere cadet to come and talk to me like that on the parade-ground; it's insufferable!"

"Well, you may be answerable if he comes to grief," said Wyatt; "I wash my hands of it all."

"Silence, if you please," said Hulton; "we are not alone."

Chapter VIII
"That Young Chap's All There!"

Captain Hulton was all the time watching what was going on by the Arab, where the slight youth, full of eagerness and activity, had nearly covered his hands with foam as he loosened the tight curb-chain, which evidently worried the horse, and was nearly bitten for his pains.

Then, as he stood wiping his fingers on his handkerchief, he made one of the syces shorten the stirrups to a considerable extent.

"You are going to risk it, then?" said Wyatt.

"I don't think there is any risk," said Dick.

"You are as blind as you are obstinate, my lad," said Wyatt. "I tell you it is a terrible risk; give it up."

"It wouldn't be acting like a soldier," replied the lad earnestly. "The men are all looking on, and even if I felt afraid I shouldn't dare to back out. But I don't feel a bit afraid; and who wouldn't long to ride a horse like this?"

"I wouldn't, for one," said Wyatt. "Well, good luck to you, then, my lad; but mind, for the brute's as full of tricks as a monkey."

"I'll mind, but I wish I'd a whip instead of these spurs. That will do!" he cried sharply to the syce, who had finished altering the last buckle.—"Now, then, old fellow," he cried, going to the Arab's head and taking hold of the snaffle on either side, "it's of no use; I'm going to ride you, so none of your tricks."

The horse whinnied and threw up its muzzle as the lad resigned it to the groom. Then, without a moment's hesitation, he took up the snaffle-rein, seized his opportunity when the off-side groom made the horse sidle towards him, thrust his foot in the stirrup, and heard Wyatt utter a kind of gasp as he sprang into the saddle, while the syces darted back to avoid the coming plunge.

Every eye was fixed upon the group, and the gunner who had been thrown smiled grimly at the sergeant, as much as to say, "Wait a minute and you'll see."

The horse uttered an angry squeal as he felt himself once more backed by a stranger, and then gave himself a tremendous shake as if to dislodge saddle and rider by bursting off the girths; but, finding this of no avail, he reared up till it seemed as if he must go over backward, and repeated the action again and again. But Dick sat fast, and gave and bent as if he were, as the sergeant said, a portion of his horse.

**He reared up till it seemed as if he
must go over backward.**

"Bravo! Well done!" muttered the captain. "By George! Wyatt, the boy can ride."

"Ride!" whispered the lieutenant in husky tones. "Look at that."

For the horse, disappointed at the failure of its efforts, began once more to bound off the earth; but there was no better result, the young rider bending and giving like a cane, but always sitting slightly bent forward as the beautiful creature made another of its graceful bounds.

"Well, I'm blest!" muttered the sergeant.

"He'll begin to buck directly," whispered the gunner who was using one hand to softly rub his back.

But this did not follow till a few more bounds had been made: and then it was after two or three angry squeals, the animal's back being arched, head and tail down, and feet drawn together for the necessary springs, each coming more quickly after the last, while every one who watched felt to a certainty that the rider must be thrown at the next leap, and the gunner wondered that the lad had not come off at the last.

But Dick's mettle was roused; and, in spite of being nearly dislodged, he gripped the saddle fast and gave with his steed's muscular efforts, getting fast again in his seat before the next effort.

Ten or a dozen of these mad leaps were made, the horse squealing fiercely as he bucked; but Dick was still in his seat when the Arab tossed up his head again, swerved to his right, and, laying himself out like a greyhound, went off at speed along the parade-ground for the opening at the end, and with his rider sitting well down to this comparatively easy work, disappeared like a flash.

"After him, Wyatt!" cried the captain. "Poor lad! I ought not to have let him mount.—You, too, Sergeant,—Follow them, Smith."

The three set spurs to their horses in the same order as their names were uttered, and went off in single file in full pursuit, while a thrill ran along the ranks of the artillery-men, who had to hold in their horses, which participated in their riders' desire to join in the chase.

The road ran straight away from the gateway for about a mile, and then turned off at right angles to where a bridge crossed the river; and Dick soon saw that if his swift steed tried to turn and make for the bridge, going at such a racing speed, they must for certain have a mishap. He was quite cool now, felt easy in his saddle, and knew that he could keep there no matter how the pace was increased. It was wildly exhilarating, and he had to repress the desire to urge the horse on and on. He looked back, and far behind he could see the dust flying in a cloud where evidently some one was coming in pursuit; but it was only a momentary glance, and then he was looking straight ahead so as to make out his course.

This was soon done. He had only to make the horse swerve a little to his right and there was the open country, where a long stretch of closely-cut grassland parallel with the river offered good going, and over which the horse might gallop till he could pull him in.

But to reach that land there was a broad dike to cross; and if, going at such a speed, the horse failed to clear it down they must come.

There was no time for thought. The great dike had to be cleared, and not many seconds later they were flying through the air, to land on the opposite side; and the horse uttered a tremendous snort as he stretched out more, and made the wind whistle by the rider's ears as he tore on faster still.

"This doesn't seem like mastering him," thought Dick, "for he has mastered me; but I said I could ride him, and I can. I wish I knew the country so that I could make a round and take him back regularly done."

He bore gently on the rein, increasing the pull by degrees; but the horse's head was stretched straight out now, and, when it came to the hardest drag upon the reins, it had very little effect upon the swift creature, who tore along as fast as ever.

"Have your own way, then," said Dick quietly; and thoroughly enjoying the pace now, he contented himself with trying to guide his mount and avoid doubtful-looking places and jumps that were too exciting, finding, to his great delight, that the horse was amenable to the lightest touch in this direction; while, when they had raced on for about a couple of miles, he began to slacken of his own accord.

A few minutes later the horse was fully under control, yielding to every touch, and stopped short, turned, and began to canter gently back till the little party in pursuit was sighted, when, apparently tamed for the day by the run, he suffered the fine charger Wyatt rode to range up alongside, and took no heed whatever of the two which fell into rank behind.

"My dear boy," cried Wyatt hoarsely, "I've been expecting to come upon all that was left of you every minute since the brute bolted."

"Have you?" said Dick, looking at him curiously. "It was nothing; one only had to sit fast."

"Nothing? Well, perhaps you're right, but you gave us a tremendous scare."

"I'm sorry," replied Dick. "But I hope you won't have the horse sent away. I'll buy him if the price isn't too much."

"We shall be glad to let him go cheaply, but you'll never dare to ride him."

"Why not? I dared to ride him when he was quite strange to me; and, of course, when he knows and is used to me it will be quite a different thing. He only wants plenty of work and proper using.—Don't you, old fellow?" he cried, leaning forward to pat the beautiful, arched neck.—"Look, Mr Wyatt: I'm hardly feeling his mouth, and he's as quiet again."

"But the brute has such a temper."

"Don't call him names!" cried Dick merrily; and, turning, he rested his hand upon his saddle, to call back to the old non-commissioned officer behind, "I say, Sergeant, don't you think I've got on well with my riding after only one lesson!"

"You managed him wonderfully, sir!" cried the sergeant; "but I can't have you riding in the troop like that. You looked like a jockey at a race, with his shoulders right up to his ears."

"That's complimentary," cried Dick. "Never mind; you shall teach me to ride with my shoulders down.—I say, you," he continued to the gunner; "I hope you are not much hurt!"

"Forgot all about it, sir. Had something else to think about."

"Why, the horse seems to like you on his back," said Wyatt after they had been cantering steadily enough for a time.

"I hope he does," said Dick. "I like to be there."

"Walk!" shouted Wyatt, and the four horses dropped into the quiet pace at once, being kept to it till they came in sight of the great gateway, outside which a vedette was stationed ready to turn their horses and pass in.

"Gone to report our coming. They won't need to send an ambulance, my lad," said Wyatt. "Look here, Darrell, you've done something to-day, and I want Hulton to see what you can do. You ride on two lengths ahead, and go in first at a walk."

"No, no; it will look so foolish."

"Obey orders!" cried Wyatt sternly. Then, changing his tone from the military to the friendly, "It may mean the keeping of the Arab for you if Hulton sees that you really can manage him." Then aloud, "Forward. Trot."

Dick had gone on to the front, and at the word the horses increased their pace.

"Give him a word or two, Stubbs," said Wyatt, reining in a little so that the sergeant and gunner could come up level; and the sergeant shouted:

"Don't bump your saddle, Mr Darrell. Elbows back, sir; heels down; drop your right hand, and ride with the horse."

Dick stiffened himself directly, and rode in through the gateway in regular military style, falling into it naturally, but flushing uncomfortably as he saw at a glance that the troop was drawn up as he had left it, and the captain, with the trumpeter behind, sat motionless on his horse.

Dick rode on straight for his commanding officer, the Arab going over the ground as if he hardly touched it with his hoofs; and the next moment discipline was forgotten, every man on the parade-ground bursting forth into a tremendous cheer which nearly drowned Wyatt's loud "Halt!"

The next moment Hulton had ridden up to the young subaltern's side.

"I congratulate you, Mr Darrell," he said quietly. "I suppose you would like to keep your mount?"

"Oh, yes, sir," said Dick eagerly.

"You had your riding-lesson this morning?"

"Yes, sir."

"And you seem to have given us one since. Believe me, I am very glad you are not hurt. Give the horse up to the syces now."

He made a sign, and the two white-clothed grooms hurried up, showing their teeth and glancing admiringly at one who was evidently about to be their new sahib.

But they were not alone, for unconsciously the lad had made himself the hero of the hour, gunners and drivers to a man subscribing to the dictum that a youngster who could ride Morrison's horse like that was made of the right stuff for the troop.

"Yes," grunted the oldest corporal, who was considered a judge; "he isn't much more than a schoolboy, but that young chap's up to the mark."

Chapter IX
A Boy at Home

Dick did it as modestly as he could, and his words were as simple and natural as a boy's need be, when he was questioned at the mess-table about his ability to ride and knowledge of horses; but it all had to be dragged out of him in replies to questions.

"Oh," he said, "I had something to do with horses for so long a time back. I must have been quite a tiny little fellow when my father used to take me up before him, and set me astride on his horse's neck. I remember that the scrubby mane used to tickle my legs dreadfully. And I often toddled into the stable to feed the horses with fresh grass. My mother used to be frightened, but my father said the horses would not trample on me; and they never did. They used to reach down to look at me with their great eyes, and blow into my neck."

"So that you became quite used to horses very early?" said the captain.

"Oh, yes; I never remember feeling afraid of a horse."

"Your father kept good ones?" said Wyatt.

"Splendid ones to go, but he was only a country practitioner, fond of hunting, and he never gave much for one, I should say; but he was always one of the first flight in a run."

"And he taught you to ride quite early?" said the captain.

Dick looked at him with rather a puzzled air.

"I don't think he ever taught me," said the lad thoughtfully. "He used to tell me to stick in my knees and hold tight. I rode so much that it came natural."

"What was the first horse you had?" said Wyatt.

"It was a donkey."

"A bull, Darrell!"

"No, no!" cried Dick, laughing; "but I had many a ride on the old bull at the farm close by. You have to keep your balance there, for your legs are stretched out, and you can't hold on with your knees."

"But you couldn't go to the hunt on a donkey," said Wyatt.

"Oh, but I did for two years; but then it was something like a donkey!" cried Dick, warming up with his old recollections. "He had a horrible temper, and he'd kick and bite, and try to wipe you off by rubbing against posts or walls; and when that wouldn't do he used to squeal something like these Arab horses, and lie down and roll over and over."

"What did you do then?" asked Wyatt.

"I waited till he got up and jumped on again."

"A nice brute for a hunter."

"He was," said Dick, growing excited. "As soon as he found that he couldn't go back to the field, he'd give in and canter off. The worst of it was, he used to spoil the saddles so with rolling. But you should have seen him go."

"Donkeys do go," said the captain dryly; "they've a pace of their own."

"Oh, yes," said Dick; "but old Thistle used to go after the pack like a greyhound. He was thin-legged and light, and he could jump like a buck; and when a hedge was too big he'd scramble up the bank, squeeze through, leap down, and be off again. We used to go over and through places which plenty of the gentlemen on their big hunters wouldn't tackle. It used to be capital fun."

"Ever have any falls?" said Wyatt.

"Oh, lots; but I never used to get much hurt. I didn't mind. Old Thistle came down with me once in a ditch, and rolled over me. He broke my arm, though."

"Father mend it?"

"Oh, yes; it soon grew together again. When I was bigger I had a pony; but he was never so fast as the donkey, and couldn't keep up so long."

"Indeed?"

"Nothing like it. That donkey would keep up to the end of a long run, and when it was over, and his saddle was off, he'd just have a roll and be ready to go on again."

"After the pony came a horse, I suppose," said the captain.

"I never had one of my own, but my father had a large practice and had to go very long distances. He always kept three horses, and I could have one of them whenever I liked. I used to ride round with him to visit his patients. He never cared about riding then. He had all the accidents to attend that happened at the hunt."

"How was it you didn't turn doctor?" said Hulton.

"Wanted to be a soldier," said Dick shortly. "I used to want to have a commission in the cavalry; but my father said he had no interest to get me a commission, and I must go to the Company's college at Addiscombe, and fight my way up so as to get into the horse brigade."

"And you were a lucky fellow to get appointed so soon."

"Yes; but my father knew Sir George Hemsworth, and he promised to help me if I could show a good set of testimonials from Addiscombe."

"And I suppose you did?" said Captain Hulton.

"I don't know," replied Dick quietly. "I tried all I could; but I was dreadfully disappointed to find I had to go into the foot artillery first."

"Thought you ought to have been appointed to the command of a troop of horse right off—eh?" said the captain.

Dick shook his head.

"I wasn't quite so stupid as that, sir," he said quietly.

"No, that you wouldn't be, Darrell," said the captain, smiling. "Well, I'll tell you something. We were dreadfully disappointed when we found Sir George had interested himself in your being appointed to our crack troop, and Wyatt, there, said it was an abominable shame for some pampered scrap of a boy to be put into an important place, when hundreds of clever, experienced officers would have been glad to have such a feather in their caps."

"Here I say—gently!" cried Wyatt, who had sat at the table staring. "I didn't say that it was you."

"Was it?"

"Of course it was."

"Ah, yes, you're right—I did," said the captain coolly; "but you agreed to it."

"Yes, I agreed to it all."

"But we think differently, Darrell, now we have found out what sort of a fellow you are; and I'm speaking for old Wyatt here and myself when I tell you frankly that we're very glad you've joined us, and may it be many, many years before we part."

"Oh, thank you, Captain Hulton," cried Dick warmly. "You've made me feel that I—yes, that I—I—I can't say any more."

"Nobody wants you to, my lad," said the captain warmly. "We want acts, not words. You've done a thing to-day that has won over every man in the troop, and henceforth you'll feel, I hope, that you are among friends."

"I do!" cried Dick warmly.

"You mustn't mind Wyatt. He's a queer fellow, but he means well."

"Here, I say—gently!" cried the gentleman named: but the captain went on as if no one had spoken:

"He's big and old, but he's a mere boy—not a bit older in brains than you are: but if you keep him in his place, I dare say you two will be able to get on together."

"I say, I'm not going to stand this!" cried Wyatt.

He took his friend's bantering remarks so seriously that Dick burst out laughing, making the lieutenant look annoyed for the moment; but by degrees a smile began to dawn upon his face.

"He sees the joke at last," cried Captain Hulton. Then gravely: "Look here Wyatt; I want to talk to you about that ugly business.—It will not interest you, Darrell. It is something which occurred before you joined—court-martial."

Dick took this as a hint that the matter was private, and he turned to converse with the next officer at the table—a sub-lieutenant in the detachment of foot artillery, very little older than himself.

Chapter X
His Monkey Up

The preliminaries were soon settled, and Dick was seizing every opportunity to, as he said, "go round to the stables and have a look at my horse."

But "my" horse was far from perfect, and no one knew it better than the young officer himself.

He was a keen, observant fellow, and it did not take him long to notice that Burnouse was gentle with one of the late Captain Morrison's syces, while the sight of the other was enough to make the animal roll back his eyes and bare his teeth.

Wyatt, big and old as he was, to fully justify Captain Hulton's words that he was quite a boy still, showed it by attaching himself thoroughly to his young brother-officer, treating him just as if he were of the same age.

"I used to find it so dull, Dick," he said once in confidence, "before you came. Hulton's a splendid chap, and I quite love him like a brother, but he's such a serious old cock. No fun in him for a companion. You and I are going to get on together, you know."

"I hope so," said Dick; "only I'm precious young, Mr Wyatt."

"*Mr.* Wyatt! Look here, young fellow, drop that; we're brother-officers. You're young, but you'll soon get over that. A fellow who can ride as you do, and drop into your place in the troop, with the men looking as proud of you and as smiling whenever you come on parade as if you were the very fellow they'd ride after anywhere, needn't talk about being young. Age has nothing to do with a man being a smart soldier. Look here; we're all glad you've joined, and there's an end of it."

But there was no end of Wyatt; he was always after his new brother-officer, and thoroughly enjoyed going with him to the stables to have a look at Burnouse, who, to do him justice, thoroughly hated him, and would not let him go near.

"Look here, Wyatt," said Dick one morning.

"I'm looking, old chap. What is it? He seems as fit as he can be, and as nasty-tempered as ever."

"Yes; that's what I wanted you to notice. Did you see him show his teeth then at Dondy Lal?"

"Yes—just as if he'd eat him."

"He wouldn't eat him, but he'd worry him if he could."

"Without salt," said Wyatt.

"Well, have you seen Ram Dad go to him?"

"Yes; and seen him take hay out of his hand."

"Well, what does that prove?"

"That he likes Ram Dad better than Dondy Lal."

Dick said no more, but he was uncomfortable; and, on thinking over the matter, he felt that he should like to discharge Dondy Lal, who, with his fellow seemed to have come with the horse as a matter of course, and looked upon him as his new sahib, it being considered quite natural that an officer should have plenty of servants.

But Dick felt it would be an injustice to discharge a man upon mere suspicion; and, as he could not stoop to watch, nor question the man's fellow-servant, matters remained in abeyance till fortune was kind to the horse one morning, when his master had risen extra early to go on to the riding-school for his lesson from Sergeant Stubbs.

It proved to be too soon, so Dick turned off in the direction of the officers' stables to have a look at his favourite, when the loud trampling of feet and the sound of an angry voice delivering a tirade of abuse sent a thrill through the lad, and he hurried to the door, where the suspicions he had formed that the horse was brutally ill-used were at once confirmed.

For there, close to Burnouse's stall in the half-dark stable, about a dozen of the native grooms had collected—to the neglect of the other officers' horses—to stand grinning and looking on at the scene taking place.

As Dick passed through the door into the long, gloomy place, he was just in time to see his horse rear up as high as his halter would let him and rise on his hindlegs, striking out with his fore-hoofs, and snorting angrily at Dondy Lal, who, armed with a pitchfork, was standing just out of reach, teasing the animal, and striking it with the handle of the fork on head, neck, or leg, whenever he could get a chance—sharp, cruel blows, all dexterously given, and with just sufficient force to cause pain without leaving traces for his master to see.

Dick's Hindustani was not perfect, and it was hard to make out exactly what was said amidst the jabbering and laughing; but the lad grasped enough to know that this was an exhibition got up for the amusement of the other syces, and to show how cleverly the Hindu scoundrel could torture the noble beast without getting hurt.

Dick was educated to be an officer and a gentleman, but the natural sturdy British boy in him boiled over on the instant.

"Ah, son of Sheitan, take that!" and there was a loud rap.

But it was not Richard Darrell who uttered the words in Hindustani, but Dondy Lal: and the rap was caused by the sharp application of the fork-handle across one of the forelegs which were vainly striking at the tormentor.

But there was an echo, followed by a rush and a scuffle.

The echo was caused by Dondy Lal's head striking against the wall of the stable, consequent upon Dick's charging through the semicircle of syces and delivering a fine, straightforward blow from the shoulder, backed by the weight of his body, right on the bridge of the man's nose, sending him against the wall, from whence he dropped to the floor.

If a thunderbolt, or a shrapnel-shell from a six-pounder, had fallen in the midst of the group, they could not have dispersed more quickly; and the next minute there was a loud *cissing* arising from different stalls, where men were industriously rubbing down their masters' chargers, and a sharp rattling of a bucket in the hands of Ram Dad, who trembled as he busied himself with water and brush.

"I thought so!" cried Dick savagely; and there was a loud neigh as the horse dropped upon all fours panting, and stamping with one of his hoofs. "What is it, old fellow? Have they been ill-using you? The scoundrels—the dogs!"

It looked dangerous with the horse in such an excited state, for his master went close up and began patting the netted neck and talking soothingly.

But the beautiful animal had sense enough to know friends from foes; and, as if getting rid of his anger by stamping furiously, he lowered his crest, snorted and whinnied, and submitted to his master's caress.

"You, Ram Dad!" cried Dick fiercely; "how dare you stand there and let that black scoundrel ill-use my horse?"

"Dondy Lal Ram Dad's sahib, sahib. If Ram Dad say a word, Dondy Lal hit him with the stick, and not the horse."

"You miserable coward!" cried Dick, as he went on caressing the horse and passing his hands softly down the bruised legs, with the effect of making the animal stand quite still; "why didn't you tell me?"

"Dondy Lal tells things sahib, or give Ram Dad poison. Kill Ram Dad, same as sahib kill Dondy Lal."

"What!" cried Dick, starting in alarm to gaze down at the syce, who was lying perfectly motionless by the wall, with the light from the door shining full upon his dark face, showing that the eyes were puffing up and the blood running down over his mouth, chin, and neck, to stain his white garments.

"Yes, sahib: kill, quite dead."

Dick stood gazing at his prostrate servant for a few moments quite aghast, till his strong common-sense began to teach him that such a blow as he had delivered could not have caused death; and the horrible dread which had begun to assail him passed away.

"The cowardly scoundrel is shamming," thought Dick.

"You think he's dead?" he said softly.

"Yes, sahib, quite dead. Ram Dad fess doctor?"

"No," said Dick sharply. "I'll soon see whether he's dead. Here, Burnouse!"

He rushed to the horse's head and began to unfasten the horse's head-stall, but before he could unbuckle a strap Dondy Lal uttered a cry of horror, sprang to his feet, and ran, leaving Ram Dad grinning with delight.

"Now you go on with your work," cried Dick sharply; "and if ever I find you ill-use my horse, I'll thrash you till you can't stand."

"Ram Dad never hurt the sahib's horse," protested the man. "Burnouse good friends. See."

He raised a hand to pat the horse, which gave a gentle snort.

"But you were cowardly enough to stand by and see the poor brute knocked about."

"Ram Dad never dare say a word, sahib; Dondy Lal too big man."

"Has this been going on long?" asked Dick.

"Will the sahib tell Dondy Lal?" whispered the syce cautiously, after a glance round to see whether the other grooms could hear.

"I'm never going to let him come into the stable again," said Dick between his teeth. "Now tell me."

The man nodded.

"Yes—long time. Hate Burnouse. Make him fight with stick."

"That will do. Now you go on, and mind you never strike that horse, for I should be sure to know."

Dick went back to pat the Arab, and then hurried away for his lesson.

Chapter XI
Black Bob

In the intervals of the riding, Dick told the sergeant what he had seen.

"The black, niggerly scoundrel!" growled the old soldier. "We're not supposed to strike the natives, sir, but if I'd been you I should have knocked the blackguard down—or tried to."

"I did," said Dick quietly.

"Try to, sir?"

"No; I knocked him down."

"Glad of it, sir," said the sergeant, smiling grimly. "It's a pity, though, because the scoundrel will go and talk it over with some of the meddling baboo fellows, and they'll advise him to make a complaint."

"What! after ill-using my horse?"

"Oh, he'll swear that he didn't, sir."

"But he did; and there are all the grooms who were present to prove it."

"Oh, they'll swear anything for him, sir. But don't you worry about that; only pay what's owing to the nigger and let him go.—'Tention! I wish, sir, you'd make a bit more of a try about stiffening yourself up; it's getting time you made some show."

"Why. I thought I was pretty well all right now, Sergeant."

"But you're not, sir. You give too much to your horse. You don't keep stiff. I'm having a deal of trouble with you."

"Very sorry, Sergeant, but I don't come off," said Dick, smiling.

"No, sir; I'd almost rather you did, for then you'd learn our ways quicker. I have just the same trouble with you that I had with that Bob Hanson."

"Hanson? Bob Hanson?" said Dick thoughtfully. "Isn't that the man I heard Captain Hulton talk about?"

"Yes, sir; no doubt. No man in the regiment has been more talked about than he has."

"A court-martial, wasn't there?"

"Yes, sir; and he was under punishment. A precious narrow escape he had of being flogged."

"Ugh!" ejaculated Dick. "Horrible!"

"'Tis, sir; but what are you to do with a man who will do wrong?"

"Try kindness."

"And be laughed at, sir. Tell a man who breaks out, and does everything a soldier shouldn't do, that he has been very naughty and mustn't do so any more. No, sir; that won't do."

"I know the man—fine, dark, handsome fellow."

"Well, I suppose he is good-looking; but handsome is as handsome does, sir."

"But I noticed him particularly yesterday when we marched out."

"Very likely, sir," said the sergeant gruffly; "and I noticed you."

"Well, of course you would."

"Sitting all of a heap in your saddle like a wet monkey, sir."

"Get out! I was not!" cried Dick indignantly.

"You weren't sitting like a soldier, sir. It made me wild to see it, after the pains I took with you, walloping about in your saddle just as if you were at home in quarters rolling in an arm-chair."

"But we were riding easy," cried Dick.

"I wasn't, sir. I was riding downright uneasy, and as if the saddle was stuffed with thorns. I like a man to rest himself in a long ride, but I don't like him to forget that he's a soldier."

"No; you want us all to be as stiff as if we had been starched, Stubbs."

"Well, sir, it looks soldierly, and makes the natives look up to you. You see, we're such a handful to all the millions and millions here, that I think we English ought always to be seen at our best. But, 'tention! We'll have that gallop again, sir. You don't sit up as I should like to see you yet, sir."

"That'll come in time, Stubbs. Your way always makes me feel unsafe in the saddle."

"That's because you haven't drilled enough. Now then, sir. Forward at a walk—trot—gallop!" shouted the sergeant so that the rafters rang; and the old horse used for the lessons went round the building at full speed five times before the command "Halt!" was called.

"Hah!" exclaimed the sergeant, with a loud expiration of the breath and a grim smile showing on either side of his heavy moustache; "how long have I had you drilling, sir?"

"Just a month, Stubbs."

"Yes, just a month. I don't flatter people, sir."

"You just don't, Stubbs," said the young officer. "You've bullied me sometimes as if I were a raw recruit."

"Oh, that's my way, sir, to force the teaching home; but I hope I've always been respectful to a young officer I felt proud to teach."

"Ah, well, suppose we call it respectful, Stubbs. You've worked me precious hard."

"All for your good, sir: all for your good. Look at the consequences. As I say, I never flatter anybody. I wouldn't, even if I was teaching one of a king's sons. But I do say this, that I'm proud of you, sir. I never saw a beginner do that gallop better than you've just done yours."

"Then I can pass now, I suppose?"

"Oh, no, sir, not yet. You've got the right form, but if I don't keep you at it you won't grow stiff in it. You'll begin to bend and bulge and dance about in your saddle again. Wait a bit."

"Oh, very well, I suppose I must; but it comes hard when I know I could challenge any man in the troop to sit an awkward horse."

"Oh, yes, I dare say, sir; but that's just sticking on—it isn't riding like a soldier."

"Have it your own way, Sergeant. But, I say, what about that fellow Hanson? He rides splendidly."

"Yes, sir—now. When he first joined he could stick on a horse well enough, but he always seemed to be reaching forward to see what was between his trooper's ears."

"He always looks to me the smartest soldier in the troop."

"That's just what he is, sir."

"But you speak in a way that sounds as if you meant he was the worst."

"And that's just what he is, too, sir," said the sergeant, with a chuckle.

"Best and worst! Then I suppose one must strike the happy medium, and go half-way."

"Well, you see, Mr Darrell, it's like this: as far as smartness and cleverness, and being well up in his drill, and a thorough good soldier, goes, Bob Hanson would, if marks were given, take the prize. But if the prize was given for a man being the most out-and-out scamp—as big a blackguard as ever stepped—there isn't a man in the whole brigade, as far as I know, as could hold a candle to him. There isn't a man in the troop as has such a bad report against him. He's had twice as much punishment to get through as half-a-dozen of the other rough ones; and it's got so bad that if he don't look out he'll find himself tied up to the triangles some fine morning, stripped to the overalls, and a chap standing by him with the cat."

"Ugh!" ejaculated Dick. "Horrible!"

"That's right, sir; it is horrible. I don't like it, and the officers hate it; but, as I said before, what are you to do with a man as will ask for it? We must have discipline."

"Oh, but imprisonment, or bread and water."

"What does he care for imprisonment, sir? He just lays himself out for a long snooze; and as for bread and water, he told his comrades that it did a man good, and he was better than ever when he came out of the cells the other day. Oh, the officers have tried everything with him, because he really does behave well in action. One feels as if one would like the whole battery to be made up of Black Bobs; but as soon as the fighting's over, back he goes to his old ways."

"But he looks so well."

"There isn't a better set-up man in the army, sir, and that's why the officers have let him off scores of times when other lads would have been punished."

"What a pity!"

"Pity, sir? It makes me wild with the fellow. I've done everything a non-com could to one of his men. I've spoke kindly and praised him, and held him up often as a sample of what a soldier should be to the other men; but you don't catch me doing it again."

"Why not?" said Dick. "I'm sure kindness is sometimes better than severity."

"Sometimes, sir; but it isn't in this case, and I found I'd made a regular fool of myself."

"What! by trying kindness with the man?"

"No, sir; but by speaking like that 'fore the others. The lads were all drawn up in line, and as soon as I had held Black Bob up as a sample, a big grin began at one end of the line and ran along it to the other. But there—I've done with him now. I began being kind to him because I thought he meant to make himself a good soldier, but it was of no use. So I tried bullying; but you might as well bully a stone image in one of the Hindu temples. You'd do just as much good. I will say this, though: if I was in a tight corner with a lot of the enemy about me, I wouldn't wish for a better comrade to back me up. Fight? Yes, he just can!"

"It is a pity, for he doesn't seem to be a common man."

"Not he, sir. He's been a gentleman, that's what he has been. Lets out Latin and Greek and furren languages. Knows more Hindustani than any man in the troop; and writes such a hand that they wanted him to be under the adjutant—but they were sick of him in two days. He's one of those fellows as have kicked over the traces at home, just when the team was at full gallop, tangled his legs, and come down quelch! And him being a leading horse, he brings the whole team down atop of him, and upsets the gun and the limber, and then there's a row. His commanding officer comes down upon him savage for not minding how he rode; and when his officer has done, every one who has been hurt begins, and the next thing he hears is that he's to be tried by court-martial—sociable court-martial, you know, sir, as he wasn't in the army then. No, that's wrong; not sociable—social. That's it. Then there's all the evidence gone through, and every one comes to the same way of thinking—that he isn't a fit man to ride in the team again—and they drive him out. They've done with him; and after they've cut off his buttons and facings, they send him about his business."

"Yes, I understand," said Dick; "he lost caste with his friends."

"That's it, sir; just as a nigger does out here. Then, you see, sir, as there's nothing else for him to do, he does a wise thing—he goes to Charing Cross or King Street, enlists in the Honourable the East Indy Company's service, goes through his facings at Warley, and then comes out here to be picked out for this troop; and it always seemed to me that it was the wisest thing a young man could do when he'd gone wrong through being high-spirited and not able to hold himself in. He can't manage himself, so he comes into a service where he's managed and taught how to behave himself, and has the chance to rise to an officer and a gentleman again."

"Could one of the privates rise to a commissioned officer, Sergeant?"

"Of course, sir, if he has it in him. Look at me. I've rose to sergeant-major, and I'm not a fool. I know I shall get no farther, because I'm only a common man who never had much schooling. But here's Black Bob, born a gentleman; he's got breed and learning, and the look of an officer. He has the ways, too, of a man meant by nature to order and lead other men. If he'd set to, there was nothing to prevent him rising to be a general. But, instead of trying to make up for the past, he settles down to being a blackguard; and when a gentleman has made up his mind to that, he makes the blackest sheep you can breed. He's so clever, and knows so much, that your everyday Tom or Jack's nothing to him. Doesn't matter what sort of scamps they are, they are reg'lar lilies to your gentleman. No, sir; I've done with Black Bob. He's past cure; but he's a good soldier when it comes to a fight, and that's all I can say for him."

"It sounds very, very bad, Stubbs."

"Horrid, sir. I've only one hope for him."

"What's that?" said Dick sharply.

"That one of these days he'll come to his end in a big fight when he's at his best."

"At his best?"

"Yes: doing one of those things as would have brought him promotion over and over again if he'd been any one else. I've known him go along full charge at a dozen to cut a comrade out. I've known him bring a wounded chap out of a tight corner with the bullets rattling about like hail, haul him up across his horse, and gallop back. I've known him jump down to give up his horse to save his officer; and I don't know how many times we've give him up for a dead un on the field, cut to pieces as we've thought, and he's turned up again all right. Fight? There isn't a man like him in the army when there's work on the way. He saved me being cut up one day in a scrimmage, when we were surprised and surrounded by a lot of those ghazee chaps with their long knives, and hadn't had time to limber up and gallop off. I never forgot that, sir, and I've stood between Master Bob and punishment many a time when I'd have given other fellows away."

"Then he can't be a bad man, Stubbs," cried Dick earnestly.

The sergeant chuckled.

"What are you laughing at?" cried Dick sharply.

"I was only thinking, sir."

"Thinking? Of what?"

"Of you, sir. You've reg'larly seemed to tame a horse as none of us could manage; you'd better see now if you can't break in Black Bob."

"I will," cried Dick, "if ever I have a chance."

"Then I wish you joy of your job, sir," growled the sergeant, pulling out an old silver watch from his fob by means of a steel chain. "And here have I been chattering like an old woman for a good half-hour over your time for a lesson, and the trumpet will be blowing directly for the men's breakfast. Dis—mount!—Here, run that trooper to the stables," he cried to the syce waiting.—"Morning, sir. Hope you'll make another man of Bob Hanson."

Dick nodded shortly, and strode thoughtfully away to his quarters. But his thoughts were not of the welcome morning meal, nor of meeting Wyatt, with whom he was to make arrangements for joining in the exciting sport which goes by the butcherly title of "pig-sticking"—an ill-chosen name for dashing charges with a lance at one of the fiercest animals of the Indian plains. But the coming hunt, the wild excitement in anticipation, and the wonder whether he would be able to handle his spear without bringing upon him the derision of his friends, all fell into abeyance, so full was he of the account the sergeant had given of the black sheep of the troop.

"It seems to have taken away my appetite," he said to himself at last. "Why, I've got Black Bob on the brain."

Chapter XII
Wyatt's Sermon

A second month had seemed to fly since Dick had joined his troop. There was so much to do. At the end of the first month he was in the thick of all the drill-practice, and playing his part well, for he picked up the cavalry evolutions and gun-practice with ease, winning plenty of praise from his brother-officers, while the men were delighted with the young subaltern, and had a bright look for him whenever he rode up to his place.

It was hard work, too—wild galloping over rough ground, with the guns and limbers behind their teams, bumping and leaping as the troop tore along, with the horses literally racing to some point of vantage. Then the bugle would ring out, the horses would stop pretty well all together, the men leap from the saddles, and the gunners dismount from their horses, which were held by their companions; then with amazing celerity the gun-trails would be unhooked, swung round in this direction or in that, to go into action, loaded and fired—with blank-cartridge, of course. Then the trumpet sounded, the trails were hooked on again, the men leaped back to their places, the trumpet rang out once more, and away they went, raising a cloud of dust as they dashed along, the wonder to Dick being that so few accidents occurred, for the officers, as a rule, made a point in practice of riding for the roughest ground.

"Nothing like it, Dicky," said Wyatt one day when, after a long series of dashes here and there, a halt was called, and the men sat at ease wiping their streaming faces. "We've got to be prepared for everything and to go anywhere."

"That we can," said Dick, who had been wildly excited by the gallop.

"That we can!" said Wyatt, his face assuming an air of disgust. "There's a pretty sort of a fellow! Our troop would go anywhere."

"That it could," said Dick shortly.

"Well!" ejaculated Wyatt—and again, "Well! this is a smack in the face. I shall have to tell Hulton. Here have I been priding myself on our having broken you in to our ways, and made a gunner of you that we could be proud of, and you talk like that."

"I don't see anything wrong in what I said," said Dick wonderingly.

"Don't you? Then I do. It's very evident that you have not half learned your duty yet. Look here, my lad. We are emergency men, expected to go wherever our general orders, and we do it."

Dick laughed.

"Worse and worse! Here, I give you up, Dick."

"Nonsense! Suppose, the enemy was on the other side of a deep river. We couldn't get through that."

"We should, somehow."

"But we couldn't. The guns would sink, and the cartridges be spoiled."

"Like your new uniform."

"Shouldn't be wearing it to fight in," said Dick.

"But look here; we should make for the nearest bridge or ford."

"Suppose there was none," said Dick.

"Bah! I shan't suppose anything. I tell you we should go anywhere. I'm not going to chop logic with you—you argumentative little beggar."

"Then, again, we couldn't charge a fort or stone walls."

"No, but we'd close up and batter them down. Look here, young fellow; you're one of us now, and what you've got to believe is that our troop of horse artillery can do anything, and do it."

"Oh, all right," said Dick merrily: "I'll try. I suppose we've done for to-day. I'm hot and tired."

"Rubbish!" cried Wyatt. "We're never hot and tired. Always ready's our motto. Talk like that after a field-day! What would you do if we went into action?"

"I don't know; get so excited, I suppose, that I shouldn't have time to think."

"Of course you would. And now, look here; I'll tell you something if you promise not to chatter about it."

"I don't chatter; but I'll promise. What is it?"

"There's something on the way."

"Is there? What—war?"

"Oh, we don't call our little fights wars, and I can't tell you what is coming off, but Sir George dropped a hint to Hulton that he was to see that we were in perfect readiness."

"Well, we always are."

"Yes; but to be on the *qui vive* as to ammunition, tents, baggage, and provender."

"Oh!" ejaculated Dick, and his eyes kindled as he sat there upon a knoll with his troop, gazing round at the two or three native regiments, a squadron of cavalry, and the foot artillery and their heavy guns, which had taken part in the field-day.

"It may be only a false alarm," said Wyatt, "but I thought you'd like to know; only you mustn't begin to howl about feeling hot and tired if we have any real work to do, nor yet think about running away."

Dick bit his lip, and then said huskily, "Am I likely to feel disposed to run away?"

"Perhaps so, the first time."

"Did you?"

"What?" cried Wyatt fiercely, as he turned upon the calm, imperturbable face looking in his. "Did you mean that as an insult, Mr Darrell?"

"No," said Dick, his eyes twinkling with mischievous exultation. "Did you?"

"Got me!" said Wyatt, shaking his head and chuckling softly. "Hist! look out. Here comes the general."

Captain Hulton gave the word, and in an instant the men were rigid in their saddles, with the line as regular as if they were on parade, for a little knot of horsemen came cantering up, the general and his staff a short distance behind.

He drew rein in front of the troop, and sat talking to the captain for a minute, and then walked his horse slowly along the line, keenly examining everything.

At the end of the line he turned and rode back, and this time Dick, who had often felt annoyed at the want of recognition on the part of his father's old school-fellow and friend, flushed with pleasure, for Sir George checked his horse.

"Ah, Mr Darrell," he said quietly, "you there! Getting used to the rough work?"

"Yes, Sir George."

"That's right. You seem to have a good mount. — How do, Mr Wyatt?"

He backed his horse a few yards, stopped, and raised his voice so that the whole troop could hear:

"Very good indeed, my lads. Capital."

Then he turned his horse and rode away, followed by his staff.

"He didn't say much," said Dick in a low tone.

"Soldiers never do say much," replied Wyatt; "but I never heard him say so much before. My word! Old Hulton will be pleased."

"I say, though: do you really think there is something on the way?"

"Yes. Are you sorry?"

"Sorry? No. I shall be delighted. It will be such a change."

"Yes," said Wyatt dryly, "it will be a change; so make the most of your comfortable quarters while you can. Next week you may be sleeping on a heap of stones after a supper of nothing to eat and a pannikin of dirty water."

Chapter XIII
Hanson Plays the Fool

But the weeks rolled by without change, save that Dick felt himself quite at home in the troop, and was able to hold his own with the rest.

He had more than once asked Wyatt if there was any fresh news, invariably to receive a shake of the head and the reply:

"One never knows."

Sergeant Stubbs had reported his pupil as having passed well through the riding-school routine; and this was the principal thing he had to master, for he had come out from college a trained soldier, and his year in a company of foot artillery had prepared him well for his new appointment.

"I shall be glad when we get away from this constant drilling," said Dick one morning, with a yawn. "I don't think I want to fight, but I should like for us to be going to some of the big cities, so that one could see the rajahs with their grand show and jewellery. I've been out here in India all this time, and seen so little. I say, Wyatt, that was all nonsense about our being ordered up-country."

"Perhaps so; one never knows. You'll see enough some day if you wait patiently," continued Wyatt; "and after you've seen a rajah sitting like a figure of Buddha, dressed up in muslins and cloth of gold, and flashing with diamonds, in his howdah, you'll think what a stupid old woman he looks, and be ready to bless your stars that you weren't born a rajah or nawab or gaikwar out here, but an English gentleman, which, after all, is the finest title under the sun."

"Oh, I don't know," said Dick slowly; "there's something very attractive in show."

"Can't be very comfortable to be going about dressed like a woman."

"I shouldn't dislike one of their jewelled swords."

"Tchah! Our service-blade is worth a hundred of them. Why, there's no grip to them; and as to the jewels, they must be always getting knocked out of the settings. All very well to have under a glass case. I say, did you hear about your friend the Black Diamond?"

"Bob Hanson? Yes," said Dick gloomily. "I was in hopes that he was turning over a new leaf."

"Not he."

"It's having leave to go out in the native quarters and getting that abominable arrack. That dose of cells ought to set him right again. Let's see; he was out again this morning, wasn't he?"

"Oh, yes," said Wyatt derisively; "he was out again last night. Haven't you heard?"

"Heard? Heard what?"

"Oh, of course: you went with Hulton to the Forty-fifth mess last night, and wouldn't know."

"Know what?" said Dick impatiently. "I never did know any one so slow at telling a story. Is this one?"

"Gently, young fireworks," said Wyatt coolly, "and I'll tell you. Black Bob was to have been out this morning, sober and wise after his last escapade. But he must have had some spirits smuggled in through his cell window, I expect; for, instead of waiting patiently, he must let the stuff get into his head; then he watches his chance, and after knocking at his cell and getting the sentry to open, knocks him down, and makes a bolt of it."

"Oh, the fool, the fool!" cried Dick angrily.

"Good boy," said Wyatt: "strong, but just. That's just what he is."

"But has he broken barracks?"

"Not he, my dear boy. The sentry objected to being knocked down, so he sat up and fired his carbine."

"He hasn't shot the man?"

"Not he. I dare say he felt savage. Being knocked down hurts a fellow; but, with all his blackguardism, the boys like Black Bob because of the way in which he can fight. Lots of them know how he stands by them in a scrimmage. The sentry only fired his carbine; then the sentry at the gate fired and turned out the guard, and my lord was caught."

"Did he go buck quietly to the cell?" asked Dick.

"Did he do what?" cried Wyatt, bursting into a roar of laughter. "You should go and look at the guards' uniforms. Tattered, dear boy, tattered. The leg of one fellow's overalls was torn right up from bottom to top, another had his jacket dragged off, and two men have got pairs of the most beautiful black eyes you can imagine."

"Tut, tut, tut!" ejaculated Dick.

"Oh, yes, he went very quietly back to the cells, but they had to sit on him first, three of the lads, for about half-an-hour till he cooled down; and then they had to give him the frog's march—four of them to carry him like on springs, while four more marched alongside, ready to jump on the frog if he tried to hop."

"I never saw that done," said Dick; "they each take a wrist or an ankle, don't they?"

"That's it, Dicky, and turn him face downward; and its wonderful how a fellow like that can kick out just like a frog, and drive the bearers here and there. But they got him back safe to his cell, and pitched him in. He's a beauty! Aren't you proud of him?"

"It's disgraceful!" cried Dick angrily. "Did he hurt the men much?"

"Can't give fellows black eyes without hurting 'em," replied Wyatt, swinging his big legs about as he sat on the table; "but the boys don't bear him any malice for that. What they don't like is having their uniforms damaged."

"What will happen now?"

"Master Bob will have to take the heroic remedy reserved for bad boys."

"What do you mean?"

"Pussy," said Wyatt, twisting his abundant moustache.

"The cat? Flogging?"

"That's it, and serve the beggar right. And if that does no good, we shall have to make him a present of his uniform and his liberty after a pleasant little musical ceremony, but his buttons and facings will be cut and stripped off. Don't like it, though. Looks so bad before the native troops. I'd rather they put him out of his misery at once."

"What! shoot him?" cried Dick, with a look of horror.

"Yes; the poor beggar's irretrievably bad. It would be a soldier's death. Better for him than letting him go on disgracing himself, his corps, and the position of the British army out here."

"It's very, very horrible," said Dick sadly.

"So it is, dear boy; but what can we do? As I've told you before, he has been let off no end of times. Ah, there goes Hulton to have Master Bob haled up before him. Ta-ta."

Dick waited anxiously for the result of the military, magisterial examination of the previous night's incident, and in due time he encountered Wyatt again.

"Well?" he said anxiously.

Wyatt laughed.

"Oh, they're giving him another trial."

"They're not going to flog?"

"No. Double allowance of cells, and the doctor is to take him in hand. The poor beggar must be a bit off his head, I suppose. Diachylon says, though, he's as right as any man in the troop."

"Who's he?" asked Dick wonderingly.

"Old Sticking-plaster—the doctor. So Bob's got off again. Bread and water. Not savoury fare. The water's so bad."

An hour later Dick encountered the sergeant striding along, making the wind whistle with his big silver-mounted riding-whip, while his spurs jingled loudly.

He halted and saluted as Dick drew near.

"Heard about Black Bob, I suppose, sir?" he said.

"Yes, Stubbs; it's a bad business."

"Bad isn't the word for it, sir. Wish to goodness he'd desert."

"What? Why, his punishment would be ten times worse," cried Dick.

"Yes, sir," said the sergeant, twisting up his fierce mustachios; "much worse."

"Then why do you wish that?"

"Well, sir, between you and me, you can't punish a man till you catch him."

"No; but he would be sure to be caught."

"India's a big place, sir," said the sergeant.

"Of course it is, but no English soldier could hide himself without being caught sooner or later."

"Depends upon them as is looking for him, sir."

"What? Oh, I see, you mean that the men wouldn't try to find him."

"That's it, sir. I believe the boys would all go blind when they went after him, and come back time after time to report that they hadn't seen him."

"They wouldn't find him, then?"

"That's it, sir; and the officers wouldn't say anything. They don't want to punish the men."

"Of course not, unless they are obliged."

"Of course, sir. They want the whole of the troop to shine as bright as their helmets and buttons before the people here. It's our character that carries everything. You've seen, sir, how the authorities, from the Governor-general downward, encourage the officers and men in their sports as well as the fighting, pig-sticking, hunting, and tiger-shooting, and the rest of it. They like the native princes and the people to think that there's no one like an Englishman, and that makes 'em contented with being ruled over by us. There's a tiger killing the poor women and children about a village, and the Hindu chaps run away. English officer hears of it, and he gets up a hunt. Perhaps he rides on an elephant; perhaps he walks the brute down, and shoots him. Don't matter what it is, we're there—the best riders and the most daring over everything; while, when it comes to one of our little wars, and a rajah brags that he's going to drive us out of the country, he collects his thousands, and comes to drive us; and the general laughs, sends a hundred or so of us, and we drive him. 'Tain't brag, sir; we do it. We've done it again and again, and before long you'll be seeing for yourself."

"Ah!" cried Dick eagerly. "Then you've heard news?"

"Only rumbles, sir. There's a storm brewing somewhere, but it hasn't broke. But you may make sure of one thing; that sooner or later we shall have one: so, if I was you, I'd give orders to the armourer to grind my sword up to the finest edge and point."

Dick nodded, and looked thoughtful.

"That's a thing, sir, that we neglect, and the natives don't. An Indian's proud of his sword, and gets it made of the finest steel. Why, a man might almost shave with some of the tulwars they wear. I think Government ought to see that we have as good, but it don't."

"Where do you think the war will be, Stubbs?" said Dick.

"Don't know, sir. Haven't an idea. I only feel that there really is something coming."

"With real fights instead of sham, Stubbs?"

"That's it, sir; and that's why I want to see you carrying sword that isn't all show."

Chapter XIV
Out of his Cage

The first thing Dick did on retiring to his quarters that night was to take his sword out of its case and admire its appearance once more. The next, to draw it and hold it close to the lamp, about which the night-moths were buzzing and a mosquito was sounding its miniature cheerful horn.

The brightly-burnished blade flashed in the soft, mellow light, and Dick thought it was very beautiful; but now, for the first time, it struck him that it was shockingly blunt.

He was devoted to his profession, and proud of being a soldier, but he had never had a bloodthirsty thought. But now a fresh train of ideas had been started by the old sergeant's words. That beautiful, specklessly-bright blade, with its damascening, was meant to cut; and it was perfectly plain that, though it might have divided a pear or a pumpkin with a very vigorous blow, it would not cut it; while, as to the result of a thrust with the point, its effect would have been almost *nil*.

The idea seemed rather horrible—that of cutting flesh, or running an enemy through; but Dick felt that it was too late to think about such things as that. He was a soldier, and he had his duty to do.

And besides, in all the sword-exercise and fencing, he had been most carefully taught to look upon his sword as a weapon of defence as well as of offence.

"If we come to fighting at close quarters at any time, I've got to take care of myself," thought the lad, "so you'll have to be sharpened up."

He was in the act of sheathing his blade, and had it half back in the scabbard, when the report of a carbine rang out across the barrack-yard.

Clang! went the sabre as the hilt was driven home, and, quick as thought, the young officer began to buckle on the belt; but before he had raised it to his waist another carbine raised the echoes of the place, the shouting for the guard to turn out followed through the open window, and, as soon as the belt was fastened, Dick caught at his sword, hooked it up, put on his cap, and hurried down.

"That you?" cried Wyatt from out of the darkness.

"Yes. What's the matter? Enemy?"

"Enemy! Nonsense! Black Bob again for a tenner."

The lieutenant was right, as they found after doubling to the cells. The prisoner had broken out again after once more outwitting the sentry and knocking him down: and, worse still, they found on reaching the gateway, where a sergeant, along with the guard, was standing with a couple of lanterns, that the sentry had been knocked down there as well, and the prisoner had passed out.

Wyatt heard all this as they came up, the sergeant being engaged in bullying the second sentry with all his might.

"You might have stopped him if you had tried, you mop-headed idiot!" cried the sergeant.

"How was I to stop him?" retorted the man. "I gave the alarm."

"And let the prisoner escape. It was your duty to have fired at him," roared the sergeant. "I want to know what the officers are going to say."

"Why didn't you fire at him?" cried Wyatt angrily.

"Beg pardon, sir," replied the sentry, drawing himself up as he recognised his officer. "I'm pretty good at firing-practice with carbine and pistol."

"It doesn't seem like it, sir," said Wyatt sharply.

"I should have brought him down, sir," said the man apologetically.

"Well, that's what you were placed here for.—That you, Hulton?"

"Yes. What is it?"

"Hanson broken out and escaped."

The captain uttered an angry ejaculation, gave orders, and men with lanterns were sent in pursuit, divided into three parties, with one of which were Wyatt and Dick.

"He's gone," said the former angrily. "Hiding in the native quarter somewhere—the scamp! It's like hunting for a needle in a bottle of hay."

"Hi! Here: this way, lads," cried the sergeant in front with a lantern, by whose light Dick indistinctly caught sight of a figure in shirt and trousers rising from below in the ditch.

Then there was a scrimmage, joined in by three or four men, and the man of whom they were in search was thrown and handcuffed, a pair being conveniently handy in the sergeant's pocket.

"This is a slice of good luck," said Wyatt as soon as the prisoner was secured. "Now then, let the fellow rise, and take him back.—Get up, sir."

"Can't," growled the prisoner savagely.

"Lift him to his feet," cried the sergeant. The prisoner was dragged up, and it was noticed that he stood on one leg only.

"Here, he has been hurt," cried Dick. "Look at that leg.—What's the matter, Hanson?"

"Sprained," said the man surlily.

"How did you do that?"

"Jumping down into the ditch. You wouldn't have caught me if it hadn't been for the sprain."

"He's only shamming, sir," said the sergeant. "He can walk."

"I think not," said Dick quietly.—"You are hurt, Hanson?"

"Oh, yes, sir," said the man bitterly, "I'm hurt. Just my luck."

"Hold the lantern lower," said Dick, going down on one knee.

"Take care, sir; he'll kick you," cried the sergeant.

"Yah!" roared the prisoner, turning to the speaker savagely.

"He won't kick," said Dick coolly, bending over to take the man's ankle between his hands after turning up the trouser-leg.

"Well?" said Wyatt quickly.

"Bad sprain, and swelling up already," said Dick quietly.

"Fetch the ambulance," said Captain Hulton, who had come up on seeing the lights stationary.

"Oh, I can hop back to the cells, Captain," said the prisoner in a voice full of bravado.

"Silence, sir!"

"It strikes me, Dick," whispered Wyatt, "that he'll have to hop somewhere else before he has done."

"Carry him back to the cell," said Hulton sternly.

A couple of the guard stepped to the injured man's side.

"All right, boys," he said in a low tone. "I've got no more fight in me; I give in."

He threw his arms over the men's shoulders, and somewhat after the fashion of giving a ride in a sedan or "dandy-chair," as children call it, the prisoner was raised from the ground and borne back to his place of imprisonment.

"He ought to have a doctor directly," said Dick as he and Wyatt followed some little distance behind the party bearing the prisoner.

"Who says so?" said Wyatt.

"I do."

"And what do you know about it, chicken?"

"I know that he has fallen heavily upon his foot and given the ankle a bad wrench. It's about double its proper size now, and requires immediate treatment."

"Don't think so. It has done him good. Tamed him a bit."

"But you don't want the man to be lame?"

"Never said I did, dear boy. But what should you do?"

"Call in the doctor."

"But if there were no doctor?"

"Apply bandages and lotion at once."

"Humph! Suppose a chap had a leg taken off by a twelve-pound shot and there was no doctor, what should you do then?"

"Apply a tourniquet well on the femoral artery, and do what I could to check the bleeding."

"Humph! Suppose a fellow had a bullet through him anywhere?"

"Plug and bandage the wound."

"Sword-cut?"

"Depend on what and where it was. Most likely put in a few stitches to draw it together, and then apply strapping."

"All right," said Wyatt; "we're often right away from a doctor, and some of us get into trouble, so just you stick by me, Dick, in case I go down."

Dick laughed.

"I suppose what you say is all right."

"Oh, yes," said the lad confidently. "That is what my father would have done."

"But your father was never in a battle."

"In the battle of life every day," said Dick.

"But he never treated a man who had had his leg taken off by a shot."

"No; but he has treated poor fellows who have had their legs taken off by machines."

"Well, no sword-cuts?"

"Worse ones—made by scythes."

"I've got you this time! No holes made by bullets?"

"No: but I went with him once to see a poor fellow who had had an iron rod driven through one arm."

"Bravo, old fellow—Well, has he quieted down?" This to Hulton, who was coming away from the cell door.

"I've sent for the doctor."

Chapter XV
Wyatt's Old Father

The prisoner's injury proved to be so slight, and his conduct so bad upon his being brought before his officers and those of the other regiments in barracks, that at last it was decided that a severe punishment must now follow the many breaches of discipline of which he had been guilty; and the sentence was no more than might have been expected, for in those days there was less hesitation over meting out punishment in the army than there is now.

Dick shuddered when he heard it, and Wyatt looked at him grimly.

"No use to make a face at it, my dear boy," he said. "He deserved it, and ought to have had it a twelvemonth ago."

"Oh, yes, I dare say; but we all deserve more than we get."

"Speak for yourself, Dicky, boy. I feel particularly good; nothing more on my conscience than a general feeling of laziness, and a stone too much weight."

"But to be flogged!" cried Dick.

"Well, yes, it does sound bad, and of course it hurts; but Master Hanson has been bidding for it month after month."

"But such a degrading punishment!"

"Ye-e-es," drawled Wyatt; "but then all punishments are degrading. They are meant to be—so it seems to me."

"It seems so hateful!"

"Of course: and the man flogged won't like it. Don't suppose in the good old times men liked to be cut short with the axe and block. The moral is, don't do things which entail punishment."

"Do you often flog men in this troop?"

"My dear boy—no! I've been with it seven years, and we never did such a thing before; and we shall none of us know how to go about it. Let's see;

the drummers do it in the foot regiments. Seems a comical idea—beating a tattoo on a man's back. Ought to do it with the drumsticks."

"Don't laugh at it, Wyatt," cried Dick angrily.

"Certainly not, old fellow. But, really, we shan't know what to do. Who's to flog? The drummer can't, because we haven't got one. The trumpeter, I suppose."

"It is horrible and disgraceful."

"So it is, dear boy; but what are we to do? We don't want to lose the man, and we can't let him go on as he is going."

"It will make him worse, Wyatt, and he'll be nursing up a feeling of revenge."

"Not a nice baby, that, for a man to nurse. But I hope for better things. Do him good."

"No, no, no!"

"Don't jump to conclusions, dear boy, till the remedy has been tried. But, really, I begin to feel a good deal like my father said he did—dear old fellow!—though I never believed it before."

"What did he feel? Tell me."

"Oh, it's nothing—nothing much," said Wyatt, tugging at his big mustachios. "Your pater ever lick you?"

"Never," said Dick emphatically. "He was too fond of me."

"Of course. My father was too fond of me, you know, but he gave me a tremendous thrashing once."

"Stick?"

"Riding-whip. Hurts more."

There was a dead silence after these laconic remarks, broken at last by Wyatt drawing a long, deep breath and saying "Ha!"—making it sound twice as long as "Constantinople" uttered very slowly with a comma after each syllable.

Then Dick sighed, and said, "Oh dear!"

"Yes," said Wyatt, "I was an awful young scamp when I was a boy."

"Don't believe it," said Dick shortly.

Wyatt turned upon him quickly, and sat looking him full in the eyes for a few moments, a pleased expression gathering in his big, manly face.

Then he reached out his hand and shook his young friend's hand.

"Thank ye, Dick," he said, warmly. "I like that. Does a fellow good. But I was, you know."

"I dare say you were thoughtless and got into scrapes, played tricks, and that sort of thing; but you're such a big, honest, straightforward, manly sort of fellow, with the heart of a boy, that I can't believe you ever did anything very bad. I say, I beg your pardon, Wyatt," added Dick hastily.

"What for?"

"Speaking out so freely, and saying you were like a boy."

"I like it, I tell you. It's true enough. I'm big and old enough, but I don't feel so, Dick. Ever since you joined you seem to have been quite a companion."

"You've treated me as if I were."

"Of course I have. You see, we meet half-way. I'm a youngish sort of fellow, and you're a regular, thoughtful, old man kind of chap with plenty of brains. That's how it is, I suppose."

Dick smiled.

"No," said Wyatt thoughtfully; "setting aside bits of mischief—pranks, you know—I don't think I ever did anything very bad; but the dear old governor was down upon me once for telling him a lie. He said it hurt him more than it did me when he gave me the thrashing, but I didn't believe it then. I do now, for if Bob Hanson is flogged, I believe honestly it will hurt me more than it does him."

"Did your father ever thrash you again?" asked Dick, looking at his big friend anxiously.

"No," said Wyatt, turning away his head and beginning to whistle a march very softly and solemnly.

"What a pity! And so you told him a lie?" said Dick sadly.

"No!" thundered out Wyatt.

"Ah! you didn't?" cried Dick, leaping up to lay his hand on Wyatt's shoulder. "I am glad of that."

"Thank ye, old man," said Wyatt. "It was all a big mistake. He thought I had."

"But why didn't you tell him—why didn't you explain?"

"Stupid, proud, young fool," said Wyatt gruffly.

"What a pity!" said Dick. "But he soon knew, of course?"

"No," said Wyatt slowly, "he never knew. He came out here to India soon after in command of his regiment, and the next thing we heard—"

He stopped short, and Dick stood looking down at the back of his head, as he went on slowly whistling the march again, his companion listening in silence.

"Know that tune, Dick, old chap," he said huskily, and without looking round.

Dick nodded; he felt as if he could not speak.

"Ah, yes, of course you do," continued Wyatt, though he had not glanced round and seen the nod—it was as if he felt the sign. "It was at the storming of Ghazeebad. The dear old dad led his men through the breach, and didn't drop till the colours were planted on the top of the main works, and the boys were cheering like mad. That was the march they buried him to, Dick. The dear old dad! A braver man never stepped."

"And he never knew that it was all a mistake—that he had punished you wrongfully?"

"No," said Wyatt. "I ought to have written and told him on my word of honour that I had not told a lie. Yes, I ought to have done that, Dick, instead of feeling ill-used and proud."

He turned round as he spoke, and met Dick's eyes gazing at him wonderingly, as the lad seemed to be gaining a new reading of his big friend's character.

"There," he said, smiling sadly, "it was all a mistake;" and he added simply, "But he knows it now, Dick—the dear old dad!"

They sat together without speaking for some minutes then, and Wyatt was the first to break the silence.

"Yes," he said, "I'd give anything sooner than that poor, weak, stupid fellow should be flogged, but the big-wigs have said it, Dicky, my boy; and that isn't the worst of it."

"There is no worse," cried Dick angrily.

"Oh, yes, there is, dear boy; we shall have to go out to a grand parade and see the brutal business done."

"I won't," cried Dick fiercely.

"Yes, you will, old lad. Duty, discipline, and the rest of it."

"I'd sooner resign my commission."

"No. It's for an example to the men; it's part of the regimental rules, and we can't break them ourselves. As to throwing up your commission, I should like to catch you at it! Why, it would be playing the sneak to go and leave us in the lurch just when we're going up-country."

"Then it isn't all talk? We are going up-country?"

"I suppose so. Going to help some rajah chap whose next-door neighbour's trying to nibble away his territory, or something of that kind. Anyhow, it means fighting."

"But I can't sit there and see that man flogged, for somehow I like him, Wyatt."

"Well, it is a bad business, Dick; but duty, old fellow, duty, you know. There, don't let's talk any more about it. Only makes one feel low-spirited."

They went out for a stroll about the barracks, which meant a look in at the horses, when Burnouse acknowledged his new master's presence with a whinny whose friendly sound was spoiled by an ugly, vicious way of laying back his ears.

"Don't do that, stupid," growled Wyatt; "I'm not going to hit you with a pitchfork. Think he's better now that Dondy Lal's gone?"

"I'm sure he is," said Dick.

"That's right. Let's go and have a look at the elephants. Wonder whether we shall have them with us. I like elephants."

They strolled over to the great stables where the huge beasts were chained by one leg to short, picket-like posts, and stood swaying their heads about and writhing their trunks.

Dick's friend held out his proboscis directly, but the lad had nothing for him, and the great beast seemed to understand it and to be friendly all the same, passing the end of his soft trunk about the visitors' arms, and suffering it to be held before the pair went away.

"Yes," said Wyatt in his big, simple way, "I like elephants. Wouldn't mind keeping one for a pet, even if he ruined me for his prog. I do wish, though, they went to a better tailor's."

"Went where?" cried Dick, laughing.

"Better tailor's. Their trousers never seem to fit."

Dick and his big friend parted soon after, Wyatt having an appointment to see Hulton about some business connected with the troop, leaving Dick with two important matters to think about—the possibility of going up-country and seeing service, and the horror of the punishment to be meted out to a man in whom he could not help taking a great deal of interest. He went over these themes for some time, connecting the former with the sword that he meant to have sent to the armourer that day.

That night, when he went to bed, a fresh train of thought commenced in connection with Wyatt, and he dwelt long upon his friend's words, and the glimpse he had caught of what the man really was.

"I didn't know," thought Dick, as he dwelt long upon the sad page in the lieutenant's history, "but I began to like him directly, and I believe he began to like me. He must, or he wouldn't have been so friendly. It seems so strange, too, for we make a curious pair. I am right, though—big, brave man as he is, he is quite a boy at heart."

Dick lay thinking then, his mind back upon the punishment, and the horror of being paraded out in the open space yonder to see that horrible flogging.

"Could I do anything to stop it?" he thought, and this kept him wakeful for another hour; while, when in the silence of the hot night he did drop asleep, it was to have the imaginary scene of the preparation for the punishment all before his eyes, while he looked on, saying to himself:

"Can't I do something to stop all this?"

Chapter XVI
A Special Pleader

Dick woke up the next morning with the words at the end of the last chapter seeming to ring in his ears, just as if he had spoken them aloud.

There was early parade that morning, and some dashing evolutions were performed with wonderful accuracy, for his share in which Dick received some friendly words of praise from the captain.

"You promise to be a smart officer some day, Darrell," he said. "Keep at it, and you'll do."

At another time the young officer would have gone in to his morning meal with an extra flush upon his cheeks—one not caused by the sun; but the praise fell upon almost deaf ears on this occasion, for Dick had gone through everything quite mechanically, his mind being occupied with the trouble that was to come off, and the thought that, even if Sir George Hemsworth was the general in command of the forces in that district, he was still his father's old school-fellow and friend.

"He can only bully me," thought Dick. "I'll risk it, come what may."

"Anything the matter, old fellow?" said Wyatt over breakfast. "Not ill, are you?"

"Oh, no: bit hot and tired."

"Go and lie down after breakfast. Get flat on your back. Takes the ache out of it splendidly. Wonderfully restful."

Half-an-hour later Wyatt growled to himself as he caught sight of Dick crossing the parade-ground in the hot sun.

"Ugh! you obstinate young cub! What's the use of my trying to play father to you if you don't take my advice, eh? Now, where's he going? He can't want a walk. Why, he's going to the general's quarters. What does he want there?"

Wyatt sat thinking for a few minutes.

"Of course! I forgot. Knew the boy's father. Old man don't take much notice of him, though. Perhaps it's all right. Favouritism's bad, and George is just; I will say that. Sent for him, perhaps. Didn't tell me."

But Dick had no such thing to tell his friend, while he shrank from telling what he could have told, feeling perfectly sure that Wyatt would have tried to veto it.

Dick had, after screwing himself up to the sticking-point, gone straight across to the general's, interviewed the aide-de-camp on duty, sent in his card, and the officer came out to say Sir George would see him as soon as he had finished a letter.

The letter must have been a very brief one, for before the aide-de-camp and the visitor had got half into an account of the slaying of a wild boar with spears the general's bell was heard.

"That's for you, Mr Darrell," said the staff officer, "*entrez!*"

Dick went in, and the keen-eyed, grey-haired gentleman in white, seated at his writing-table, rose and shook hands.

"How are you, Richard Darrell?" he said. "You are growing much like what your father was as a boy. Hah!"

He paused for a few moments, looking at the young man thoughtfully. Then he was the stern, businesslike officer again.

"Now, Mr Darrell," he said gravely, "you wished to see me on particular business. As few words as you can, please, for I am much occupied over despatches from up the country. What is it—a petition?"

"Yes, Sir George," said Dick, speaking with military precision; "I have come to beg that Private Robert Hanson of my troop may not be flogged."

The general frowned, and stood looking at the young officer sternly; but Dick's eyes did not for a moment blench.

"This is a strange application, Mr Darrell," said the general sternly—"an extremely young subaltern applying to me, his general officer, to alter the sentence pronounced, after a proper trial, upon a man who for a long period has gone on breaking the regulations of the service. It is a most unheard-of proceeding on the part of a young officer."

"Yes, sir," said Dick: "I feel that. I know it is, but I do not come to you as the general in command, but as my father's old school-fellow and friend."

"Your father's old school-fellow and friend has nothing to do with the matter, sir," replied Sir George sternly. "It is the officer in command here who has signed and approved of the sentence. Young man, I never allow friendship to bias my duty to the Government who have trusted me."

"Of course not, Sir George."

"Then why did you come to me as your father's friend?"

"Because I was young and ignorant, Sir George, I suppose, and in my eagerness to save that poor fellow."

"Exactly. You are young and impulsive, sir. This is not at all correct."

"I beg your pardon, Sir George. I have done wrong in the way I came," said Dick earnestly. "Let me come to you, then, as my officer whom I wish to obey."

"But this is not in proper form, Mr Darrell. You should have written."

"I suppose so, sir."

"Well, as you are here, tell me what induces you to come and plead for this poor fellow, as you call him."

"Because I have seen so much of him in the short time I have been with the troop, Sir George. He is such an excellent soldier—one of the smartest men we have."

"All that has been taken into consideration, Mr Darrell, again and again, and taken in extenuation of some of his failings; but he has gone too far now. The man is a thorough wastrel."

"But I think there is some good in the man, Sir George."

The general shrugged his shoulders.

"You must have microscopic eyes, Mr Darrell. His officers, who have had long experience of the man, have failed to discover it."

"He has behaved very bravely in action, sir."

"Yes; I am told so. But cannot you see, Mr Darrell, the necessity for preserving the character of your corps—how it must be kept in the highest state of discipline?"

"Yes, Sir George, of course; but—I don't know how it is—I have felt attracted by this man. He is a gentleman, evidently, by birth and education."

"Have you become at all intimate with him, Mr Darrell?" said the general sharply.

"Oh, no, Sir George; I have never spoken to him except to give orders."

"Has he written to you begging you to help him?"

"No, Sir George. It is because it is so sad for a man like that to sink so low as to suffer such a horribly degrading punishment."

"I am glad it is that, Mr Darrell," said the general coldly. "Then I am to presume that you take great interest in the men of your troop?"

"Oh, yes, sir!" cried Dick earnestly.

"And that you would put in a petition for any other man who was in a similar trouble?"

"I think I should, sir."

"Well, Mr Darrell, this is a very disorderly proceeding on your part, but I feel that it is through a certain natural enthusiasm in a young man, who has certainly distinguished himself since he has been out here by his sterling endeavours to make himself an energetic officer, and, therefore, I feel disposed to try and meet you in this matter."

"Oh, Sir George!"

"Silence!"

Dick drew himself up to attention, and the general went on.

"I may tell you, Mr Darrell, that I signed this man's sentence with extreme reluctance, and it was not until everything had been tried that these extreme measures were decided on; but we cannot have the force disgraced. To be brief, I will leave this matter in your hands. If you can bring me this man's word as a soldier that he will from this time forward begin earnestly to amend, I will let him off the degrading portion of his sentence."

"Oh, Sir George!" began Dick excitedly.

"That will do, Mr Darrell. See the man, and come back to me at once. I am very busy: good-morning."

Dick saluted, and turned to the door at once.

"One moment, Mr Darrell," said the general, bending down to write. "Knowing what I do of the man from old reports. I do not think you will succeed. If your kindly effort does not bear fruit you need not return. Here is a pass to the man's cell."

Sir George gave the young man a short nod, and took his place at his writing-table; while Dick hurried off to the cells, anxious lest he should encounter his brother-officers, who would question him about his proceedings.

A few minutes later the cell door was being unlocked, and he stepped into the gloomy place where Hanson was seated upon a bench, nursing his injured ankle, with the light streaming down upon him from the little barred window.

The man stirred slowly as the door was closed behind his visitor.

"Well, is it time?" he said in a low growl.

"For your punishment? No; not yet."

"You, Mr Darrell?" said the man wonderingly as he started up.

"Yes, Hanson; I've come to see you about this terrible punishment."

"Terrible? Bah! It has been coming a long time. I'm sick of it all, and want to wind up. Let them flog me. I suppose they will now?"

"Yes; I believe the sentence is to be carried out to-morrow morning, Hanson."

"A good job, too. Let them flog me, and as soon as I get about again I'll shoot the general, and they may hang me out of my misery."

"I came to talk to you quietly, Hanson, not to listen to mad words like those."

"Mad men say mad things."

"But you're not mad," said Dick quietly. "What you say is folly."

"Is it?" cried the man desperately. "Wait and you'll see."

"I shall never see that. But we're wasting time."

"Why did you come here—sir? There, I suppose I must say 'sir' to you—boy."

"Speak naturally while I am here, Hanson. Yes, I am a boy yet; but you were a boy once."

The man started slightly.

"Yes," he said mockingly, "I was a boy once."

"And very different then."

"Look here, sir," cried the man, "if you've come to preach, you may save yourself the trouble."

"I've not come to preach, Hanson," said Dick quietly, "and I have no wish to hurt your feelings by asking you how it was you went all wrong as you did; but isn't it time all this came to an end?"

"Yes; and it's coming to an end, and pretty soon, too, if they flog me."

"They will, Hanson, for certain now, and I have come because I would do anything sooner than see it."

"What is it to you?"

"Something horrible to see a man of your birth and education—a gentleman—flogged."

"Hold your tongue!" roared the man fiercely, and the sentry unlocked the door quickly and threw it open.

"Shut that door," said Dick quietly to the sentry; "there is nothing the matter."

The man obeyed, and the occupants of the cell stood facing each other for some moments, the prisoner breathing hard, and the visitor struggling hard mentally to acquit himself of what was a very difficult task.

"That will do, my lad," said Hanson at last. "You mean well; you've always behaved well to me, but you are doing no good. You don't know, and you couldn't understand. I suppose you have been sent."

"No; I obtained leave to see you, and I have come just as I would to see any man of the troop who had been hurt."

"Ah, you're young," said the man hoarsely.

"So are you, Hanson," said Dick quickly. "You can't be above six or seven and twenty."

"Ha, ha!" laughed the prisoner; "why, I feel seventy, and want to get to the end of the miserable business. I've tried times enough to get killed."

"Yes! We heard how brave you are in action."

"Brave!" cried the man mockingly. "Bah!"

"Look here, Hanson," said Dick gently, "you called me a boy just now."

"So you are. A fine fellow to set over seasoned men!"

Dick winced, but went on quietly: "You can't be more than ten years older than I am. Isn't it time to turn over a new leaf?"

"There's only one left in my book," said the man scornfully, "and that has 'finis' printed at the bottom."

"Nonsense, Hanson! Come, turn it over. Don't let's have this horrible, degrading scene, with you, one of the smartest soldiers in the troop, the principal actor."

"Smartest soldiers in the troop! Humbug! The biggest black," cried the man scornfully.

"Both true," said Dick.

"Who said that?"

"Every one says it. I've heard the captain and Mr Wyatt say it a score of times. Old Stubbs, too."

"Then you've been sticking up for me?"

"In some things—yes. Why, it was only yesterday Captain Hulton said there was not a finer soldier in the troop. Yes; and he said it went against his grain to see a brave man treated like a dog, but that discipline must be preserved for every one's sake."

"Ah, it's all too late—too late, sir."

"Nonsense, Hanson! It's never too late to mend."

"Yes, it is, sir, when the stuff's all rotten. I've gone to the bad, and I'm done for, and the sooner I'm hung and out of my misery the better."

"You think so now because you're sentenced to be flogged."

"Yes; and that's the last straw."

"I say, Hanson, weren't you once a gentleman? Tell me."

"Silence!" cried the man fiercely, and the sentry once more came to the door.

"Nothing: all right."

"Don't you ever speak to me again like that," said the man in a hoarse whisper.

"Very well, I will not: but I know now, and I shall think as much as I like."

"There, go now, sir, before I get mad."

"No: you will not hurt me."

"You don't know that."

"Yes, I do. You respect me too much."

"It's a lie. I hate you for your youth and good looks and luck, and the way in which other people spoil you, boy."

"Nonsense! You do like me, and if we were in action you'd do anything to save me from being hurt."

The man uttered a low growl like some savage animal, but his dark eyes softened, and he turned away his face from the light which streamed in through the bars as Dick went on:

"The natural result of knowing that is that I've got to like you."

The man gazed at him mockingly.

"What!" he cried. "You, an officer, and I the most blackguardly private in the troop?"

"I meant as a brave man and a good soldier, and it hurts me to see such a one as you going to the dogs."

"You don't know what you're talking about this morning, boy," said Hanson bitterly.

"Boy? I am your officer, Private Hanson."

"Yes, sir, I was forgetting myself; and I shall forget myself more if you stay, so please go."

"That's what I want you to do," said Dick earnestly.

"I want you to forget what you are now, and be what you used to be."

The prisoner drew his breath hardly, as if he were in pain.

"I want to be a friend to you as much as I, an officer, can be to one of our men."

"Look here, sir; you were sent here to me this morning by the captain?"

"He does not know I have come, Hanson."

"What! Look here, is that true?"

"Don't insult me by asking such a question, sir," said the lad, flushing. "I had to beg for permission to come. I tell you it hurt me horribly when I knew you were sentenced."

"Yes, the brutes—the cowards!"

"No. They were your judges, and you had done things which deserved punishment. They said if it had not been that you were such a brave soldier, the court would have sentenced you to be drummed out of the regiment as a disgrace."

"Let them do it!" growled the man.

"I thought about it a great deal, and then I went to the general and begged him to let you off."

"Didn't he threaten to kick you out of his quarters for an insolent young puppy?" said the man mockingly.

Dick winced, but mastered his anger.

"No; he looked astonished at first, and then he behaved to me like a gentleman, as I want you to behave to me, Hanson. You can if you like."

"Yes, I can, my lad, and I—no, no; be off, and leave me. Let them flog me, and that will be the end of it. I'm too great a coward to shoot myself."

"No, you are not," said Dick quietly. "You've got pluck enough to do anything but be a coward. You haven't pluck enough for that."

"What! Is it to be a coward to make an end of one's self?"

"You know that as well as I do. Now, understand this once for all. I came here entirely through my own efforts. No one prompted me; no one helped me. I've tried to do my duty since I've been a soldier, and it seemed to be the right thing to go and ask the general to let you off that degrading punishment. So I went, and, as I told you, he was surprised, but he was not angry; and he finished by saying that if you would give your word as a soldier that you would turn over a new leaf, he'd look over the past, and give you another chance by cancelling the sentence of flogging."

The man's face grew hard and drawn, and it was as if the little weak good left in him was making a desperate struggle against the bad and being crushed, when Dick took a step forward.

"Promise me, Hanson," he said; "don't let's have our troop degraded before the people by one of ours being flogged."

"I can't promise, boy; I can't," groaned the prisoner desperately. "I've gone too far."

"For the sake of the good old past, Hanson."

"Do you want to drive me mad, boy?" roared the man fiercely.

"No. You know that," cried Dick. "There, look here; fate has made me your officer, boy as I am, and you one of my men."

"Yes, that's it," said the man bitterly, and he sat lower, with his fingers clutching at the flesh of his bare breast through his open shirt.

"I ask you, then, as one gentleman might ask another—promise me Robert Hanson, that you'll make a brave effort to start afresh."

The man sprang from his sent and stood with every nerve quivering gazing from the hand Dick had held out to him to the lad's face and back. Then, with a gasp that was almost a groan, he seized Dick's fingers and held them in a tremendous grip for a few moments.

"I promise," he said hoarsely. "It's like one coming to snatch a man back when he was sinking for evermore."

The tramp, tramp of the sentry was heard outside, but there was a dead silence in the cell, as those two stood there with the bright light streaming in through the iron bars, till the prisoner let fall the hand he had grasped, and turned sharply round, to stand with his back to his officer.

"Go now, Mr Darrell, please," he said in a hoarse whisper.

"Yes, I'll go now," said Dick softly, and he took a step forward to lay his hand upon the prisoner's shoulder. "All this is between us. No one will ever know from me what has been said here."

Dick turned and rapped at the door, which was opened at once, and he passed through, hearing the clang and rattle of the lock and bolts as he strode away, making for the general's quarters, hurrying his steps as he saw a syce holding a horse at the foot of the steps.

He was none too soon, for before he was across the great parade-ground the general came out and mounted, fortunately for Dick, turning his horse and moving in the direction which brought them face to face.

"Ah, Mr Darrell!" he said, reining up; "want to see me?"

"Yes, Sir George. I've just come from the prisoner's cell."

"Well?"

"He promises, Sir George."

"Indeed? But will he keep his word?"

"Yes, Sir George; I'll answer for him."

"You are a foolish, sanguine boy," said the general, smiling; "but we'll see.—Come with me."

He turned the horse's head and walked him back to the door of his quarters, where he alighted and threw the reins to an orderly. Then, leading the way back to his room, he removed his glove and sat down at the writing-table, where his pen ran rapidly over a sheet of paper.

"There," he said when he had blotted and folded it; "I am not young and sanguine like you, Mr Darrell, but I am glad to have the opportunity of stopping the degrading exhibition we were about to have; and let me say, too, equally glad to oblige a young officer whose career I have been noticing ever since he joined."

Dick reddened, and faltered a few words.

"That will do," said the general, nodding pleasantly; "but recollect this—you have undertaken an onerous task. You promised me to be answerable for this man."

"I did, Sir George, and I honestly believe I can."

"Of course you do. Well, I shall watch the progress of your efforts—mind that. There, I have work on hand. Take your letter to Captain Hulton. I have given your protégé a clean slate, so that he may start free, and I shall expect you to turn him from the brute he has been into a credit to his troop."

"A clean slate, Sir George!" stammered the lad. "Will he have no punishment to undergo?"

"No, Mr Darrell; as a soldier I never do anything by halves."

He walked to the door, mounted, and rode away, leaving Dick half-suffocated, for he had succeeded beyond his wildest hopes.

"Oh," he cried to himself as he hurried off with his letter, "if Hanson will only mend!"

Chapter XVII
On Service

"Here, Dick, lad—bit of news for you," said Wyatt a few hours later, after giving a heavy thump with his fist on the door, and then striding into his friend's room.

"Indeed!" said Dick quietly, and without showing a sign of knowing what it was. "Good or bad?"

Wyatt screwed up his mouth, and shook his head at his companion.

"How precious innocent we are," he said. "But it won't do."

"What's your news?"

"Bob Hanson's let off."

"I'm glad of it," said Dick.

"Won't do, I tell you. You mean morsel. Didn't I see you sneaking over to the general's quarters this morning? Didn't you go from there to the cells. Didn't you come away and go straight to Hulton with the general's despatch."

"Yes—yes?—yes."

"Well, you might have told me, Dicky."

"I did not feel that I ought to say a word to any one."

"You told Hulton?"

"Not a word. I only gave him the general's order, and came away."

"Well, never mind; I'm very glad, and I forgive you this time. But that isn't the news."

"What is, then?"

"Serve you right not to tell you, only I won't be mean. We march to-morrow."

"To-morrow!" cried Dick excitedly. "Where to?"

"Soojeepur."

"Ah!"

"Up in the hill country, my lad."

"Are we at war, or is it to a fresh station?"

"We're not at war; but, as far as I've heard, the Rajah is. But you heard before?"

"Yes," said Dick. "With some neighbouring chief."

"That's it. Well, the Company wants to keep on good terms with him, and we're going up to help his highness. So the Company does not want an enemy on his borders, but a friend. So see to your traps. I expect we shall get the route to-morrow, and march in the evening."

"How far is it?"

"Oh, not far—six or seven hundred miles. Get your fellows to work over your packing. Got much to do?"

"No—very little. I could be ready to-night."

"I say, though, have you ever had that new sword of yours ground?"

"No; I've been meaning to have it done for days."

"Get it done at once. Here, send one of your fellows for the armourer, so as to catch him before he knows, or he'll be too busy."

Dick summoned his servant and sent for the man who acted as armourer in the troop, and the bright new weapon was brought out.

In a very short time the man had received his orders to bring the weapon back in a couple of hours, and he looked inquiringly from one to the other; but, obtaining no information, he went off, and brought the sword back keen of edge and point.

Then Wyatt spoke.

"Heard the news yet, Smith?"

"No, sir; nothing stirring that I know of."

"Ah, well, you'll get some; so look out."

Before the man had reached the barrack-yard the news was running from one end of the cantonments to the other; and as the two officers looked out, they saw half-a-dozen men hurrying up to the man who had just quitted them, speaking eagerly, and Wyatt laughed.

"Master Smith has got his work cut out for the next few hours," he said. "Never mind, you've had your first go, so you needn't mind."

"Are you pretty well prepared?" asked Dick.

"Oh, yes, I'm ready enough. Been expecting the order, you see; and the less one takes on the march the better. There'll be an early parade and inspection, of course."

"What regiments are going with us?"

"None. The elephant-guns are to follow, but not for a week. We shall have it all our own way, and it will mean promotion, I hope. Perhaps I shall get my troop; and if I do you'll come with me, Dick?"

"That would mean leaving this troop?" said Dick, aghast.

"Of course. But you and I would soon make another as smart."

"Think so?" said Dick thoughtfully.

"Oh, yes. I don't profess to be clever, but it always seems to me that if two fellows make up their minds to do a thing and stick to it—if it's possible—they'll do it."

"Yes," said Dick still more thoughtfully, "I suppose so."

It was late before he lay down to rest that night, for there was more to do in preparations than he had anticipated. For instance, there was the letter home, announcing his departure up-country on service—a letter which took a long while to write, and set him thinking, taking, as it did, much of the holiday aspect and excitement out of the coming trip. For now he began to realise that it meant something more than show. He was going to face the realities of a soldier's life, and the possibilities of his never coming back alive.

Dick did not go to sleep quite so easily that night, and when the bugle was sounded he seemed to have hardly closed his eyes.

But there was no time for thought in the early grey of the morning. The bustle and hurry of preparation was going on all round. There was the trampling of horses, the clink of spurs, and the rumble and rattle of gun-wheels, limbers, and ammunition-wagons.

Soon after there was a familiar whinnying sound outside, and he ran to the window, to look down and see Ram Dad in spotless white walking Burnouse up and down, ready for his master.

"Who's going to feel dumpy when he has a horse like that?" muttered Dick as he turned away and stood before the glass, giving the finishing touches to his dressing, ending by buckling on his sword.

"Wish I were bigger," he said to himself; "I don't seem to grow a bit," — which was strange; but at that time the lad's ideas of growth were that he ought to increase in size as rapidly as a melon.

The opening of the door behind him interrupted his meditations, and he turned to see the smiling face of his body-servant, who had brought him his morning coffee.

"Will the sahib take Hakim with him to Soojeepur?" said the man.

"Of course. Don't you want to go?"

"Hakim would go everywhere with the sahib," replied the man, "if the sahib will promise that his servant shall not be killed."

"I'll promise that I will not kill you, Hakim," said Dick, smiling.

"Then his servant is satisfied and happy. Will Ram Dad go too?"

"Oh, yes. Look here, Hakim; you will see that my things go with the officers' baggage, and look out for yourself."

"The sahib's servant has been on the march before," said the man importantly, "and he will see to everything."

"That's right," said Dick, hurrying through his coffee and biscuit, for he was none too soon. Then, running down, he reached his horse just as Wyatt came up.

"Morning," said the latter, with a very sleepy look in his eyes. "Humph! your charger looks well. Don't seem quite so ready to eat you now, or to kick you into the middle of next week."

"Oh, no; we're getting great friends. — Aren't we, 'Nouse," replied Dick, patting the beautiful neck and rubbing the muzzle extended to meet his hand.

"Yes, he looks civil enough, but I wouldn't trust him. There, mount, and come along. Here comes Hulton."

The troop was already drawn up in heavy marching order, and directly after they moved out on to the parade, where the general and the staff soon after rode on to the ground. There was a careful inspection, and the men were dismissed long before the sun made its power felt, the general having expressed his satisfaction with everything.

Those were busy hours which intervened till just before sunset, when the order to march was given, and the troop rode out from the town, escorted by a squadron of one of the native cavalry regiments and a band, for a short distance, before the final farewells were said, and they broke into a trot to overtake the long train of baggage-wagons which had set off a couple of hours earlier; for, in spite of everything being cut down, the necessities for a lengthened expedition, with tents, servants, grass-cutters, provender, and an ample supply of ammunition and spare horses, sufficed to make what seemed to Dick an appallingly long display.

Long before midnight, though, they were encamped, with everything, consequent upon the admirable state of discipline, in perfect order; and Dick sat with his brother-officers and the doctor in their mess-tent by day, and lay in their sleeping-tent by night.

The guard had been set, and it was Dick's duty to visit the posts about the camp that night. To his surprise, he found Wyatt awake, ready to roll off his camp-bed and make the round with him.

"Don't mind my company, I suppose?" he said.

"Glad of it;" and they went round the little sleeping camp together—an attractive walk by the light of the great full-moon.

"Looks quite nice," said Wyatt, "and no fear of an alarm."

"Alarm—no!" said Dick, laughing.

"I was thinking of being in the enemy's country, with a force ten or twenty times as strong as our own on the *qui vive* to wipe us out. Keeps you from feeling sleepy, my lad."

"Have you ever been in that position?" asked Dick.

"Often," was the laconic reply. Then, after a pause, "Perhaps we may be next month."

It was a long, monotonous march, with the customary incidents: troubles about water, native servants breaking down with illness, real or fancied—oftener, the doctor said, the latter. Then the dreary plains began to give place to hilly country, the air was less heavy, the woodlands more beautiful; and, after a week or two of this, hills began to appear in the distance—hills that would in Europe have been dubbed big mountains.

The marches now were for the most part along winding valleys, with sparkling rivers near the roads, which became more difficult for the guns and wagons: but this was balanced by the beauty of the scenery and the invigorating nature of the air.

"Fellow can breathe out here, and Hulton says Soojeepur is more beautiful and higher up than this."

"This valley is beautiful enough for anything," said Dick as they rode on one evening. "Why, there ought to be tigers and leopards in these jungles."

"Lots," said Wyatt.

"And fish in the river."

"Heaps," said Wyatt; "monsters sixty and seventy pounds weight. You and I are going to have some shooting and fishing by-and-by, old lad, if we find time. But Hulton's right."

"What about?"

"He says we're in for it."

"In for what?"

"Who knows? It's as he says—we've got to depend entirely upon ourselves; for, if we have to do any fighting, and the other side's too strong, we shall have to pull up our boots and tighten our belts."

"Surely we shall not be in such a position as that?" said Dick.

"Who can tell? Perhaps the Rajah's chaps haven't much go in them, and will leave us to do the fighting. There we are. Suppose we send for help; it will take a month for the messenger to get to cantonments, and a month for the help to come, and during that time they could eat us all but our boots."

"But if things went against us we should have to retire."

"Retreat, eh? Yes," said Wyatt thoughtfully; and then he broke out suddenly, to Dick's amusement, with a capital imitation of the Irishman in the old anecdote, "'Och, your honner, I've tuk a prisiner.'

"'Bring him along then, Pat.'

"'Plase yer honner, he won't come.'

"'Come without him, then.'

"'Plase, yer honner, he won't let me.'"

"Suppose that's our position, Dicky. It seems to me that we're going right into a trap, and mayn't be able to get away again. I don't think we ought to have been sent."

"Why, you're not afraid?" said Dick.

"Not a bit, lad; only thoughtful. I say we oughtn't to have been sent, because this isn't the sort of country for horse artillery. We want to be out in wide plains where there's room to gallop. Here, for instance, we could do nothing but sit on our horses while the enemy lined the sides of this valley with sharp-shooters to pick us off."

"Perhaps Soojeepur may turn out to be a plain country."

"Hope it is," said Wyatt abruptly; "but I don't think it is. We ought to be rifles, not what we are. Here's a pretty place for an ambush. If the Rajah's enemies know we're coming they'll be collected up yonder, and as soon as we get near enough they'll begin playing a game of skittles. We shall be the skittles, and the rocks the balls."

"I say," said Dick merrily, "would you mind going to the rear, to ride beside Captain Hulton?"

"Yes, I should mind a good deal. I've been riding with him, and he's as obstinate as a pig."

"Oh!"

"I said we ought to send out the advance-guard farther, and double the rear-guard."

"And what did he say?"

"Told me to mind my own business; that we were not in an enemy's country, and that I was getting quite an old woman."

"Well?"

"I didn't like it."

"It did not sound pleasant. But you don't think there is anything to mind, do you?"

"I don't know that there is, young un, but it may have got about that we are coming, and if I were our friend's enemy, it is the very thing I should do."

"What—try and cut us off?"

"Of course. There's more done by scheming than hard work, they say, and I'm sure there is in war. Five hundred men attacking an enemy's rear at a critical time will do more towards producing a rout than five thousand fresh troops attacking the front. It's the sudden and unexpected that does so much in a battle."

Dick nodded and looked grave.

"What shall we do?" he said.

"Obey orders. Hulton's in command."

These last words were spoken in so decisive a way that Dick said no more, and rode on in silence; but for the rest of their ride, whenever a valley narrowed into a gorge, he watched the sides anxiously in search of marksmen waiting to dispute the way.

But he searched the sides in vain, and after encamping two more nights, the valley they were in debouched in a fruitful plain stretching far and wide, to snow-capped mountains glittering in the brilliant sunshine: while, as the officers halted to gaze down in wonder and admiration, they could trace the serpentine course of the widened-out river stretching far in all directions, fertilising the plain, and meandering on like a ribbon of silver, till many miles away they could see, through the wonderfully pure air, the gilded minarets and walls of an extensive city.

"Yonder's Soojeepur," said Hulton, riding up. "Now then, Wyatt, will there be room enough there for us to manoeuvre?"

"Yes, yes, dear boy," cried Wyatt enthusiastically. "Splendid! Magnificent! Miles of galloping-ground. Ready to begin now if the enemy would come in sight."

"There you are, then," cried Dick, rising in his stirrups; "look yonder."

He pointed right away, and his companions shaded their eyes, and made out in the distance the glint of arms in the sunshine; and, as the order was given to halt, the officers made out that a large body of horse was coming in their direction.

Satisfied of this, the captain gave the order for the troop to advance, the baggage-train being halted where they were, with the few men appointed for their guard.

"Now then, Dick," said Wyatt as they trotted on, "this is right. Hulton wants to get us more out in the open. Yes, that's right; he's making for that low mound, from which we could sweep the plain in all directions. That's soldierly. See?"

"Yes, I see," replied Dick; "but these may be friends coming to meet us."

"Of course they may, and we shall be none the worse for being prepared. But, by the same rule, they may be enemies, and we shall be all the better for being ready to receive them."

In less than an hour all doubts were solved by the advance of a little detachment of well-mounted men, who announced that the Rajah was coming himself to meet his friends with all his horse; and soon after the glittering array in attendance on the great chief, mounted in a silver howdah upon a huge elephant, nearly covered with cloth of gold, and with tusks painted and banded with the precious metal, rode up.

It was a sight which riveted all eyes—the Rajah's officers glittering with jewels and splendidly arrayed, while the Rajah himself, a handsome, dark-eyed man, was in simple, snow-white muslin and white puggree, his sole ornament being a diamond clasp over his forehead, from which rose a delicate white egret plume.

It was like a procession of hundreds of years before, many of the mounted men wearing small steel caps with spiked top and face-guard, while from all round the back depended a protective curtain of the finest chain-armour. Many of them, too, wore shirts of mail, fitting tight to the body, and without exception they carried light, curved tulwars and round shields.

In undress uniform, covered and begrimed with sweat and dust, it seemed to Dick that their troop cut a sorry figure beside the Rajah's force; and he looked sharply from one to the other of the haughty-looking chiefs on their handsome but undersized horses, fully expecting to see an air of sneering contempt upon their faces as they looked down upon the little auxiliary force which had come to join them.

But he soon saw that he was wrong. The Rajah and his party were men of war, and their eyes glittered with satisfaction as they roamed over the splendidly mounted, stalwart, picked men who rode with the guns, knowing, as they did from hearsay, what a tremendous power these light six-pounders were in the hands of the highly-drilled troop. They knew that the troop meant work, and possibly the saving of their country from a dangerous foe; and there was no mistaking the spontaneous, wild burst of welcome given in long-continued acclamations, which were repeated again and again as the mahout flourished his gilded ankus, and forced the great elephant to kneel so that the Rajah might reach down to shake hands with the officers.

"Something to write home about," thought Dick as he drew off his gauntlet to grasp the thin brown hand extended to him, when his turn came to meet the flashing dark eyes and pleasant smile turned upon him.

"I am glad to welcome you, sir," said the Rajah in excellent English, though with a strange intonation. "I would ask you to come up into the howdah to sit with me, but I have already asked Captain Hulton. Another time. It does not matter, for you have a beautiful horse, and you ride him well."

"I am glad to welcome you, sir," said the Rajah.

Dick was hot before; now he glowed, and found himself wanting in words when the Rajah loosed his hand.

The next minute the captain was mounting by using the elephant's trunk as a succession of steps, the intelligent beast helping him so that, with the aid of the mahout's hand and the friendly grasp of the Rajah, he climbed to the howdah; the elephant heaved and rolled like a boat among waves; and, at a word from the Rajah, his force divided and drew up on either side, facing inward for the troop to pass between them and then close in behind.

Wyatt took the command as the captain's horse was led by one of the men.

"Gallop back," said the former, "and order the rear-guard and train to advance at a trot, Darrell;" and, extricating himself from the crowd of horsemen, Dick sent his charger flying to the rear, a burst of exclamations following him as he passed, while half-a-dozen dark-skinned, fierce-looking horsemen chipped spurs to their steeds' flanks and followed him at a gallop.

His mission was soon accomplished, and the train came rumbling along; while, still followed by his self-formed escort, Dick galloped back to take his place by Wyatt, who was at the head of the troop, following close behind the Rajah's elephant, in advance of which were one half of the horsemen, the other half being in rear of the train.

"What do you think of this, Dicky?" said Wyatt as they rode slowly on towards the city.

"Very jolly," was the reply.

"Well, don't get swelled head over it, young un. I'm thinking that if this is going to be the sort of thing, we shan't want to go back to Roumwallah, Calcutta, or anywhere else."

"Why?"

"Because we are going to be the greatest people in the Rajah's army, and we shall want to stay."

"Nonsense!"

"Oh, no, it isn't. In about a month old Hulton yonder, perched up like an idol in a temple, will be made field-marshal; I shall be a general; and as for you—oh, you shall be my aide-de-camp."

"Thank ye," said Dick.

"Oh, I shall behave well to you if you're a good boy. What are you thinking about?"

"I was thinking it strange that nature should have given elephants such ridiculous little tails as that in front."

"Get out! You weren't."

"I was, really. Look at it whisking about. It's quite absurd."

"Humph, yes; but the brute shuffles along pretty well. I'm glad it's old Hulton the chief has got up there instead of me. I'll be bound Hulton wishes himself back upon his horse."

"Shall we camp out to-night as usual?" said Dick after they had ridden a little way.

"I'm beginning to think not," said Wyatt; "the chief isn't poor, that's certain, and the place yonder looks big. I expect we shall have a palace apiece, and be left to toss up who is to entertain the doctor. Really, though, I expect we shall find some kind of barracks and stables set apart for us."

A couple of hours later the procession was crossing the river by a well-built bridge, held by a strong force of sturdy-looking men in white, armed with crooked, heavy knives and shields; while the road leading to the principal gate was lined with the Rajah's troops—swarthy, active-looking men, but with weapons of the most antique kind, principally long-barrelled matchlocks.

"But they look as if they've got some fight in them," said Wyatt.

"Yes," said Dick; "those little dark fellows seem as active as cats."

"And they are," said Wyatt. "Hillmen, that's what they happen to be. I say, though, the Rajah has plenty of subjects."

For the narrow, bazaar-like streets and the housetops were crowded with people, who seemed to devour the new-comers with their eyes, till suddenly, in a long street kept by troops, one side of which was formed by a building with a carved gateway, the procession halted, the elephant knelt, and Captain Hulton rose.

"Pass the word along for the captain's charger," said Wyatt sharply, and the next minute one of the gunners hurried forward with the led horse in time for his chief.

The captain rode up to his brother-officers.

"That building is our barracks," he said, "and the place is ready for occupation, so we will move in at once. Set sentries at the gates, Wyatt. By the *way*, the Rajah tells me that a meal is ready for the men, and he asks our company at the palace to join him."

"We can't all go," said Wyatt quietly.

"No, so I have excused you. Darrell, you will come."

The captain moved away.

"I'd rather stay and help you, Wyatt," said Dick.

"I believe you, dear boy; but you must go. We shall soon settle down. The sergeants and corporals work well, and when you come back the place will seem as if we had been in possession a month."

Chapter XVIII
A Royal Dinner-Party

"Nearly ready, Darrell?" cried Hulton.

"Yes, and waiting for you," was the reply as the captain entered the lad's quarters and looked round critically.

"Humph! you've got better rooms than I have."

"Like to change, sir?"

"Not I. So long as I've a good bed I don't mind. Bless us! how smart the boy looks! Shall I do?"

"Do? Yes; you always look well and manly, sir. But how are we going to find our way?"

"Oh, I'll find the way; but I wish we were not going to walk through the dust, on account of one's shoes."

They were not going to walk, for there was the trampling of horses and jingling of accoutrements heard in the courtyard, and Hakim entered.

"The sahib's elephant is waiting," he said.

"Eh?" cried the captain. "What elephant?"

"The Rajah's, sahib; come to fetch."

"Hah! that's something like a host." cried Hulton.

"I was just going to see if we couldn't have palanquins."

They recognised the elephant as the one the Rajah had ridden that day, but the howdah and trappings were changed, though they were magnificent enough as it was; and as soon as they appeared, the great beast was guided forward from where it stood in company with a dozen of the Rajah's mounted guard, who saluted the officers.

At a word from the mahout and a flourish of his ankus the elephant knelt, a ladder was placed by a couple of servants, and the two officers mounted. Two of the guard placed themselves in front as the elephant rose, and the rest formed up behind as they set off across the courtyard and through the gate, riding in state through the streets, with the people collecting on either side to see them pass.

"It's a much finer city than I expected to see, Darrell," said the captain. "Plenty of temples—a pretty good sign that the Brahmin priests have a strong hold over the people. Look; there are a couple coming along. Humph! Scowls for us instead of welcome salutes. That means something."

"Don't like the English," said Dick.

"Yes, that is evident. Look here, Darrell; I want you to keep your eyes and ears open while we are at the palace, so as to pick up all you can, and then we will compare notes afterwards. Look at that, too."

This remark was made as they passed a crowd at the entrance to what appeared to be a temple. Up to this point, saving the two priests, every one they passed had given them a smiling welcome, or gazed with eager curiosity at the new-comers; but now it was evident, from the scowling looks which greeted them, that the crowd was inimical.

"There's lesson the first, Darrell," said the captain.

"It means keeping our men well in barracks, in case of their getting into trouble."

Before they reached the Rajah's palace they had further evidence of the fact that they as strangers had as many enemies as friends in the place. Then for the time all was forgotten in the warm welcome they received from their host, who gave them a dinner which was a strange combination of his own native style and English, but mingled with an evidently earnest desire to make the guests satisfied with their reception.

He spoke capital English, as had been before noticed, and in the course of conversation he said:

"I used to hate your people, and look upon them as enemies and intruders, till I awoke to the fact that in this world of change matters were altering—that our old superstitions and follies must pass away before the spread of European civilisation. I am not going to criticise the acts of the great Company, but I look upon it all as fate, and I want my people to think as I do, throw aside the bad old past, and welcome the newer and better."

"And what do they say?" asked Hulton: while Dick listened with keen interest to all that was said, reading, as he did, that the young Rajah was a gentleman of high aspirations and keen intelligence.

"Unfortunately, I find I am making many enemies," the Rajah replied. "My mother reproaches me as a degenerate son of my father, and sides with the Brahmins, who hate me and my rule."

"Because you wish to improve your people," said Hulton.

"Exactly. And because I wish to be friends with the Company, and march with the times. She wishes to do what my father would have done, she tells me—oppose the advance of the Company and help to drive them back into the sea, and go back to the old days of tyranny, superstition, and vice."

"Which would be folly. She cannot have any idea of the British power."

"She is a woman," said the Rajah sadly—"one of our women, brought up in ignorance and seclusion. Help to drive the English into the sea! It is absurd."

"Yes," said Hulton; "absurd. As the enemy of the Company, the result would be that your raj would be lost. As the Company's friend, you will always reign and your country will progress."

"All this I know," said the Rajah; "but, as I told you, my mother sides with the Brahmins, who feel that under the new order of things they will lose their horrible, tyrannical hold upon the common people, and keep them in ignorance and slavery no longer."

"And what about the Rajah of Singh?"

"I fear it is by the invitation of people near me that he has declared war. It is hard, when one tries for the good, to find enemies springing up on all sides."

"And friends too," said Hulton.

"Yes," said the Rajah, smiling, "and brave friends. Yesterday I was in despair, for I thought the help I had asked from the Company would never come. Now I live again, and am content."

"Is the Rajah of Singh very strong?"

"Just about as strong as I should be were all here faithful to me; but there are so many that I cannot trust. With you here, though, I feel his equal."

"I'm afraid," said Hulton quietly, "that the Rajah, your enemy, will lose his possessions, for in declaring war against you he has declared war against the Company; and if we are not enough to defeat him, more and more will be sent until the task is done."

"You make me live again," said the Rajah excitedly. "I always felt that the English would see justice done, and it would be an injustice for another to take the country I inherited from my fathers."

"Certainly it would, and you have nothing to fear, sir."

"You will not be offended if I speak and say something that is in my mind?"

"Of course not, sir. What is it?"

"I thought the number of troops my English friends have sent were very few."

"Yes, but they are highly-trained men, sir; and there are the guns. But I understood, on leaving Roumwallah, that more troops with heavier guns were to follow."

"It is good," said the Rajah, smiling with satisfaction.

Then coffee and pipes were brought, in which Hulton and the Rajah indulged; and in good time the elephant was brought round, and, after many expressions of friendship on the part of the Rajah, his guests returned to the old palace which had been turned into a barrack for the time.

"Well," said Wyatt before Dick retired for the night, "how are you, O festive one?"

"Tired out, and want to go to sleep," said Dick, yawning.

"Oh, come! none of that nonsense," cried Wyatt. "Here have you been feasting on cake and wine, drinking sublime coffee, and smoking rose-water hubble-bubbles, while I have been hard at work, shaking the men down into their quarters, and giving orders about the stowing of the baggage; and now, when I want to hear a little about your sports and pastimes, what's what, and the rest of it, you yawn in my face and want to go to sleep."

"Can't help it."

"You must help it. Wine good?"

"Didn't like it. Sickly, sweet stuff."

"Victuals and fruit?"

"Splendid."

"And the coffee?"

"The nicest I ever tasted."

"Then I'll go next time. Did you smoke?"

"Of course not."

"Well, what about the state of affairs here?" Dick told him as nearly as he could everything that had passed.

"Hah! Then we shall have some fighting."

"Think so?"

"I do, my boy. This Rajah Singh will be kept well informed about our coming, and you will see that he will strike at once before more troops come. He'll think, as the Rajah does, that we are so few that the sooner he begins the better; and, if he gives us a chance, he'll catch a tartar. He doesn't know what our troop can do."

"We are few, though," said Dick thoughtfully.

"Yes, we are few; but that doesn't matter. We only want plenty of room. By the way, though, Dicky, the city seems to be pretty strong with its big walls. I hadn't time to see much more than we did when we rode in, but I had a peep. As for this old palace, there's plenty of water, and, given enough provisions and forage for the horses, we could stand a siege; for it is a fortification in itself—only one entrance, and that through those big gates. Take it altogether, I think we are in for some fun."

"Yes; it looks bad," said Dick.

"Bad, you young heathen! Then why, in the name of common-sense— why did you turn soldier? Here we are with plenty of friends, and a splendid suspicion of danger sandwiched in amongst them in the shape of conspirators like mamma, the dowager, and her Brahmin friends."

"Yes; we noticed several of those scowling at us as we went to the palace."

"Hulton said something of the kind just now, but I couldn't get much out of him. He was grumpy and thoughtful. I don't think he much likes the idea of what he has to do. He's brave enough, but I think he likes to be led better than leading others. There, go to bed."

"Thank you; I will," said Dick eagerly.

"You may sleep soundly for I shall visit the posts to-night and see that no one goes near the ammunition with a light."

"Where is it, then?" said Dick anxiously.

"Just below these rooms. I was obliged to have it put there temporarily. We'll make one of the places across the yard there a magazine to-morrow. Good-night."

"Good-night," said Dick, who had suddenly grown wakeful.

"You shan't be blown up, Dicky," continued Wyatt; "we can't spare you."

"I wish he hadn't said anything about that powder being underneath," muttered Dick as he undressed, after examining his charpoy, with its delicate muslin mosquito-curtains.

But he threw himself down with a weary sigh, thoroughly enjoying the elasticity of the laced-string bottom of the bedstead; and, powder or no powder, in less than five minutes he was fast asleep.

Chapter XIX
In Action

It was hard for a brief space for Richard Darrell to grasp the fact that he was not in cantonments at Roumwallah when the trumpet rang out in the grey dawn and echoed round the courtyard—for the change was sudden from deep sleep to wakefulness.

But the appearance of the bed-hangings and the strangeness of the place brought all back with a rush, and he leaped out of bed to run to the window and look out.

There in the courtyard, backed by the dark shadows, stood the six guns, looking pearl-grey with dew, and by them the fine, stalwart figure of one of the gunners in fatigue uniform, his sabre hooked up and carbine resting in the hollow of his arm, marching slowly up and down.

Away to the left was the lofty, dark arch of the gateway, made high enough to allow for the passage of a fully caparisoned elephant with the roofed howdah and ornament; and there, too, was a sentry pacing his beat at right angles to the man by the guns, who for some reason once more attracted Dick.

He stood gazing hard at the man, trying to make out his features; but it was too dark yet.

"It must be," thought Dick; "and—yes, that settles it—he limps slightly. It is Hanson."

Dick began to wonder whether the man would keep to his promise; and somehow the recollection of all that had passed kept the thinker's brain actively employed during the time he was dressing, with the full intention of taking advantage of the cool freshness of the morning to have a stroll about the place.

By the time he was dressed the men were giving the final touches to the guns, which glistened in the morning sunshine, free from every speck of dust; from the long double range of stables the whinnying and stamping of horses was heard, while the camp-servants and others were busily rearranging the baggage and ammunition-wagons along the front of the stabling, formerly, no doubt, the site of much more important buildings.

The first man he met on descending to the courtyard was Sergeant Stubbs, who looked full of business, but found time to salute.

"Was not that Hanson on guard by the guns, Sergeant?" asked Dick.

"Yes, sir," said the old sergeant, shaking his head. "It's him, and it ain't him, if you can understand that."

"Find him changed?" said Dick eagerly.

"Changed ain't the word for it, sir. There's something wrong with him. I ain't a sooperstitious man as believes in fetches and warnings and that sort of thing, but if Bob Hanson gets something at our next set-to, I shouldn't be much surprised."

"I should," said Dick shortly—"very much."

"Yes, sir," said the sergeant respectfully, "you would be, I dessay; but, begging your pardon, sir, one thinks very differently when you're one side o' twenty to what you do when you're the other side o' two twenties."

"Morning, Darrell.—Morning, Sergeant; you're beginning to get a bit ship-shape," said Wyatt, coming upon them suddenly.

"Yes, sir; soon be right now. Saves a lot of time having no tents to set up or strike. These'll make better quarters than our old ones as soon as we're shook down."

"No doubt," said Wyatt.—"Which way are you going, Darrell?"

"To the gate, and to have a stroll round. Come?"

For answer Wyatt walked with his young companion to the great gate, and then stopped short.

"Don't go out yet, my lad," he said quietly; "and when you do go, have some one with you, and carry your side-arms."

"Think it's necessary?" said Dick sharply, as he gave a wondering look at the very serious aspect of his companion.

"Yes. Give up this morning's stroll, and let's go up here and have a walk along the roof, or battlements, whichever you like to call them."

"Very well," said Dick in rather a disappointed tone.

Wyatt noted it, and entered a side archway just large enough to admit one, Dick following him up a narrow stairway to the terrace-like roof of the old palace, the place being furnished with a good breastwork and quite open, so that they could walk right round the courtyard.

The sun was now rising, and they had a good view of part of the city with occasional glimpses of the walls by which it was ended.

"Better than I thought for," said Wyatt after being silent for some time. "Last night I was afraid that the other buildings were nearer, and would command this place in case of trouble, but we command them."

Every man knew what he had to do, and did it with the precision taught by long practice, so that there was not the slightest confusion; while already, when the two officers descended, the people from the town and neighbourhood were bringing in fruit, vegetables, and other provisions as if to a market, and the mess-men and cooks had their quarters fitted up, and were hard at work.

That morning the officers' table was liberally supplied by the Rajah, and the meal was eaten in peace, everything being satisfactory—even the doctor's report, he having no one on the sick-list—nothing to do.

"I think we may congratulate ourselves on our progress so far," said Hulton.

He had hardly spoken when there was the trampling of a horse and the loud challenge of sentries, regardless of which latter a man dashed in through the gateway at full speed, and drew rein so suddenly that he threw his horse upon its haunches.

The officers hurried to the window, and the rider, seeing them, drew a paper from his cummerbund, spurred his horse up towards where they stood, a floor above him, stuck the paper on the point of the lance he carried, and held it up to Hulton.

"Look out," said Wyatt quickly. "Treachery, perhaps. He may thrust."

"It means his death if he does," said Hulton firmly, for two sentries had run up and caught the horseman's reins.

As he spoke he took the paper from the point of the lance, unrolled and read it aloud to his companions:

"'To Captain Hulton.—My spies bring word Rajah Singh with strong force approaching fast.—Doon.'"

"That's plain English," said Hulton sharply. Then to one of the sentries he shouted the one word, "Trumpeter!"

The men were already on the alert, the dashing in of the messenger having brought them out from barrack-room and stable, and there was no need to search for the youth whose presence was needed. Foreseeing that his services might be required, he had been to fetch his instrument, and now came running across the courtyard, received his orders—and the messenger's dark eyes flashed with excitement as he sat up like a bronze statue, keenly watching everything. Then the trumpet sounded its call, making the walls echo, the first blast seeming to electrify the place, as it drew forth sounds even from the stables, where the horses whinnied, snorted, and began to stamp.

"Now, gentlemen," said Hulton sharply, "I want the Rajah to see how quickly we can turn out."

To one unaccustomed to such a scene, it would have been marvellous in its celerity and freedom from confusion. A few minutes had scarcely elapsed since the coming in of the messenger before the horses, already harnessed, were being led out and attached to the gun-limbers, and the officers' chargers were being hurried by the syces to the flight of steps leading up to their quarters.

But the buzz of preparation was not confined to the old palace, for already there was the trampling of horses in the streets outside, and armed footmen were hurrying by the gate as if to a gathering of troops elsewhere.

"The alarm comes soon, Wyatt," said the captain, buckling on his sword, "and it is a pity that we are so strange. The Rajah has generals, I suppose; and we know nothing of where the attack is expected."

"Of course you will act quite independently of the Rajah's men, and as seems best."

"Of course," said the captain, going once more to the window, as he drew the chin-strap of his helmet beneath his chin.—"Capital!" he exclaimed. "Well done!—Come, gentlemen, or we shall be last."

He led the way to a little terrace at the head of the steps, where the trumpeter, already mounted, sat close by the messenger, waiting, the latter's horse looking startled and uneasy at the flashing helmets close at hand and their scarlet, waving, horse-tail plumes; but his rider steadied him, and once more horse and man stood there like a bronze group.

Meanwhile the sergeants were hurrying here and there, seeing that everything was ready, and then came to a standstill.

This was the signal for Hulton to spring upon his charger. The buzz of preparation had given place to a silence broken only by the uneasy stamp of a hoof and the champing of bits, while the windows and doors of the different buildings were thronged by the white-robed servants who would be left behind.

"Can you remember the way to the palace taken by the elephant last night, Mr Darrell?"

"Yes, sir," said Dick sharply.

"Lead," said the captain laconically. Then, after a final look round, he signed to the trumpeter, whose notes rang out, and every man stood at "attention."

Another blast, and gunners sprang on horse or limber as the three drivers to each gun mounted.

Another blast, and the advance-guard marched with Dick, the messenger trotting without orders to his side; and all filed out beneath the gateway into the narrow street, the gun-wheels, limbers, and ammunition-wagons rattling and rumbling, while way was made for the strangers.

A note rang out from behind, and the troop broke into a trot, Dick feeling doubtful of finding his way through the intricate streets and lanes; but some object which had struck his attention overnight always came to his help, till he successfully performed his task, and reached the wide opening in front of the palace.

As they were debouching on to this place at a trot, Hulton cantered up alongside of the leaders, for he had grasped the position at once.

"We should only be crippled here, Darrell," he said. "Lead the men to the bridge, cross the river, and out on to the plain."

This was easily done, for a broad avenue of trees led from the palace to the river gate and the bridge over which they had entered the town.

The road was pretty clear, so the trumpet was sounded again, and the troop broke into a gallop, tearing along till the gate, whose tower was manned now with troops, came into view; and through this they dashed and over the bridge, where quite a crowd of mounted men could now be seen.

These were all in motion, apparently without discipline or motive; but as Dick rode on he could see that they were not without a leader, for several brilliantly dressed officers were amongst them, and the Rajah himself was present on his elephant.

The horse artillery troop bore off a little to the right, thundering by this body of irregular cavalry—apparently about a thousand strong—swept round them into line, and, at the trumpet-sound, halted as perfectly as if on parade, when Captain Hulton cantered up to the Rajah's side.

"How quick you have been!" said the latter involuntarily.

"Quick, sir?" replied Hulton; "and yet we were last."

"Yes; but my people were out here before the messenger was sent to you. Listen now; the enemy is coming by the open road from the north. I have left all my footmen to hold the walls of the city, and I propose marching to meet these people and attack them at once. You can take the lead, or follow, whichever will be best."

"Neither will be best, sir," said Hulton gravely. "To be of most service I must be free. We can help you better by riding in advance on either flank where-ever it is open. But, tell me, are there any mountain-passes beyond the forest there?"

"No; open ground fit for cavalry. If we are forced to retire, make for the city at once. We can hold that."

"And we shall be of no use," thought Hulton as he saluted the Rajah and rode back to the troop, fully determined to act as he thought best, and not to be shut up in the city if it was possible to maintain himself and his men outside.

Giving the order to dismount, to rest the horses for a few minutes, he had a short consultation with Wyatt, telling him all he had heard from the Rajah.

"He must go on his own way," he said in Dick's hearing. "It will be a fight quite in the old fashion, as they have always fought, but it will be against an enemy who fights in the same way; so, if they are not too many, our bit of civilised warfare may turn the tables on the Rajah's side."

A few dozen more mounted men came galloping up to join the Rajah's force, and then he evidently made preparations for an advance.

"He is wrong," said Hulton, "for there are narrow roads and jungle yonder, while here he has room for his cavalry to act."

Then, seeing that the Rajah was sending out detachments to feel for the enemy, and two more at intervals to act as supports, the captain felt better satisfied, knowing that the attack on the part of the enemy could not occur without due warning; while, to make the best use he could of the guns, he moved the troop up to a little hill, which gave him a commanding view of the country for a couple of miles round—the detachments of cavalry sent forward coming once more into view—but the glass showed no sign of the enemy.

Wyatt came to where Dick was seated once, looked at him sharply, and nodded.

"It may turn out to be a false alarm," he said. "Humph! Hulton thinks so too," he added, for the order was given to dismount, so as to ease the horses as much as possible, and keep them fresh for any work they might be called upon to do.

Then half-an-hour passed, and this grew into an hour, during which the Rajah's men changed their position again and again, but, as in accordance with Hulton's notions, they kept well out in the open; and Dick was watching the restless movements of the body, where every man seemed to be acting according to his own ideas—there being no signs of cohesion or mutual support—when he found that the old sergeant was close to his elbow.

"I expect these fellows can fight, sir," he said in a low voice. "You've never seen anything of the kind, I suppose?"

"Nothing but sham fights, Stubbs," answered Dick.

"Ah! there'll be nothing sham about this, sir. I expect the enemy will get well within reach, and then make one big charge, if our side doesn't begin the business; and then they'll all brush up, and it'll be hand-to-hand lighting, scattering all over the field, and giving us a very poor chance, for we shan't be able to fire for fear of hitting our friends. Look, sir, look!" he said sharply. "Your eyes are keener than mine. Can you make anything out yonder, a mile away, by that patch of wood?"

"Cavalry," said Dick excitedly.

The officers had caught sight of the movement, and Hulton's orders were given sharply. The men sprang to their saddles, the guns were wheeled round, unlimbered, loaded; and Dick's heart began to throb heavily as the movement developed, and they could make out a detachment of horse galloping back towards them, followed by another and another—evidently the parties sent out in search of the enemy.

There was no doubt of this being the case, for, directly after, a cloud of horsemen came into view in full pursuit; and, from a movement in the neighbourhood of the Rajah's elephant, it was evident that all this was seen, for fully half of his force began to gallop forward in support of their friends.

"That's what the captain was afraid of, sir," said Stubbs. "Before long they will all be mixed up together, and there'll be no telling which is which. They ought to keep retiring and leading the enemy on, so as to give us a chance. Hullo, what does this mean?" he said aloud, and he looked anxiously in the captain's direction.

It meant that, however inexperienced the enemy's chief might be in European tactics, he was a better general than Rajah Doon, for the attack was to be made from two quarters at once, and the horse artillery troop was to have its chance of doing good after all.

Hulton saw the danger at once—a serious peril not yet noticed by the troops about the Rajah's elephant.

For a large force of mounted men had suddenly come into view away to the left in the most unexpected way, so that the attack was about to be delivered in front and rear; and if the Rajah's men proved unable to hold their own, there was the possibility of a disastrous business, the only way of retreat being over the river, and there was no infantry to hold the front of the bridge while the mounted men crossed it into the shelter of the town.

"Looks bad for us," thought Dick, who in imagination saw the troop and their guns helplessly wedged in amongst the irregular horse.

But there was no more time for thought; Hulton's orders were being obeyed. The front was changed, and the little battery faced round towards the approaching cloud of horsemen, who were about to deliver their attack at a gallop before the Rajah's troops could recover from their surprise.

From where the young subaltern was seated he could command every movement, and though wanting in the steady rush of a European cavalry charge, the enemy's horse kept well together quite a thousand strong; and Dick's heart palpitated as he loosened his sword in the scabbard, and then saw to his pistols, for it seemed to him that before many minutes were over the enemy would be upon them, riding them down.

But the surprise was to the foe, whose leaders were under the impression that they would sweep away the little group of horses and men stationed upon the hill.

Hulton waited till the enemy were only a few hundred yards away before giving the word to fire. Then *thud—thud—thud*—the guns began to belch forth their clouds of white smoke, and the rapid reloading went on, so that the regular intervals could be preserved, the discharge of number six being followed by that of number one, ready again, but with a different charge.

It was horribly exciting, and the young subaltern had ample time to see the effects of the fire. The disorder began in the approaching body with the first discharge, horses and men coming to the ground at every shot; but there was no check in the rush—men leaped their horses over those who fell, and a wild yell now smote the ears of the troop, heard well above the roar of the guns.

But as the first gun delivered its second round, this time with grape instead of round-shot, the havoc caused had its due effect; while as the five more discharges followed, tearing through the densely-packed crowd, there was a few moments' check; but finding the firing suddenly cease, the hesitation passed away, and, with fierce cries of rage, the enemy dashed up the slope, and charged straight through the dense cloud of smoke, dispersing it in all directions.

A yell of rage burst forth as they encountered a second surprise. For as the second discharge roared from the guns, the order to limber up was given, and while the enemy was still a hundred yards away the swift battery was in motion, and, covered by the smoke, swept off down one side of the hill and away at right angles, to take up a fresh position nearly a mile away.

Then was the time for the Rajah's force to have delivered their charge, while the enemy was halting in a state of confusion, but it did not come; and as soon as the enemy had recovered from its surprise, there was a rush made in pursuit of the battery, which halted, turned, and poured in another half-dozen rounds, and was off again, with the guns bumping and leaping as the horses stretched out and raced over the ground.

No less than six times did Hulton bring his battery into action from different parts of the field, playing terrible havoc in the enemy's ranks, and then his work seemed to be done, for, as had been foreseen, the battle had become a cavalry mêlée, or, rather, a series of single combats, friend and foe being hopelessly intermingled. But one thing was plain enough from where the artillery were seated, waiting for another chance to be of service. In spite of the terrible losses they had sustained, the enemy was steadily pressing the Rajah's people back towards the river and the bridge, Hulton raging as he felt how helpless he was to produce a diversion.

"Why hasn't he a regiment or two of foot there to cover the retreat?" he cried. "There would have been plenty of time for them to man the walls afterwards. Can you suggest anything, Wyatt?"

"No," was the reply. "It's what I expected. We've done our work, and ought to be getting over the bridge now."

"If we were there now we should be jammed. Look at them; they're beginning to fly, and our retiring would have a terribly bad effect."

"There must be another gate and a bridge on the other side of the city," said Wyatt. "What do you say to following the river-bank?"

"I don't want to leave the ground. We ought to be covering the retreat," cried Hulton angrily.

"That's quite right," said Wyatt; "but we should injure friends more than foes, and we ought to be moving off. No; look!"

He pointed away along the course of the river, and as Dick followed the direction of his hand, it was to see that a fresh body of cavalry was coming up in the direction Wyatt had proposed for their retreat; while, to add to the peril, from the same direction the white cotton garments of a strong body of foot could be seen following the horse.

That gave something to do, and, rapidly unlimbering, the approaching horse and foot were soon thrown into a state of disorder, and their advance for the time being was checked. But fresh peril threatened. The enemy had gathered together away to their right, and the guns had to be slewed round for a fresh discharge; but before half the volley had parted, a body of about fifty horsemen came on at a gallop, opening out right and left so as to avoid the next discharge.

There was no time for limbering up, and drivers and horse-holders prepared to defend their dismounted comrades to the death.

But as the horsemen opened out they shouted wildly, and a revulsion of feeling swept through Dick as he grasped the fact that they were friends, who reined up ready to help them.

The gunners sprang to their places again, and once more the guns spoke out to their front and to their left flank, where the fresh horse and foot were coming.

"Is there another bridge?" cried Hulton in Hindustani to the leader of their reinforcement.

"Yes; but we could not reach it now," was the reply.

"Then we must charge right across the field."

"No, no," cried the leader; "there is the ford."

"Hah! could we take the guns across?"

"Yes. Follow us."

"Wait!" shouted Hulton, and six more discharges were sent at the hesitating enemy, the smoke rising densely and again covering their retreat. For, before the enemy could realise what had happened, the battery was limbered up and in full retreat towards the river, the leader of the little body of horsemen taking them diagonally down to the stream, his men dashing in at a gallop, for the fresh body coming from the open bridge now grasped what was about to be done, and came on with a rush to capture the guns.

There was no hesitation on the part of the troop. As the horsemen dashed in, sending the water flying, in rushed the men with the leading gun, the water rising above the axles of the wheels and foaming round them, as, of necessity slowing down, the horses tore through the river, a good hundred yards wide, the drivers making every effort to get their teams through in safety.

Fortunately the water shallowed as they neared the farther bank beneath the walls; unfortunately the enemy's foot reached the bank that had been left soon after the last gun had been dragged in, and opened a dropping fire from their long matchlocks, the bullets rattling on the gun-carriages and making more than one horse plunge wildly.

It was only a matter of minutes, and then the enemy's fire slackened before a fierce rattle of musketry opened upon them from the walls, effectually covering the retreat of the troop, once more on firm ground—a well-made road running along beneath the walls, leading to a gate, through which the battery passed—while the firing grew louder in the direction of the bridge.

"Going to make for the old palace, and defend ourselves there?" said Wyatt, riding up abreast of Hulton.

Dick heard the question, and looked towards his leader, seeing him slowly turn his face towards his brother-officer, and then raise his hand with his sword hanging by the knot from his wrist, to take off his helmet, before drooping forward over his saddle-bow.

"Ah!" exclaimed a familiar voice close to Dick's elbow, "the captain's hit;" and the old sergeant spurred forward to Hulton's other side to keep him on his horse.

"Forward!" rang out Wyatt's order, and then he shouted to one of the horsemen to guide them to their quarters.

"Pass the word for the doctor," said Wyatt then hoarsely.

"He's badly hurt, sir," said the sergeant. "They've got him on the limber of the last gun."

"Tut, tut!" ejaculated Wyatt; and then he was silent till the gateway of the old palace was reached, and they filed into the yard, where the guns were placed so as to cover the entrance, and Captain Hulton and six of the men were helped into one of the rooms, turned for the time being into a hospital; while directly after, by a strange irony of fate, the doctor, to whom they should have looked for help at such a time as this, was lifted carefully off the blood-stained limber and borne in last.

"Sergeant," cried Wyatt, "gallop to the bridge and see what is being done there. The Rajah may need a couple of the guns to sweep it."

As he spoke, the heavy report of a cannon told that one of the pieces mounted at the main gate was being brought into action.

The sergeant went off without a word; and as the men stood to their guns, ready for anything that might befall them now, Dick followed Wyatt into the hospital room.

"Now, Dick, lad," he said hoarsely, "you are a doctor's son; for heaven's sake, bring all you know to bear. Hulton first."

The lad was already unbuckling his belt; his heavy helmet followed, and, with a strange feeling of horror and dismay attacking him now after the wild excitement of the fight, he bent down over Hulton, who lay upon a charpoy, perfectly insensible, and with his face of a strangely pallid hue, contracted, too, as if by approaching death.

Chapter XX
Playing the Doctor

In answer to the call made upon him—a tremendous call at such a time—Dick carefully removed the captain's jacket, soaked with blood, back and breast telling plainly enough the kind of wound with which he had to deal; and, as it was drawn and ripped off, there was a sharp rap upon the floor, from which Wyatt stooped to pick up a ragged jezail bullet, which, discharged at so short a distance, had passed right through the poor fellow's chest.

Wyatt looked at Dick inquiringly.

"I am not doctor enough to know," whispered the lad. "I can only plug and bind the wounds. A vital part may not be touched."

Wyatt's lip quivered slightly under his great moustache, but he said nothing, only looked on, while one of the men proved himself an able aid in producing lint and bandages from the doctor's valise.

"See to the doctor next," said Wyatt in a low voice. "I must leave you directly."

"Yes," said Dick; and as soon as his first patient was finished he turned to the doctor, who was just recovering from his swoon.

He smiled wistfully at Dick as the lad approached his bed and looked at him inquiringly.

"Badly hurt," he said. "Back of my head and across my side. The fellow cut at me like lightning, but the sergeant ran him through."

"Don't talk much," said Dick, "but guide me, and tell me what to do."

"You know as well as I can tell you, Mr Darrell," the surgeon answered bluntly. "I saw part of what you did for the captain. Most unfortunate—most unfortunate," he murmured, and he fainted again from loss of blood.

Just then the sergeant came in quickly, and made for Wyatt to deliver his report, the heavy firing endorsing all he said.

"Rajah in safe, sir, with the greater part of his men; others made off together, with enemy in pursuit. They've got the gates closed, and the guns at work sweeping the bridge, and the Rajah says there is no need for you to send help."

"You saw the Rajah to speak to, then?"

"Oh, yes, sir. I went straight to the side of his elephant. He says the engagement is over for to-day, and the enemy beaten off."

"Humph!" growled Wyatt. "Seems more like our being beaten in."

"Yes, sir. He said, too, that he should like to see Captain Hulton as soon as he could come."

"Then he will have to wait some time," muttered Wyatt. "Here, stay with Mr Darrell, Sergeant. Do all you can to help him, and then see to the men who are well enough being moved. We must have another room for them."

Wyatt stepped to the wounded men, said a few encouraging words to them, and then, telling his brother-officer he would be back as soon as possible, he went out to see to the prospects of defence, in case the enemy should obtain a lodgment in the city.

"What can I do, sir?" said the sergeant, crossing to where his young officer was busy with the wounded men.

"Anything, Stubbs. Hold this poor fellow up while I see to his wound."

"Right, sir. Who is it? Oh, it's you, Dundas.—Slit the linen right down, sir; that's the way.—How are you, my lad?"

"Bit sicky, Sergeant.—'Tar'n't much, is it, sir?"

"I hope not," said Dick. "The bullet is embedded in the muscles of the back. I will not attempt to extract it—only stop the bleeding."

"Pretty sort of a fellow you are, Joe Dundas, to get a wound like that," said the sergeant, holding a brass basin of water for the amateur surgeon to use. "I should be ashamed of it!"

"I am, Sergeant," said the man, smiling.

"Let it be a lesson to you, my lad. Never turn your back to the enemy. Always show 'em your face."

"Shouldn't keep our guns long if we did, Sergeant," said the man grimly.

"Do I hurt you?" said Dick.

"Well, it isn't what one might call pleasant, sir. Not the sort of thing a man would choose to amuse him."

"But you can bear it?"

"Oh, yes, sir, I can bear it."

"Because I find I can touch the bullet, and it will be better out."

"Out with it, then, sir," said the sergeant; "Joe won't mind. Nasty ragged kind of bullets these are which they fire from their matchlocks, and they irritate."

"That hurt you, Dundas?"

"Yes, sir; but you go on," replied the man, who had winced from the pain he suffered.

"Yes, go on, sir," growled the sergeant. "You're too easy with him. He's a man—not a gal. Never mind making him squeak. Our last surgeon used to say it did good and set up a healthy action."

"Hah!" whispered the man through his set teeth. "That was sharp, sir."

"Yes, but I've got the bullet," said Dick.—"Now, Sergeant, bathe away, and the wound will soon heal."

"Oh, yes.—You needn't lie up, Joe, my lad."

"Not going to, Sergeant."

"You can sit out in the yard for a few days and smoke your pipe, or go in and talk to the horses. And, if I was you, I should let one of the fellows in the bazaar drill a hole through that bullet and put a bit of gold wire through it, so that you can wear it on your watch-chain."

"Yes," said the man gravely.—"Been awkward, I s'pose, sir, if it had gone a bit farther?"

"Very," said Dick, who could not help feeling amazed at the calm way in which the stalwart gunner seemed to trust him.

"Heart, sir?"

"I think so."

"Ah, you'd know, sir," said the man. "It's a lucky thing for us chaps that you joined."

"Why?" said Dick, who was busy with a bandage.

"Well, sir, you see, you can lead and fight and at the same time you was born a doctor—so I've heared."

Dick laughed. "There," he said, finishing his task. "Now lie on your side, and go to sleep if you can. I hope Doctor Robson will soon be well enough to see to you."

"Thank ye, sir; but I mean to be well before he is," said the man cheerily.

Dick attended man after man with his assistants till they came to the last, who was lying on a charpoy with his face averted.

"Now, my lad," said the sergeant, "your turn. Yours a bullet too?"

The man slowly turned a face blackened with sweat and gunpowder, and looked up in a dazed way at the speaker.

"Bob Hanson!" cried the sergeant. "Why, I didn't know you were one of the men hit."

"Yes, Sergeant, I've got it this time," said the man grimly.

"Well, I'm sorry, my lad, for I never saw a gun better served than yours was to-day. Bullet in the back?"

"Two," said the man slowly. "I was hit twice before we got to the middle of the river."

The wounds were painful, but they were superficial, the bullets having glanced from the rib-bones, and with care it only meant a fortnight in hospital, as Dick was able to announce; and while he was busy over the bandaging, the sergeant looked on, frowning. Hanson bore what must have been intense pain without flinching, and the young officer mused as he worked upon the strange accident which had brought this man completely helpless under his hands.

He was just finishing when Wyatt returned, to approach the beds and speak a word or two with each of the wounded.

"Painful, but not serious," he said, repeating Dick's words. "I'm very glad, my lads, for we can't spare you."

He laid his hand on Dick's shoulder, and walked with him to the window.

"Thank you, my lad," he said gravely. "We must drop the boy now, Dick, and accept this big responsibility."

"We?" said Dick.

"Yes, *we*! I've got the burden of all this suddenly thrust upon my shoulders, and I feel that I must have help. Hulton will be fit for nothing this side of a month."

"Well, look at me with my responsibility. I never before felt so much like an impudent boy as I have done this last hour, playing surgeon with these wounded men."

"Not much play in it, Dick, lad," said Wyatt sadly. "Well, little un, we're in for it, and we've got it to do. I know you'll stand by me like a man."

"Yes, *like* a man," said Dick, "but only as a boy."

"Never mind that. Now tell me—poor old Hulton will get better?"

"I think so; but he has a bad wound, and ought to have proper treatment."

"Don't worry about that, lad. You will be able to get bits of advice soon from Robson, and put them into practice. Then you've got nature to help you, and she's a grand nurse when her patients are healthy men, so don't let what you have to do worry you. Things will come right. Now I want to talk. I have seen the Rajah."

"Ah! what does he say?"

"All cock-a-hoop. Ready to hug me. He says he never saw anything so grand as the way in which we pursued his enemies. It will be a lesson to the Rajah of Singh that he will never forget, he says."

"But we were beaten."

"Yes, he owns that; but, as he says justly, his enemies were four times as strong, and though he has lost some of his men, the enemy have done nothing. The city is safe, and strong enough to set Singh at defiance. Horsemen are of no use against stone walls, and there is an abundance of stores and plenty of water, so that he has nothing to fear but treachery."

"Treachery?"

"Yes; he says he has so many people about him that he dare not trust. Finally, he says he looks to us to keep him safe upon the throne."

"To us! The English—the Company?"

"No, to us—you and me."

Dick laughed.

"Ah, you may grin, my lad; but he means it. He told me he had taken a fancy to you."

"Means nothing," said Dick. "These Indians are all smiles and flattery."

"Some of them, but I don't think this Rajah is a humbug. He has seen a good deal of our people, and he is very downright. He told me he was sorry to hear that so brave an officer as Hulton was wounded, but that he did not take to him much, for he was too haughty and supercilious to him."

"Yes," said Dick thoughtfully, "Hulton was a bit stand-offish to him."

"Yes; that's his way, poor fellow. The Rajah said that though he was in trouble, and we belonged to the conquering race, he still felt that he was a king, and Hulton seemed to look down upon him."

"He said all that?"

"Every bit, in other words. And here's what I liked, Dick. He said all that he knew of me was from seeing me in the field with the men, but he felt that I was a brave English gentleman."

"Hear, hear! So you are."

"Don't be a fool, Dick," said Wyatt shortly; "this is serious."

"Well, I was never more serious in my life."

"Gammon! And he said that if I would stick to him—"

"That he didn't," said Dick. "Not an Eastern style of expression."

"Get out! You know what I mean—that if I'd stand by him well with the men, I should find him a very true friend."

"And what did you say?"

"Only that we were sent to do our duty, and that we'd stick to him like trumps."

"Did you explain to him what a trump was?" said Dick dryly.

"No, I didn't; but I shook hands as if I meant it; and he made a face, for I gave him a grip such as he isn't used to, for my paws are rather heavy, and he has a hand thin and soft as a girl's."

"Poor fellow!" said Dick. "I've felt that squeeze of yours. Regular walnut-crusher. Was that all?"

"No; I began to find fault with his majesty about what happened to-day, and pointed out what he ought to have done."

"How did he take it?"

"He smiled, and said I was quite right, but that out here they are not used to fighting like we do: that his men could fight like furies behind stone walls or in hand-to-hand fighting on horseback, but we had shown him to-day what might be done: and he ended by saying. 'Stand by me, and help me.'"

"And you?"

"Well, I said we would; but I don't like it, Dick."

"Why?"

"Because, as I've said before, we're out of place."

"We weren't this morning."

"No, not out on the plain, but towards the end; and if Mr Rajah Singer or Scorcher, or whatever his name is, had been a soldier, he'd have made a better dash at capturing our battery. Just now I feel ready to wish we were infantry officers, with five hundred bayonets at our backs. What are we to do—use the guns from the walls?"

"No," said Dick with energy; "make sallies, and next time we go take rations for a day or two, so that we can hold out, and not be bound to retreat into the town."

"That isn't a boy talking, Dick," said Wyatt sharply as he clapped his companion on the shoulder. "You make me see daylight through the smoke. I was quite disheartened at our being caged up here. Yes, we'll do something yet. Now then, have a look round at your patients, doctor, and then come with me."

Chapter XXI
Sergeant Stubbs Opens his Eyes

Hulton was sleeping and the men were lying fairly restful, but the doctor was awake and eager to know of everything that had been done.

Dick told him as much as he could, the doctor nodding his satisfaction.

"Good," he said at last. "Your father must be a clever man, Darrell. Now, do your duty by me."

"How?" said Dick, smiling.

"Tell me to leave off talking and go to sleep, so as to lessen the fever that is sure to supervene."

"I'll ensure that by going away, and leaving this man to keep watch," said Dick: and the next minute he followed Wyatt out into the yard, where the men of the troop were seeing to the cleaning up and oiling of the guns and carriages, while the syces were busy over the horses, which were dry now, and none the worse for the galloping they had gone through, save two which had bullets in their haunches. Fortunately the bullets were small, and had penetrated but a little way, and the farrier of the troop had decided that the poor animals would be fit for work in a day or two.

While the officers were inspecting the horses, the fire that had been going on by the bridge gate slackened, and then died out, but scattered shots which had been heard at intervals on the other side of the city increased now to a roar, broken by the rattle of musketry.

News soon came in that the enemy had been making a fierce attack upon the other gate, and had been repulsed, while now the firing died out, and it was evident that the fighting was over for the day.

Soon after the Rajah, followed by a retinue of his officers, made his appearance at the great gates, and was challenged by the sentry. The guard turned out, and a message was sent to Wyatt, while the Rajah sat frowning in his howdah, and the officers who accompanied him scowled and looked furious, each man seeking the Rajah's eye, as if asking leave to cut down the insolent Englishmen who blocked the way into the Rajah's own palace, the place where his father had held his court.

But they were not kept waiting long; Wyatt and Dick came quickly out to the gate. The Rajah and his retinue were ushered in, and taken about the old place, where everything had been so rapidly transformed.

It was evident that the Rajah and his followers were duly impressed by the orderly and businesslike appearance of men, horses, and weapons; and, after the way all had behaved that day, some of the scowling officers' faces showed that, if they were not friendly towards the new-comers, they were at least disposed to treat them with respect.

It was not deemed advisable for Hulton to be disturbed, and the Rajah was content to dismount and enter the mess-room, where he warmly thanked both officers for the help they had rendered that day.

Wyatt did not mince matters; he questioned the Rajah at once as to the possibility of a fresh attack that day or night, but he was told that such a thing was highly improbable.

"But," said the Rajah, "we shall most likely have a renewal of the fighting to-morrow. I may count upon you?"

"Of course, sir," said Wyatt quietly; "that is why we are here. But I cannot help thinking that it would be better if you refrained from leaving the city. You have guns and ammunition. Why not content yourself with waiting behind the walls?"

The Rajah looked at him in astonishment.

"Would you do so?" he said.

"I belong to the Flying Artillery," said Wyatt quietly; "my work is on the open plains."

"So is mine, at the head of my horsemen," said the Rajah, with a look of pride. "If I were to do as you propose, Rajah Singh would think that I was afraid: and, what is worse, my people would think so too, and refuse to obey a king who was a coward."

Wyatt bowed.

"If he comes to-morrow, he will find me with my horsemen drawn up, waiting. You will come?"

"Of course," said Wyatt quietly; "but I should advise that your general should hold a body of your cavalry ready to attack each time our fire has thrown the enemy into disorder."

"Yes," said the Rajah, "that shall be done. It would be wise."

At this he rose to go, and walked slowly to where his elephant was waiting, with his mounted guard in attendance, all scowling and looking exceedingly fierce, as if, in fact, they fully believed that their chief was in danger, and it was their duty to attack the sentries stationed here and there in his defence.

Wyatt and Dick stood watching the party file through the gate, and then the former turned to Dick.

"What are you thinking?" he said.

"That we don't seem to have many friends here," replied Dick. "Hallo! what does this mean? One of the enemy?"

For a richly-dressed officer rode back to the gateway, and after a moment's parley with the sentries was allowed to pass.

His face as he rode up to the two officers plainly showed that he was upon no inimical mission, but the bearer of a message from the Rajah, requesting that the officers would come and dine with him that evening.

"I can't go," said Dick sharply; "I have my wounded. Besides, I was there last night."

"It is impossible for me to go," said Wyatt.

"You must go," whispered Dick. "Go for as short a time as you can. It would give offence to refuse."

"Tell the Rajah I will do myself the honour of coming," said Wyatt shortly, and the messenger rode away.

"It would have been bad policy to refuse," continued Wyatt; "and I must get the Rajah to follow out my plans if we are to help him. Look here, Dick, I'm in command of a troop sooner than I expected—worse luck!—so I must make a couple of temporary promotions. You will act as my lieutenant, and Stubbs must take your place."

"Why not yours?" said Dick hurriedly.

"Because I want you," was the reply.

Wyatt deferred his departure to the last minute, and before leaving upon the elephant and with the guard the Rajah had sent, he summoned Sergeant Stubbs and announced to him that he was to act for the time being as a commissioned officer.

"You will help Mr Darrell in every way you can?" said Wyatt.

"Of course, sir."

"And, Mr Darrell, you will have an orderly on duty ready to send me a despatch if any emergency occurs. That is all, I think;" and he mounted and rode off.

A peculiar feeling of awe came over Dick as the last echo of the horses' trampling feet died out. It was almost indescribable, for he was conscious of being horribly alone and left to his own resources in a place where he was surrounded by enemies. He felt horribly young and helpless, and as if the great responsibility was crushing him down to such an extent that he must run away from it all before matters drove him wild.

The sensation was horrible while it lasted, and in a despairing way he felt that he was hopelessly overburdened, far more so than he could bear, and that everything now was sure to go wrong.

"Suppose," he argued, "the wounded get worse, and Hulton was to die.

"Suppose the men object to having nobody in command but me.

"Suppose the people in opposition to the Rajah should seize this time for attacking us, what could I do—how could I defend the place? I must have been half-mad to let Wyatt go and leave me.

"Suppose—suppose—suppose—"

There was no end to the suppositions, for the lad's brain had suddenly become terribly active, and was suggesting a whole series of phantasmic dangers, every one of which seemed bad enough to drive him to despair.

In fact, Dick was getting fast into the state ordinarily called "losing his nerve," and he started as if he had been guilty of some crime when, after watching him for some time unseen, Acting-lieutenant Stubbs suddenly uttered a short, gruff cough.

Dick looked at him wildly.

"Did you speak?" he said, making an effort to be firm, and succeeding, for the fancies which had troubled him grew faint.

"No, sir; only waiting to see if you had any orders for me."

"No," replied Dick, giving a cough to clear his throat; "I don't think there is anything more to be done until Mr Wyatt returns."

"Beg pardon, sir, but Captain Hulton is down, and Mr Wyatt naturally takes command of the battery. It is only a question of a natural promotion being confirmed. Wouldn't it be better to speak of the commanding officer as Captain Wyatt now?"

"Would it?" said Dick.

"I think so, sir; it would be better before the men."

"But it seems like taking Captain Hulton's rank from him now he is in trouble and giving it to another."

"Oh, no, sir—not at all. Here's Captain Hulton shot down after bringing his troop safe through a retreat after a gallant fight. He won't want his captain's title any more. You may take it for certain that he'll be Major Hulton now."

"I see," said Dick quietly. "Very well, then, I do not see that there is anything more to be done till Captain Wyatt returns."

Stubbs coughed and stared. "Yes?"

"Beg pardon, sir. Not from any wish to interfere, but I've been opening my eyes and ears a good deal since I came here."

"Well, and what have you seen and heard?"

"Just enough to make me understand that the Rajah and some of his people want to be good friends with us."

"Yes; he said so."

"While his mother, all the Brahmins, and the people who believe them would like to cut our throats."

"Yes, Stubbs; there is no doubt a division of opinion."

"Which means a house divided against itself, sir—enemies in camp as well as outside."

"I'm afraid so."

"Well, Mr Darrell, under the circumstances, and as I'm made an officer, *pro tempry,* as they call it, perhaps it wouldn't be out of place if I made a sort of suggestion."

"Not at all, Stubbs," replied Dick, pulling himself a little more together. "I shall be glad to hear anything you have to say. Of course, I am not obliged to follow your advice?"

"Cer-*tain*-ly not, sir. I only say what I do because I've been seeing what the people out here are like for the last twenty years."

"Exactly. Well, what is it?"

"Only this, sir. Some of them with brains take to the English—you know, and including Scotch and Irish too—while the others, the benighted ones, taught by their idol-worshipping old priests, hate us like poison."

"Yes, I know; and they're not to be trusted."

"That's it, sir. Consequently, you never know when there may be a rush. It's just as likely as not that, when you least expect it, a mob may come down upon you and never give you a chance."

"You believe there's a prospect of something of the kind now?" said Dick quickly.

"I think there's always a chance of it, sir; and it makes me venture to say that if I was in command here, shut up in what is half an enemy's city, I wouldn't trust to a couple of sentries at the gate. You see, if we were rushed the enemy'd do a lot of mischief before we could rally and hold part of the place."

"You'd double the sentries again, then, Stubbs?" said Dick quickly.

"No, sir. I wouldn't wish to be with braver chaps than ours are, but the sort of thing I want to guard against would take place before you could say 'Jack Robinson.' And what could four of ours do against a mob of men armed with knives, who think nothing of being killed, because their priests teach that if they've only killed a few infidels—meaning us—they'll be as right as a trivet?"

"You'd double them again?" said Dick.

"No, sir, I wouldn't. I'd do something much easier, and then have one sentry so as to spare the men."

"What do you mean?"

"Simplest thing in the world, sir," said Stubbs—"I'd shut the big gates."

"Of course. How stupid! Go and give orders for them to be closed at once."

Stubbs tightened his lips and shook his head. "Not now? Look suspicious?"

"Do it directly, sir: but you give the orders sharp yourself, and as if you meant business. The men will like it. You've no idea how they notice that sort of thing, sir, and what a deal they think of an officer who seems to be always on the *kwee weeve* to keep them out of danger. It gives 'em confidence, sir, and they work twice as well. That's why our troop's so smart—the men believe in their officers."

"Thank you, Stubbs," said Dick quietly. "Yes? You were going to say something else?"

"Which I were, sir. What do you say to ordering out the squads o' number one and two, letting 'em unlimber and turn the guns to command the gateway, then load up with grape, and dismiss all but two men with lighted linstocks. You could do with one sentry at the gate then, and take a couple from the roof to balance it."

"Yes, excellent," said Dick; and the next minute the orders were being given in as manly a tone as the lad could command, the gates were closed and barred, the men summoned, the guns run into position and loaded, and all dismissed save two who stood close to the breeches of the bright pieces, armed with their linstocks, each a smouldering spark.

Everything was gone through with the greatest alacrity; and as the men went back to their barrack-room one of them said to a comrade:

"Well, talk about old head on young shoulders!"

"Ah," said the other. "He's a sharp un, and no mistake."

"He is," said the first man. "I say, you know what the niggers believe in?"

"Everything. See that great copper idol in the temple just yonder?"

"What—of the fat chap with the elephant's head? Yes; but that isn't what I mean. 'Temsy chosy,' they call it—'bout a man always being on the change after he's dead, and coming out something else."

"Oh, yes, I've heared."

"I'm going to take to that way of thinking, for it seems to me that young Dick Dare-all must have been an old fighting-general come to life again."

And his comrade said, "Yah!"

But Dick, of course, heard nothing of this, or he would have called himself, in his straightforward, honest way, a jackdaw in borrowed plumes.

It might have meant nothing, but the sentry on duty at the closed gates noticed that the street in front was twice over filled with armed men, who hung about for some time; but he attributed it to the changing position of some of the Rajah's forces, and when guard was relieved he had nothing to report. Neither was his successor disturbed till about nine o'clock, when there was the jingle of accoutrements, trampling of horses, and the soft, shuffling sound of an elephant's feet.

Wyatt had returned, and upon finding the gates closed he dismounted outside, and was admitted as his escort rode away.

"Why, Dick," he said when they met, "have you been besieged?"

Explanations followed.

"Quite right. Old Stubbs is a fine, sterling fellow—a man to be trusted. I'm glad it was done, for things are very bad here—worse than I should have imagined; and if something pretty firm is not done the Rajah will lose his throne, and then, if we're not cut up first, we shall have to fight our way back to cantonments."

"What ought to be done?"

"The safest thing would be to take off the heads of the principal conspirators; only that is impossible."

"Why?"

"Because one is the Rajah's mother, and the other the chief Brahmin. But I'm too tired to talk. Let's visit the posts and then try and get a sleep."

Chapter XXII
How the Guns Worked

The next day there was a repetition of the evolutions, the enemy having drawn off, but only to make another attack during the afternoon and receive further punishment from Wyatt's troop, which was forced, by the desperate efforts to destroy it, into a series of retreating tactics which took them miles away over the open ground, upon which they could turn and fire over and over again.

The punishment inflicted by the well-served guns was terrible, and the enemy's cavalry was never allowed to get within touch, the horse artillery galloping away to take up position as often as could be on high ground, till well on in the day, when, enough having been done without loss, it was Wyatt's intention to make for the city gates and take refuge there.

But the enemy's swordsmen were not beaten. They kept on following up with desperate pertinacity, their leaders seeing that until the Rajah's new allies were destroyed there was no chance of winning the day. Hence it was that, towards sunset, Wyatt found himself quite unsupported half-a-dozen miles from the city, and with a strong body of cavalry between him and safety.

"There are two ways open, Dick," said Wyatt as they waited, breathing their horses at the top of a slope, the enemy a thousand yards away awaiting their coming, and so posted that, if the troop advanced upon the main body, a wing thrown out on either side would close in and take them as in a trap.

Wyatt stood with his arm through his bridle, talking with Dick as he watched the enemy's movements through his glass.

"Well," said Dick, after waiting some moments for his companion to speak, "what do you say?"

"Charge through them or retreat."

"Go right away?"

"Yes; we have our rations, and can make them last."

"Camp out, and risk attacks during the night?" said Dick.

"Yes; that's the worst of it. Then you advocate charging right through?"

"I didn't say so," said Dick; "but that seems the thing to do."

"Yes," said Wyatt, closing his glass and letting it fall to the extent of the slings. "We might gallop to that hillock and give them a salvo first."

"Suppose they charged; they'd be upon us before we could limber up, and, even if we got away in time, we should only have tired the horses more and done no particular good. They only come together again like sand."

"Words of wisdom, General Dick," said Wyatt. "I tell you what—we'll spoil that trap they have been setting for us by a feint. We'll rest the horses as long as they will let us, and then move off to the left as if we meant to get round the other side of that palm-tree tope. They will send off half their men to intercept us, and as soon as they have got out of sight we'll turn, right incline, and charge straight through the rest. They'll never expect such an attack as that."

Dick nodded his satisfaction as he grasped his companion's plan.

"Yes," he said, "it will be a grand surprise, for they'll think we're retreating."

A few minutes were devoted to examining girths and the harness of the teams. Then, with the trumpeter close up to Wyatt, the preparatory note was blown, the order to mount was given, and as their movements were carefully watched by the enemy, who were seen to close up a little, the troop advanced, changed front, and went off at a steady trot away to the left, as if to put the patch of forest between them and the trap laid, and escape by getting back to the city after taking a long sweep round.

Matters fell just as Wyatt had anticipated. As soon as the manoeuvre was grasped, there was a quick movement among the great body of irregular cavalry, and about half went off at a gallop to intercept them on the far side of the tope, while the rest sat firm.

The troop kept on at their steady trot, and as the head of the troop nearly reached the far side of the patch of woodland, the trumpet rang out "Gallop!" and away they went as if racing to pass round their side first.

The effect on the enemy was electrical. They tore on like a whirlwind, and as they passed out of sight the trumpet sounded again, the head of the troop swung round with Wyatt in front, and dashed straight at the centre of the remaining half of their foes, which was just being put in motion as if to pursue them.

The term "taken aback" thoroughly exemplifies the effect of the manoeuvre, for as the enemy saw the troop bearing down upon them at full gallop—absolutely tearing over the ground *ventre à terre*—a shiver seemed to run through the dense body of horsemen. There was a movement to advance, another to retire, and again a confused attempt to open out to right and left, and then the whole body was seething, as it were, in a state of confusion; while all the time, with a strange, rumbling, rattling sound, the little column, with swords flashing out now in the evening sunshine, tore along, getting nearer and nearer, till, with a loud hurrah, the head of the troop was upon them.

But not upon a dense mass of cavalry waiting to receive their charge; for, with one impulse, the enemy broke and melted away in a wild radiation from the spot where they had stood, scattering in all directions, and galloping for their lives; while, without the loss of a man, Wyatt and his followers tore right through, making for a knoll half a mile ahead, where a halt was called, to breathe the horses and once more unlimber the guns.

There was method in all this, for that which Wyatt had also anticipated was once more about to happen.

There was nothing to fear from the half that had been dispersed. They were still in full flight, utterly broken, without cohesion, and not likely to form up into a whole again for hours. But the half that had charged round the tope of palm-trees was still in hand, and fierce for fight on finding how they had been outmanoeuvred; and as soon as they had realised what had happened, their leaders halted them, gathered them—as much as such an irregular body could be gathered—in hand, and came in pursuit.

"A couple of rounds from each gun, Darrell, lad," said Wyatt. "We shall just have time, and then off and away for home. It will sicken some of them."

The guns were loaded, and, linstock in hand, the men waited till the order was given, Wyatt pausing too long to give them time to get a second round from each gun, as Dick thought, knowing well what the consequences would be if the fierce horsemen could get among them with their keen tulwars before the troop could limber up.

But Wyatt knew exactly from long experience what his men could do, and had calculated correctly.

Number one belched forth its little storm of grape; number two followed; and before number six had been fired, number one was ready again.

As the first charge of grape made a gap in the advancing body of horse, there was a yell of rage, and they tore on faster. The second had a similar effect, the men rushing on heedless of the killed and wounded they left behind, strewing the field; but, as the other guns spoke out, confusion began to set in, and by the time number one discharged its second cartridge, men were opening out, others were drawing rein. But still a brave half of them came thundering on, and they were within a couple of hundred yards as the rest of the second round was poured into them, with such dire effect that the scared horses stopped, kicking and plunging, and the gallant charge came to an end, the leaders of the crowd hesitating, and then wheeling to right and left, and tearing off in full retreat, till the great plain was dotted with fallen and galloping horsemen, all cohesion gone, and every man fleeing for his life.

There was a yell of rage, and they tore on faster.

The next minute the order was given to limber up: but Wyatt made no effort to leave the ground for a time, waiting to rest the horses and scan the field, ready to send a round-shot bowling at the first knot of gathering horsemen that collected as a nucleus for another charge.

But not one centre appeared—it was a case of every man for himself—and, closing his glass with a snap, Wyatt rode close to Dick's side and reached over to shake hands as he said:

"Well done, us, Dick! I think we may call this the Battle of Palm Tope, and say we've won."

"It's horrible," said Dick hoarsely, as his hot hand clung to his friend's; "but how gallant, and how grand!"

"The light of discipline and skill against brute force, old fellow." said Wyatt, nodding quietly; "and I feel as if I should like to pitch my helmet in the air and cry 'Hooray!' But officers mustn't do that. Come along with me."

He led the way and rode along the line, looking anxiously in the men's faces.

"Who is hurt?" he said. "Any man want to fall out?"

There was a pause, during which no one answered. "Well done!" cried Wyatt excitedly. "Splendid work, my lads."

There was a loud cheer at this, and directly after the order to advance was given, and the troop rode steadily back, mostly at a walk, to the city, reaching the gates quite unmolested, and entering just before dark.

Chapter XXIII
Differences of Opinion

To the great satisfaction of all, everything was going well. The troop had found themselves received in silence at the gate by the Rajah's troops, and had ridden through the streets to the old palace, with the people in crowds watching their entrance; but no enthusiasm was displayed, and Wyatt said grimly:

"They look as if they were sorry that we have come back safely."

"Or as if some of them wanted to give us a warmer welcome, only they feel afraid."

"That's about what it is," said Wyatt. "They are afraid. I hope nothing has gone wrong in barracks."

His hope was satisfied, for the gates were close shut, and the guard ready to challenge them before admittance was given, Sergeant Stubbs, left in command, having nothing more to report than the fact that a large body of armed men had been hanging about the place.

"Just as if they were waiting to hear how things were going, gentlemen. And, between ourselves, I can't help thinking that if you had been worsted they would have attacked us. Not that they would have had much satisfaction out of that."

"What do you mean, Stubbs!" asked Wyatt.

The man shook his head.

"They'd have been too much for us, of course, sir," he said; "and we should have been done. But I'd got a plan ready for them in the shape of the ammunition."

"What were you going to do?" asked Dick.

"Only going to put a lighted linstock to the end of a train leading to a big powder-bag in the ammunition-wagon, sir. Pity, I thought, to let our friends have that. They don't understand our cartridges, and might have burned their fingers."

Sergeant Stubbs said this with a grim look, but it was sober, earnest determination not to die un-revenged, for there was powder enough to destroy the place and all that were in it.

Dick was warm enough with his hot ride and all he had gone through, but as soon as he had flung his rein to his syce and patted Burnouse, he hurried to the room where the wounded men lay, finding Hulton looking deadly pale, but calm and free from fever; while the doctor, in spite of his weakness, was able to make inquiries about how the day had gone.

Dick told him in as few words as he could, and soon found that every one was listening.

All at once there was a deep groan, and Dick sprang to the bed of one of the men, to find that the sufferer was Hanson.

"Arm you in pain?" he said anxiously.

"Pretty well for that, sir. Why do you ask?"

"You groaned as if in agony."

"That was not me, sir, but Jones there."

"Your wound hurt you much?" said Dick to the man in sympathetic tones.

"No, sir; but it's hard, that's what it is—hard."

"To be wounded?"

"To have to lie here and all that fun going on. Beg pardon, sir; you just dress me up again to-morrow, and then give me a stiffykit of being fit to go on duty again. I should get right quicker along with the men than lying here alongside Bob Hanson."

"I have not made a sound," said Hanson.

"No, my lad, but you've looked as if you were going to."

"There, lie still," said Dick. "I'll come and look to your bandages as soon as I've got these hot things off; and I'm not fit to come now."

Dick kept his word, and this time he had the doctor's advice to help him to ease the poor fellows lying in misery.

"We shall be better in the morning, sir," said Hanson so meaningly that Dick asked why he said that.

"We can lie and think about the troop having won."

Dick had barely finished when there was a summons to meet the Rajah, who had come to obtain first-hand an account of the fight, to which he listened with an intense display of interest, expressing his satisfaction again and again.

"How have you got on here, sir, while we've been away?" asked Wyatt.

"They made some attacks upon the gates," said the Rajah, "but there is nothing to fear from them. We are strongest there. It is in their mounted men that they are powerful and get the better of us, but after to-day I think I can laugh at them. Scouts came galloping in to say that you had won; but later on other men came in to say that you had all been cut off, and I was afraid."

"We were cut off," said Dick, smiling; "but Mr—Captain Wyatt—"

"Steady there!" growled that officer.

"Captain Wyatt," said Dick, with a little more emphasis, "cut a way for us back again."

The Rajah was for taking both away with him to the palace, but they excused themselves on the plea of being completely worn out; and he left them, to send servants with fruit and choice refreshments from his own table—a present which made Dick's eyes brighten with satisfaction as he thought of his patients lying feverish and weary in the extempore hospital ward.

"Oh, this is glorious," said Dick to himself as he threw himself on his bed at last, the night, for a wonder, being fairly cool; and, as he had a good sprawl, the refreshing sensation of the absence of muscular effort mingled with the mental feeling of a day's work well done, and he was just dropping into the weary body's insensibility, when he started into wakefulness as suddenly as if some wriggling abomination had crept into his bed and stung him.

But it was only a thought.

Still, it was strong enough to make him half dress himself, open his door, and nearly fall headlong over something soft lying outside.

"Does the sahib want something?" said the plaintive voice of his servant.

"Want something? Yes!" cried Dick angrily—"you get out of my way. Do you mean to break my neck?"

The man sighed and wisely said nothing, but thought to himself: "These English sahibs are so fierce, even when very young. He has been killing people all day—he may kill me."

But Dick was not in a killing humour; his thoughts were upon a different track—the very reverse.

"Have I hurt you?" he said more gently.

"The sahib's servant's ribs are a little sore where he was kicked, but they will get better."

"I forgot you always slept across my door. Here, show me where Sergeant Stubbs sleeps."

The man led the way with alacrity to the non-commissioned officers' quarters, for Stubbs had kept to his old place at night, and his gruff voice responded at once to the smart rap at his door:

"All right; rouse up the trumpeter."

"No, no, Stubbs; it is I. Don't make a noise."

"You, Mr Darrell, sir! In a moment," replied the sergeant; and the next moment he presented himself, drawing on his overalls. "What is it—a night attack?"

"No, no. I just remembered as I was going to sleep. What about that train to the bag of powder?"

"Yes, sir. What about it?"

"It must not be left like that. Some one might be going there with a lantern and blowing up the whole place."

"No fear, sir," said the sergeant grimly. "I swept that all away hours ago."

"Did you? Oh, that's right. I was afraid you might have left it there."

"No, sir; I know too well what powder will do."

"Then I've woke you up with a false alarm."

"And yourself too," said the sergeant quietly. "There was no need, but there's nothing like making sure."

"No, there's nothing like making sure. Good-night, Sergeant."

"Good-night, sir."

Dick felt foolish, but decidedly more comfortable, as he went down into the courtyard, closely followed by his white-coated servant. But, being there, he thought he might as well go along close to the wall, and come suddenly upon the two men on sentry at the gate, to make sure that they were well on the alert.

He had proof of it directly, for before he had gone many steps he was challenged, and the sharp click of a carbine lock, followed apparently by the echo, brought him to a stand, to give the word and pass on to his quarters and bed.

Then the night passed peacefully enough, and after many hours the lad rose, and began wondering, after his cold splash, to find himself fresh and free from weariness in spite of the previous day's exertions. His first visit was to his patients, where his time was well taken up till he was summoned to the morning meal, when he met Wyatt.

"What time do we parade?" was his first question.

"Don't parade," said Wyatt bluntly. "Rajah's scouts have brought in word that the enemy has withdrawn, but it's too good to be true."

"Then it is because we gave them such a flogging yesterday."

"Looks like it," said Wyatt, "but I can't believe it. I only hope it is, for I am sick of slaughtering men and horses as we did yesterday."

"We were doing our duty," said Dick.

"Yes; but it's such a horribly unpleasant duty."

"Better than for them to be slaughtering us."

"Well, yes; we think so, of course," said Wyatt. "But how is Hulton?"

"Better, certainly; Dr Robson says so."

"I hope he is; but I don't like to see him so white and with those dark marks under his eyes."

"Robson says it is only weakness."

"Then you must set to and make him strong."

Another message from the Rajah arrived soon after, with the news that the enemy were retiring; and before half-an-hour had elapsed Dick was summoned from Hulton's bedside to meet one of the ruler's chief officers, who had come to request that the two English captains, as he called them, would come on and see the Rajah at once.

"We must go, I suppose," said Wyatt aside to his young companion; "only I don't like being bothered like this." Then to the officer:

"Tell his highness we will have our horses saddled and come on soon."

"An elephant is waiting at the gate," said the officer respectfully, "and the escort with it."

Wyatt nodded, and, after summoning the acting-lieutenant and giving him his instructions, the pair mounted, and the escort led and followed.

"We may as well take the honours conferred upon us," said Wyatt, "but I would rather walk."

"Yes; I want to see some of the place."

"Never mind; we must be too grand for that. It makes the common people and the soldiery look up to us, and keeps up our prestige as much as the fighting."

Upon reaching the front of the palace, it was to find the wide court full of mounted men and scores of brilliantly accoutred officers waiting about, all of whom saluted the fresh-comers with every show of respect. Way was made for them when they dismounted from the howdah, and they were led at once into the Rajah's council chamber, where he was seated in state, but only to rise, shake hands with his visitors, and motion them to seats placed ready.

Dick grasped at once that a council of war was being held; and the Rajah hastened to tell them that, as the enemy had evidently become disheartened by the disastrous defeat of the previous day, and was retiring to his own district, it was considered that now was the time for following him up and dealing another severe blow.

Wyatt spoke out plainly that if another such blow could be delivered it would, without doubt, be a fine thing, but his men had worked very hard on the previous day, the horses had been a good deal distressed, and it would be far better to let the enemy retreat unmolested.

"No," said the Wazir, a tall, fierce-looking man, frowning; "it is bad counsel. The enemy should be pursued at once."

"I think it is good counsel," said Wyatt quietly. "To have been effective the pursuit should have been made last night when he was disheartened; then the retreat could have been made a rout."

"Yes," said the Rajah, nodding; "that is right."

"Is the English captain afraid?" said the Wazir, with a sneer.

"He is cautious, sir," said Wyatt hotly, and he turned to the Rajah.

"What is the road like by which the enemy has gone?"

"An open plain for the first few miles," said the Rajah; "after that a series of ravines and passes, had for horses."

"Then that quite determines me, sir," said Wyatt gravely. "In such a country as you describe, my troop would be at a terrible disadvantage. We want open country to manoeuvre."

"The English captain is afraid," said the Wazir scornfully, and he turned and smiled at some of the chiefs round about where he was standing, several of whom responded to the meaning smile, while the Rajah looked angrily upon them.

"I do not know that I need answer such an insulting remark as that," said Wyatt sternly; while Dick felt hot, and rose from his seat as he saw the Wazir take a fierce stride forward at the word "insulting."

But Wyatt turned from him to address the Rajah.

"It is quite true, sir," he said; "I am—afraid—"

He paused for a few moments, and looked round haughtily at the assembled chiefs and officials before repeating the last word.

"Afraid to needlessly risk the lives of the men entrusted to my care. I am now answerable for them, and it is left to my discretion how they are used. It would be taking them to be slaughtered where they would have no means of getting at the enemy, who would be hiding in the sides of rocky ravines and gorges."

"That is quite right," said the Rajah. "Your advice is good, Captain Wyatt. We know what you and your brave men can do, and their lives shall not be wantonly thrown away."

"Then your highness prefers to take the advice of strangers, of emissaries sent by the Koom Pahni, who will take away the kingdom left by your brave father, the Rajah?" said the Wazir insolently.

"I shall defend my territory or attack my enemies how and when I think good," said the Rajah angrily. "I shall also listen to the advice of all my chiefs and officers, as I am doing now, and take so much of the advice as I think wise."

"Then your highness means to throw over all your old friends and supporters, who have often risked their lives in your service?" said the Wazir haughtily.

"No," cried the Rajah fiercely as he rose and looked round; "I will be as faithful to my friends as my father was before me, and as stern and severe to my enemies. Listen, all of you; I am quite aware that I have many enemies here present now."

"There are two," said the Wazir, pointing mockingly at the English officers.

"It is false, sir," cried the Rajah sternly. "You are going too far. Cut for the fact that you were a good servant and adviser to my dead father, and that you are still the friend and counsellor of my mother, your head would answer for your insolent words to me to-day and your insults to these brave officers. Listen, all of you. The English are our friends, and you all know that but for them Rajah Singh would have swept the greater part of my fighting-men away."

There was a low murmur of acquiescence from many of the officers present, but as many stood stern and frowning.

"I may seem weak in patiently bearing with much that has passed, for I wish to respect those who are my mother's advisers; but I tell them here, in the presence of you all, that those who persist in supporting her unwise ideas, and aid her in bringing down upon me the attacks of Rajah Singh, are no longer my friends, but my foes."

"Does your highness consider those your enemies who wish to go out to fight for you against this invader?"

"Yes," said the Rajah sharply, "when they advise measures which must result in defeat."

"Then I feel that the time has come," said the Wazir, "when I must leave your highness's service. Those who are my friends can do what they please. I retire from this hour."

"You will give up your duties, sir, as one of my chiefs, and as the attendant upon my mother, when I tell you to do so. Till then, do your duty as my servant. That is enough. Till these people attack again there will be peace. The council is at an end."

The Rajah turned to Wyatt and Dick.

"I am sorry for all this," he said gravely. "It is in my power to silence all these unfriendly manifestations; but my visits to the seat of the government have taught me much. Still, I can be firm if it should become necessary. Gentlemen, I thank you for what you have done. You are my friends, and if any one dares to insult you again it will be at his peril. Captain Wyatt, you will come here to-morrow and give me your advice as to the best means of defending this place. From this day I make you one of the chief officers of my army."

"But Captain Hulton is my chief, sir," said Wyatt quietly.

"Captain Hulton is wounded and unable to help me. When he recovers we shall see. From now, sir, you will give what orders you think necessary for the defence or attack, and I will see that they are obeyed. Once more, the council is at an end."

The two English officers bowed and left the room, the same officer who had brought them seeing them back to the old palace.

"How many enemies have we made to-day, Dick?" said Wyatt quietly.

"None," said Dick. "Half those were our enemies before. I think we have made some friends."

"It was yesterday over the fighting, I'm afraid," said Wyatt; "but we shall see."

Chapter XXIV
Friends and Enemies

"All right, Dick, my boy; but I don't believe it."

"But I tell you the Wazir was as civil as could be, and went out of his way to explain to me that he felt now that he had been in the wrong; that he had heard such reports about our confiscating different territories that, as an old servant of the queen-mother, he felt bound to oppose our coming."

"Well," said Wyatt, "I'll give him credit for that; he did oppose us most thoroughly."

"But," continued Dick, "he says he sees clearly now how wrong he was in his judgment, and that he intends to do everything he can to assist the Rajah in his efforts to be friendly to the Company."

"Wise man," said Wyatt, laughing. "He began to feel that his head was getting shaky."

"Then you believe in him now?"

"Yes, to be a cunning old sham, Dick, whom I would not trust in the slightest degree. There's a nice—triumvirate don't you call it?—the queen, or begum, or whatever she calls herself; that old Brahmin high-priest fellow, Ganga Ree; and the Wazir. They hate us like poison, and if they can get the people to rise against us and kill us, you may depend upon it they will."

"I'm afraid some of this is prejudice," said Dick gravely, "for I can quite understand these people disliking us as strangers who, as they thought, meant to seize the country. But, as the Wazir says, they know better now."

"Perhaps it is, Dick, and perhaps they are all that is good and amiable, and I'm quite wrong. Let them prove it, and I'll go over to their side. As it is, I think I'll believe in myself and the Rajah. When Hulton gets better and takes command he will judge for himself."

"Hulton will not get better and take the command for a long time," said Dick quietly.

"Who says so?"

"Doctor Robson. He told me so this morning. He says that Hulton must go back to England for a year before he does anything more."

"Poor old chap," said Wyatt earnestly. "I hoped better things. He certainly is mending."

"Yes, but very slowly. The doctor says that he must have complete change."

A month had glided by since the Rajah of Singh's forces had returned to their own country to await the retaliation they felt sure must come; but, so far, the Rajah of Soojeepur had contented himself with trying to consolidate his own state, and to convince his people that they must accept his plans for being in alliance with the English—a task, as yet, far from being accomplished.

The old palace, under Wyatt's eye, had become a strong little fort, well provided with ammunition and provisions, so that they were well prepared in case of a siege, either from within or without the walls, though there were no signs of a fresh attack on the part of the Singh people, while the attitude of the natives within the city had ceased to be menacing. The result was that the orders respecting the men's going about had ceased to be stringent.

Dick took advantage of this in his natural desire to see all he possibly could of the place and of the people, a ramble being more pleasant now that it could be taken without seeing scowling looks, and hearing knife-armed men cursing aloud at the dog of an infidel who dared to profane the streets with his presence.

On the morning that the above short conversation took place, he rose from the table to take his puggree-covered cap from where it hung.

"Where are you going, my son?" said Wyatt, with an Eastern metaphoric style which he sometimes put on.

"Just to say a word or two to Hulton, and then I'm going to have a look at the big temple."

"What for?"

"To see it. One of the men told me it was very curious inside."

"Who told you?"

"Hanson."

"Humph! That letting-off and his wounds seem to have done that ruffian good. I didn't know that he was the sort of fellow to visit temples. What's to be seen?"

"I hardly know; only that it's a wonderful place inside, with a gigantic bronze figure of that fat Indian god with the elephant's head."

"You'll wear your side-arms?"

"Of course."

"Don't let the priests do anything to you for profaning their place. If they kill you, I promise you, though, that I'll blow the temple up, if that's any comfort to you."

"Oh, thank you; that is good of you!" cried Dick, laughing. "Now, I call that friendly."

"Don't chaff. You mind what you are about, and take care of yourself. If you are not back in three hours from now, I shall call out half the troop and come in search of you."

"Mounted?" said Dick mockingly.

"Bah!"

"And with a couple of guns?"

"Be off at once before it gets hotter. I want to go and see Hulton myself."

As the call on the captain was more to keep him from feeling dull than anything else, Dick buckled on his sword, crossed the court, acknowledged the sentry's salute, and passed out, to go up and down several crooked streets, at the end of one of which, as he was crossing from the sunny to the shady side of the way, he noticed something which made him stop short and turn as soon as he had passed round a corner, when he met Hanson, now quite convalescent, face to face.

The man looked staggered at the unexpected meeting, but drew himself up and saluted.

"There you are again, then, Hanson," said Dick sharply.

"Yes, sir. The doctor said I was not to return to duty for a few days longer, and I have a pass."

"So I suppose, or you would not be out," said Dick. "But now, look here, Hanson; no nonsense—I want the truth. For the past week whenever I've gone out for a stroll you've followed me."

"I had leave to be out, sir," said the man evasively. "I know that; but you've been following me."

"I am quite strange to the place, sir."

"That's gammon," said Dick, who in his fit of annoyance did not carefully select his words. The man was silent.

"What's that you've got buttoned up under your fatigue-jacket?"

"Pistol, sir."

"Yes; I could see it was. Loaded?"

"Yes, sir."

"And what's that stuck down inside your overalls on the left side?"

"Bayonet, sir."

"Sharp?"

"Yes, sir—very."

"Well, look here, my good fellow, I'm not a baby."

"No, sir."

"And I don't like to be treated as if I were one. Who sent you?" No answer.

"Look here; I will know the truth. Captain Wyatt told you to arm yourself and always keep me in sight?"

"No, sir."

"Is that the truth?"

"Yes, sir."

"Then who did turn you into my bodyguard?" Still no answer.

"Will you speak, sir, or am I to go back and investigate the matter?"

"I'll speak, sir."

"Very well, then, who sent you, Mr Stubbs?"

"No, sir. Only Private Hanson."

Dick frowned and stared.

"What!" he said at last. "Did you do this out of your own head?"

"Yes, sir. I beg pardon, but I am having a good deal of liberty just now as a convalescent."

"And you abuse it by taking an unwarrantable liberty with one of your officers!" cried Dick hotly.

"I hope not, sir," said Hanson, with a faint smile. "I don't think you know how dangerous it is for you to be out as you are, alone."

"Pish! I have my sword."

"A sword is of no use for parrying a cowardly stab in the back."

"Of course not; but there is no danger now the people have become friendly."

"Only on the surface, sir. The fire has been smothered down for a while, but it is smouldering, and ready to burst out the moment it is fanned."

Dick looked at him curiously.

"So you don't want me to get a knife in my back?"

"I'd sooner have it in my own, sir," cried the man earnestly. "It really is very dangerous, sir. Don't be angry with me, even if it is a liberty for a private to take with his officer. — Mr Darrell."

"Well?"

"You asked me to do something once."

"I did, Hanson; and so far you have done it well."

"Then, do this now for me, sir. I couldn't bear the thought of you going about as you do, and I couldn't sleep for the horrible thought always with me."

"What horrible thought?"

"I seemed to see you being carried back into quarters dead — murdered; and I felt that I might stop your gallant young career from being cut short — at any rate that I might try."

"Even to receiving the imaginary blow yourself, eh?"

"Well, yes, sir," said the man, smiling sadly. "I think I could be better spared than you."

There was so much sincerity in the man's tones, so much earnestness in his way of speaking, that Dick felt moved, and his manner changed.

"You've been ill, Hanson, and you are still weak."

"Oh, no, sir; I could take my place with the gun at any time now."

"I'm glad of it. But you fancy things."

Hanson shook his head.

"There is no such danger now."

Hanson smiled meaningly.

"What do you mean?"

"Only this, sir," said the man, taking a step nearer, and laying a finger on his shoulder.

"What of that—a tear in the flannel, sewn up?"

"Not a tear, sir—a cut from a sharp knife that was stuck in there from behind."

"When?"

"The night before last, sir."

"What! were you wounded?"

"Only scratched, sir. The aim was bad, and I started when I seemed to feel something coming, so that the blade went down along by my arm."

"Good heavens!" cried Dick, "we never heard of this."

"No, sir; I didn't want to be in the doctor's hands again, and my leave stopped. Besides, a bit of sticking-plaster was enough, for it was only the skin divided. I shouldn't have told anybody now, only I was obliged."

"This is serious, Hanson," said Dick thoughtfully.

"Very, sir; and it shows the need for care. I will not be obtrusive, only follow you pretty close."

"But it makes me seem like a coward."

"There is nothing cowardly in taking precautions to preserve one's life, sir."

"Well, no," said Dick thoughtfully.

"Then I may come, sir?"

"Yes, for I will not alter my plans," replied Dick. "You astound me, though."

"I am glad you feel the truth, sir. Quite half the people like us, and are for the king; but the rest are—well, sir, it's like having the ground mined under our feet, I'm sure."

Dick nodded, looked full in the man's eyes for a moment or two, turned, and went on without a word.

The next minute he was at the entrance of a large, highly ornate, and wonderfully-carved Hindu temple, into which he passed unquestioned as one of the conquerors of the place; but, glancing round, he saw several white-robed men of the priestly caste advance to stop his follower.

"My attendant," he said sharply in Hindustani, and the priests fell back, while from out of the gloom in front, where the outlines of a huge, elephant-headed monster towered up from floor to ceiling, a white-robed personage slowly approached, followed at a short distance by a train of a couple of dozen priests, to meet the visitor, who was taken round the building, the leader of the party speaking eagerly, and evidently striving to make himself agreeable to the young officer, who had more than once encountered him in the Rajah's, and knew him for the chief leader of the Brahminical religion in Soojeepur.

At first he confined himself to pointing out and explaining the various objects of interest to the visitor—the many heathen gods, their names and attributes—in a frank, easy way that made his narrative highly interesting. Then he showed and described and spoke of the value of the various precious stones which adorned the great figures, all offerings from the pious for the benefit of the temple, which was extremely rich in treasures.

But by degrees, as the objects undescribed grew less, the old Brahmin's remarks became more friendly and confidential, and he began to make allusions to their first meeting at the Rajah's palace.

"Ah," he said, "it is not long ago, but in a short time one learns so much. I looked upon you then—you and your brother-officers and people—as being terrible enemies of our religion. We had been told that you would come and ruin and destroy and take away all the treasures of the temple here. And then I hated you, and felt that it would be a good and pious thing to destroy all your lives, while now we have all lived to find that the treasures of the temple have been respected and remain untouched, and that the Rajah was right—that the English really are our friends."

Dick listened and made suitable replies, and went on conversing with the smooth-tongued old Brahmin, but all the time he recalled Wyatt's doubts and the terrible words he had heard that morning from Hanson; while, as they passed on and on through the semi-darkness, he could not help feeling how easily a blow from one of the keen Indian knives would lay him low, and how easily his body might be disposed of among the dark, labyrinthine ways of the huge temple. These thoughts, at times when they were passing through some of the most gloomy parts, were appalling; but, so sure as they came to the worst, they died out again, for he had but to glance round, and there, following him like his shadow, was the tall figure of Robert Hanson—well-armed, active, and determined—ready, if the need arose, to fight for him to the death.

Perhaps he felt the horror of his position the most when they were traversing a gallery sixty or seventy feet above the floor, one which led past the huge head and neck of the monstrous idol, and a door at the back of the figure.

For here the young officer could not help feeling how easily he might be hurled over, to fall and be dashed to pieces on the floor far below, or thrust through some one of the several openings which, for some purpose, yawned around. But, as before, there was always Robert Hanson, calm and silent, following like his shadow, and ready to give good account of any one who might venture to attack.

No one could have been more courteous than the dark-eyed, smooth, swarthy man at his side, nor more open and free in his way of speaking about the huge image and the attendant idols upon which they looked down. He seemed to wish to impress his young English companion with the idea that the temple, with its weird gloom and assumption of mystery, was merely intended to overawe the common people, and that he was too much a man of the world to expect an Englishman from his land of enlightenment to look upon all he saw as serious.

But somehow he impressed Dick in a way he did not intend, for, as they went along the silent, echoing gallery, the young officer felt more and more that his guide was treacherous and untrustworthy to the last degree—a man who, in spite of his sacred office, would proceed to any extremity to get rid of people who stood in his way. So that it was with a feeling of relief that he descended once more to the floor of the great temple, and upon being ushered into one of the rooms used by the Brahmin priesthood, who dwelt in a part of the building, he did not at all enjoy the sweetmeats and fruit provided for his refection, nor fancy a sweetish kind of wine given him in a quaint Indian cup.

At last he was conducted to the temple gates, Hanson still following close behind, the Brahmin begging him to come again, as it was his wish now that the English officers should look upon him and his brethren as their friends.

"I wish you would teach the people to feel towards us in the same way," said Dick, smiling and trying, now they were once more in the bright sunshine, to look upon the ideas which had coursed through his brain as fancies.

"We are trying," said the Brahmin; "but the people are very weak and ignorant, and you must see that, after being taught for so long to look upon the English as infidels and enemies, it must take time."

They parted apparently the best of friends, and Dick was walking back towards his quarters, when, in turning a corner, he looked sharply round and saw that Hanson was watching him intently; and, if he had been asked, he would have found it impossible to have explained why he asked his follower the following question, but ask it he did:

"Could you hear what the Brahmin said to me as I took leave?"

"Every word, sir."

"What did you think of it?"

"That I'd trust him as far as I would a tiger."

"Then it was not all fancy on my part," thought Dick as he went on. "I was right in my impressions, and I'll trust him as far as I would one of the great savage cats; but I must be civil, I suppose."

Chapter XXV
Sleeping with your Window Open

As soon as the Rajah was satisfied that his invading neighbour had quite withdrawn, he consulted with Wyatt, and expressed a wish that no further troops should be sent to Soojeepur until he made the demand.

"You and your men will be sufficient," he said; and after a short consultation with Hulton—very short, for the latter said that his brother-officer was to act as he thought best—arrangements were made with the Rajah for runners to bear a despatch to the nearest town on the frontier, where the regular communications for postal purposes could be reached.

In this despatch Wyatt gave a full account of all that had taken place, with reports of the state of the wounded and their needs, giving his opinion that the Rajah seemed to expect the troop to remain at Soojeepur permanently, and concluding with a request for a further supply of ammunition for the guns, the large use made of that which they had brought suggesting that, if the little force should remain where it was for a long period, the store might run short.

The reply to this despatch was long in coming, and in the interim matters went on with fresh displays of friendly trust on the part of the Rajah, who was daily in communication with the old palace, and constantly consulting the English officers as to improvements in his little army: but every now and then insignificant straws showed which way the wind blew, and the strangers felt that their position was, like that of the Rajah, insecure. For, though the party opposed to the friendly feeling towards the English was deferential and, to all appearance, quite in accordance with their ruler now, and the officers among them made much of the visitors, neither Wyatt nor Dick allowed themselves to be lulled into a state of security which, they felt sure, did not exist.

Hence it was that the horse artillery corps occupied its quarters in the old palace just as if it were a tiny army of occupation. It had its parades and marches out, joined in military evolutions with the Rajah's regiments of horse and foot, to the decided improvement of the latter, the officers and men being impressed by the perfection to which discipline and training had brought them, and beginning to imitate them in every way they could, to the Rajah's great and liberally expressed satisfaction.

The return despatch came at last from Sir George Hemsworth, announcing his satisfaction with all that had been done, his hope that Captain Hulton was sufficiently recovered to resume his command, and quite agreeing that there would be no need for the reinforcement, which had been already on the way, but was now recalled. For the general considered that there must be plenty of material amongst the Rajah troops for drilling into shape, especially among the irregular horsemen, who ought, without much effort, soon to be turned into serviceable cavalry.

Finally, the general announced that the ammunition asked for was on the way, with an escort of twelve horse artillery-men, ten privates, and two drill-sergeants, who would strengthen the little force, and allow of the two non-commissioned officers being devoted to the training of the Rajah's horse.

This despatch, directed to the officer in command, was read aloud by Wyatt to Hulton and the doctor in the former's room.

"No," said Hulton querulously, "I'm not fit to take over the command, and I shall not be for long enough—shall I, Doctor?"

"Well, hardly yet, my dear boy," was the reply: "and there is no need. I was obliged to get back to my work, in spite of Darrell proving such a formidable rival, but you can wait."

"Well, read the rest," said Hulton in an irritable tone.

"The rest?" said Wyatt, with assumed innocency.

"Yes; no nonsense," said Hulton bitterly; "you are keeping something back."

Wyatt hesitated for a moment or two, and then tossed the paper to Dick.

"You finish it, lad," he said.

Dick glanced from one to the other with his face flushing and eyes lighting up, for, like Hulton, he had expected something more.

"Yes," he cried eagerly, "of course Wyatt is promoted to captain."

Hulton's brow wrinkled, and his pale, thin face looked more sunken as he winced as if from a sting of pain, but for some moments he did not speak. Then a faint smile began to appear on his face, and he said sadly:

"I couldn't help feeling a bit upset, but I am not envious, Wyatt; only a weak, sick man. Shake hands, old fellow. I congratulate you. It was very bravely earned."

Wyatt eagerly gripped the extended hand.

"I can't help it, old chap," he said huskily. "I'd rather they had given you your majority—but it's bound to come."

"If I live," said Hulton sadly.

"I'll answer for that," said the doctor. "Only it must take time. Ten men out of twelve would have sunk under such injuries as yours, so no grumbling. You've done and you're doing wonders. Wait a bit, and we'll congratulate you in turn as we do Captain Wyatt. Darrell, you ought to go and announce this to the Rajah."

"No, no. Nonsense!" cried Wyatt excitedly. "I'll tell him myself next time we meet."

"You will not," said Hulton, "for I shall send him word myself. He ought to know. Write to him, Darrell, for me, and I'll sign the letter."

Wyatt made a bit of a protest, and then was silent, the letter being written and despatched by an orderly, who brought back a message that the Rajah would come and see Captain Wyatt.

The latter gentleman's countenance was so absurdly comical that, as soon as the orderly had gone back to the stables, Dick burst into a roar of laughter, whereupon Wyatt turned to him fiercely.

"Look here, young fellow," he cried, "do you want to quarrel?"

"Of course not."

"Then don't you laugh at me. It's no joke, I can tell you."

"Why, what is there to mind in the Rajah's coming?"

"Everything. It means having him come smiling here to make me look like a fool."

"Nonsense!" said Dick, laughing again.

"Be quiet!" roared Wyatt. "I won't stand it. Do I look the sort of man to stand and be smirked round and buttered with Eastern compliments? I hate 'em, and I won't see him when he comes."

"You must," said Dick. "We can't be rude to our friends."

"Then let them keep away and let me alone. I'd sooner go into the thick of a fight any day."

Wyatt looked stormy for some time before the clouds began to disappear from his countenance.

Half-an-hour later, as he was sitting with Dick talking about their invalids, who were out in the shady side of the court, and remarking that they might return to duty, he seemed reconciled.

"I shall have to go through it, Dick," he said. "The Rajah means well."

"Of course he does. He'll only say a few civil things, and then go."

An hour after there was a challenge at the gate, and the visitor arrived, dismounted, and was shown into the room which the officers had devoted to receptions. There he entered, followed by an attendant bearing something wrapped in a shawl.

This the man laid upon the table at a sign from the chief, salaamed low, and retired; while, as soon as they were alone, the Rajah shook hands warmly, and, in as English a manner as he could affect, congratulated Wyatt.

"I am very glad, Captain Wyatt," he said in conclusion, "and I want you to accept the little present I have brought in honour of the occasion."

"Oh, there was no need for that, sir," said Wyatt roughly.

"But I think there is, and I hope you will not refuse it.—Mr Darrell, will you unroll it and give it to your friend for me?"

"Of course, sir," replied the lad; and his heart beat with something like envy as he unrolled a beautiful Lahore shawl and took out a magnificent, carved tulwar, whose hilt was of silver inlaid with delicate traceries of gold, while the scabbard was deadened silver, ringed with gold and ornamented with emeralds.

"Oh!" cried Wyatt, "this is far too rich an ornament for me, sir. I beg you will not press me to keep it."

"But I do press it," said the Rajah warmly. "It is no ornament. Take it and draw the blade."

Wyatt obeyed, and as he looked down he saw that indeed it was no ornament, but a deadly weapon, with a magnificent damascened blade, and keen as a razor.

"It is light in the hand, and a stroke from that would lay one of my enemies dead at your feet. Keep it for my sake. I may want you to defend me again."

"I'll keep it, Rajah," said Wyatt, sheathing the beautiful weapon; "but I would have fought for you just as well without it."

"I know that," replied the Rajah. "Now take me in to see Captain Hulton and my friend the doctor. I am truly glad that they are recovering from their wounds."

Wyatt led the way to Hulton's room, bearing with him his present; and when the Rajah at last took his leave, he attended him to his elephant, and then, with the sword still in his hand, walked beside him to the gate, afterwards taking the weapon into Dick's room, where the two carefully examined it and had a long talk about the beauty of the gift.

"Shall you wear it?" said Dick at last.

"Yes, on state occasions, for show. It would be no use to me on service. I should never get used to such a hilt. The grip is too small, but it would be just the thing for you. I've a good mind to give it to you."

"You can't," said Dick. "It would be unfair to the donor."

"Humph! yes, I suppose so. Well, I could lend it to you; there would be no harm in that. It just fits your girlish hand. There, hang it up."

"I shouldn't like it to be stolen."

"Pooh! Who is likely to steal it?"

"Any one of the niggers who are always hanging about the gateway. I often feel a bit nervous about my gun and other tackle. Let's hang it up here over the other things. It will help to make quite a trophy."

This was done, the handsome tulwar being suspended from a nail facing the window of their sitting-room, opening out on to a terrace-like veranda, the sleeping-chambers of the two officers being on either side.

"Safe enough there," said Wyatt, standing back to admire the handsome weapon.

"Quite," replied Dick; "not much chance for any one to get by the sentries."

That evening closed in thick and dark, with a peculiar murkiness and heat in the air. It was as if the clouds had sunk low down towards the earth, and a strange feeling of oppression troubled the occupants of the room, which they shared in common.

"Wonder how that lamp managed to get here," said Wyatt as he lay back in a cane chair smoking, and as he moved slightly when he spoke the chair creaked in a peculiar way.

Dick turned himself lazily to stare at the old-fashioned sperm-oil lamp, with its ground-glass globe, and watched some of the many moths and flies, attracted by the light, commit suicide before he replied slowly:

"Present for the old Rajah, perhaps, sent up from Calcutta."

"Likely enough," growled Wyatt; "and I wish the new Rajah had sent it back before we came. Abominable thing. It's never properly trimmed, and the oil they use doesn't suit it, so that it always smells. And look at that great moth.—Go it, stupid! There, I thought so. There you are, singed and roasted, and you nearly put out the light. Now, why couldn't that idiotic thing have contented itself with flying about in the soft darkness, instead of diving down that hot chimney on to the flame?"

"It's nature, I suppose," said Dick.

"It's ill-nature, Dicky."

"Horribly tiresome," yawned Dick. "I'd shut the window, only the place would be so unbearably hot."

"Never mind; shut it, and open the bedroom doors. Anything's better than having the light put out."

Dick rose slowly and did as he was told before taking off the lump globe and chimney to clear the lamp-wick, and then replacing them and returning to his seat.

As the lamp was turned down for retrimming, the faint flickering of lightning could be seen, and a distant muttering sound broke the silence.

"Storm coming," said Dick.

"Let it come," said Wyatt; "make it cooler, and be a bit of a change."

"It must be tremendous up in the mountains."

"Let it be tremendous up in the mountains, Dicky. There's plenty of room for it to rumble round there, and if it splinters a few crags it will do no harm."

"No," said Dick, leaning back and gazing at the dimly-seen window. "We don't want it here."

"Why not? Cool the air. And a heavy rain would wash the streets; they don't smell very nice. Lay the dust, lad; it's choking."

"I wasn't thinking of the rain, but the lightning."

"What of that?"

"The powder-magazine."

"Humph! Ha! Yes; send us all flying if that blew up, Dick. Unfortunate, too. No knowing how long the fresh lot will be coming. We shouldn't be of much use to the Rajah without our guns. But we mustn't meet troubles half-way; the storm isn't here yet."

"What are we going to do to-morrow?"

"Drill," said Wyatt shortly.

"We drilled yesterday and again to-day," said Dick wearily. "Oh, I say, how hot it is with that window shut!"

"Yes, dear boy, it is hot. I feel like a mouse in a baker's oven."

"No, you don't," said Dick impatiently. "You were never in a baker's oven, and you were never a mouse."

"No. More of the elephant about me," said Wyatt good-humouredly. "I'm getting too fat."

"Yes; we want some change," said Dick impatiently.

"You think so, do you?"

"Yes; it's so monotonous here. I'm getting horribly tired of it."

"Oh, that's what you mean—not about my being too heavy?"

"Absurd! No."

"Well, what shall we do?"

"I don't know. Couldn't we get up a tiger-hunt, or go fishing?"

"Um-mm-m, well, yes, we could. Tell you what, Dick, boy. Here's an idea, and it will be more exciting."

"Yes? What?" said Dick, sitting bolt upright.

"You write a letter to Rajah Singh, and tell him he's a chuckle-headed fool of a nigger, and that if he dares show himself anywhere near here you'll punch his head."

"Bah!"

"It'll make him come down in a huff, and then we can have some more fun."

Dick rose from his seat.

"What are you going to do? Write the letter at once?"

"Bah!" ejaculated Dick; "I'm going to bed."

"Best thing you can do, my little man. You're tired, and the dustman has been shaking his bag in your poor dear little eyes, as my old nurse used to say. Be off. You have been as disagreeable as you stand high for the last hour."

"Well, it's late, isn't it? You haven't been any too amiable," retorted Dick.

"No, dear boy, I haven't. Mine is a vile temper. I think it's because I never can have my own way. There, all right, old chap; I'll go too. Turn out the lamp."

As Dick turned out the lamp the flickering lightning played through the window, showing Wyatt crossing to his chamber door, which he opened, turned, said "Good-night, old man," and closed after him.

Dick yawned heavily and went to the sitting-room door, which he threw open, disturbing his man, who, in company with Wyatt's servant, was asleep on the mat; and then, satisfied that the men were there, he closed the door again, went to that of his own room, and passed through, leaving the door of communication open.

There was no light in the slightly-furnished bedchamber, and he felt that he did not need one, for it would only add to the heat of the place; so he partially undressed before going to the open window. This looked out on the shaded terrace, and he stood there gazing out at the darkness, which was cut every now and then by the flickering lightning, the latter being followed at intervals of several seconds by the muttering of the thunder far away in the mountains to the north.

"Phew! how hot it is!" muttered Dick. "Wish I was a fish."

All was wonderfully still in the courtyard below, and the darkness seemed mysterious and strange, till there was an impatient stamp from a horse's hoof, which sounded echoing and loud. Then the stillness and darkness grew oppressive as the heat, and a peculiar nervous sensation came over the lad as he thought of their loneliness away there among strangers, and what the consequences would be if the people rose against them at a time like that. How helpless they would be against the lithe, knife-armed enemy if they surprised them in such a darkness as seemed to fill the courtyard!

As he looked down, his imagination peopled the place with fierce-eyed enemies, each armed with a keen knife, and the perspiration gathered upon his face till the drops ran together and began to run down by the sides of his nose with a troublesome, tickling sensation.

It was horrible! A night like this would be just such a one as the enemy might choose for an attack, and, with the nervous excitement increasing, the lad leaned out as far as he could, wondering why he could not hear something of the sentries.

Then the whole of the northern sky was lit up by a pale, lambent sheet of lightning, and there beneath him was the courtyard, clearly seen, with the guns, limbers, and wagons; while, before the distant muttering of the thunder could reach his ears, the regular tramp of the sentry by the gate rose to where he stood.

"I don't wonder at little children being afraid to be in the dark," mused Dick. "How cowardly it does make one seem! It must be the peculiar feeling brought on by the coming storm. Ugh! if a flash were to strike our magazine!"

Dick left the window open and finished undressing. Then, throwing himself upon the light charpoy, which felt like everything else, hot, he closed his eyes so as to have a good sleep; and, as a matter of course, although he could hardly keep his eyes open when in the next room with his brother-officer, he felt now thoroughly wide-awake and as if sleep was the last thing possible.

It was as if every nerve had been sharpened and his senses made more acute.

The familiar ammoniacal odour known as "stables" stole in from the horses across the courtyard; he could hear stridulous crickets making their sharp, shrill, tooth-comb sounds in every direction; a moth was wearing out its wings against the ceiling; and through the sitting-room from the passage outside came the heavy breathing of the men, who were quite content with the mat upon the floor.

Then there were the sentries' steps, and the fidgety movements of the horses, and the heat, and the absence of sleep, and the flickering of the lightning, and the distant mutterings of the storm, which came no nearer.

All together, and separately, every one of these trifles went on magnifying itself, till Dick felt as if he must get up and dress, so as to go out into the veranda and lie down to sleep there.

Then, all at once—nothingness, for a deep sleep had come at last.

Chapter XXVI
A Smell of Oil

"What's that?"

The question was not uttered aloud, but said mentally, as Richard Darrell suddenly unclosed his eyes and lay gazing in the direction of the window, seeing nothing, for all was pitchy dark. Cut there was the muttering of the distant thunder, the chirping of night insects, and the rustling about of the great moth against the ceiling.

What did it mean? Why should he have awakened so suddenly? There must have been a reason, and the question, "What's that?" seemed to be ringing in his ears.

"All fancy and dreaming," thought Dick wearily as he was about to turn and try a fresh position. Then there was a solution of the mystery which made it seem as if, though he slept, there was a something within him still on the watch against danger.

For all at once the open window was lit up by the flickering of the lightning, and there at the top, moving gently, were the nude legs of a man, looking black as jet against the pale, lambent light.

Then all was dark, and Dick lay chained, as it were, to the bed, thinking of his sword, which was hanging against the wall out of reach; of his pistols, equally out of touch, and useless because unloaded. His shotgun and rifle? Both in the sitting-room, at whose door lay the servants, and on the other side of which was his friend and brother-officer.

Dick's first idea was to call for help. But he hesitated, for he wanted to see more; and he did, for the lightning flickered again, and the legs he had seen were no longer hanging from the upper part of the window, but were at the side, where their owner was feeling with his toes for support on the Venetian-blind like shutters, while a slight, cracking sound told that their strength was being tested.

Dick lay breathless, with the perspiration pouring from him in the darkness, again for a time trying to nerve himself for an effort, till there was another quick opening and shutting, as it were, of the clouds, and this time he saw a dark figure gliding in over the window-sill like a huge, thick snake.

And now he realised, as he believed, what was about to happen. The question of the safety of the Rajah's present was about to be tested; for, plainly enough, its bringing had been watched, and one of the lithe, active Hindus had by some means—how, the young officer could not divine—managed to climb to the projecting shade of the veranda, and was about to carry it off!

Dick's thoughts ran fast in those moments, and he argued to himself that, if he shouted to alarm the sleepers near and the sentry below, the man would escape. It would be better, he thought, to let him pass through the chamber into the sitting-room, and then follow and trap him. For the window there was shut and fastened, and of the exits, one was guarded by the two servants, the other by Wyatt, who would rouse up at the first alarm.

To carry out his plan Dick lay perfectly still, listening and watching for the next flash of lightning, which seemed as if it would never come; but when it did, it showed him just what he expected—a dark figure, like a four-footed beast, creeping to the chamber door.

Then came the darkness again, and as Dick listened, with every nerve on the strain, he heard the door opened and an increase in the loudness of the breathing which came from the servants.

He waited a few moments, to give the marauder time to get right into the sitting-room, but not, as he thought, sufficient to reach down the dangerous weapon, and then glided out of the bed to make for the door, drawing in his breath ready to utter a loud cry as soon as he had reached it.

But in spite of his care the bedstead gave a faint creak, which was followed by a rustling in front; and as he sprang to the door, it was to come in contact with the soft, warm body of the man.

The next moment he was engaged in a wrestling match with an adversary half as strong again as himself, and, in spite of his efforts, he could get no grip of the soft, elastic flesh, whose skin had been lavishly oiled while garments the man had none.

It was a brave effort, though, in which the young officer tried hard to hold the nocturnal visitor by twining arms and legs about him as he was borne here and there, and felt as if he were trying to hold some gigantic eel.

He had succeeded in one thing though. By the dash of his attack he had driven the man back into the sitting-room, where the alarm was given, not by a cry from Dick, but by the knocking over of a couple of chairs, and then by a crash as the wrestlers struck against the table.

The next moment the man had wrested himself free, and Dick was sent staggering into the arms of some one who seized him, yelling loudly for help; and then, quite breathless, he was thrown to the floor, and two men were seated upon him, just as the report of the sentry's carbine rang out and Wyatt's door was opened, that individual roaring in Hindustani, "Give up or I'll run you through."

"Here, Wyatt," panted Dick, "make these two fools get off me. A robber! a thief! He'll escape by the window."

"Oh, it's you, is it?" growled Wyatt. "Who else is here?"

A flash of lightning showed him the two native servants slowly rising from off the prostrate lad, who leaped to his feet and ran to his bedroom window in the darkness now.

"Below there, guard!" he cried.

"All right, sir. What is it?"

"Did you hit him?"

"Didn't see any one, sir. I tried to give the alarm."

"There's a fellow somewhere about. He got in at my window."

"Nobody came down this way, sir."

"Have a good hunt. Get more lights," shouted Wyatt, as the corporal of the guard bore a lantern out into the courtyard and held it up.

"Hush! listen!" cried Wyatt; but there was not a sound, and he turned to whisper to his companion, "Sure you weren't dreaming, Dick?"

"Certain. I had him fast, but he was like a snake."

"But you may have been walking in your sleep."

"No, no! Nearly every thing is torn off me."

"Yes; but that may have been in your struggle with the boys."

"I tell you I was awakened by a slight noise, and saw a dark, naked figure creep in at the window."

"It was too dark to see such a thing, lad."

"What! with flashes of lightning like that?"

"Humph!" ejaculated Wyatt, for every thing in the room was for the moment plainly seen.

"I tell you it was a thief creeping in to steal your present."

"What!"

"And I let him get through the door of the room before I followed, so as to trap him."

"Look here, Dick, lad," said Wyatt; "I'm sorry for this. You've roused every one up."

"You don't believe me?"

"Hark at them, and look at the lanterns.—Below there—see anybody?" he shouted.

"No, sir; there's no one here."

"You don't believe me?" said Dick hotly.

"Well, old boy, you were talking about niggers coming in at windows to steal it before you went to bed, and you might have dreamed it. I think I was fancying something of the kind when I was woke up by the row."

"Oh, very well," said Dick shortly; "but I know."

"Don't be huffy, old boy," said the captain; and as a flash came in at the window he caught sight of the trophy on the wall. "I say: the tulwar's all right."

"Because he hadn't time to get it. Hff! how the beast wrenched me about! He was slippery as an eel.—Ah! Now then!" cried Dick triumphantly; "smell my hands."

Wyatt caught his brother-officer's wrists and raised the extended hands to his face. "Hallo!" he said. "Rancid oil."

"Yes; he was covered with it."

"Here, get a light," cried Wyatt. "Has either of you been oiling himself?"

"No, sahib," said Ram Dad. "It's the Sahib Darrell, all cover, and come off."

"Bring up a lantern, some one," cried Wyatt out of the window.—"But, Dick, my lad, no one could get to your window from below."

"I told you he came from above."

"That you didn't."

"Well, I meant to. He lowered himself from the top."

"May I come in, gentlemen?" said a familiar voice outside the door.

"Yes, yes, come in," cried Wyatt; and Acting-lieutenant Stubbs, in shirt and trousers, entered, with a drawn sabre in one hand, and a lantern in the other.

"Hah!" cried Ram Dad, making two jumps over the floor of the disordered room, to come down like a frog upon something before rising up again and displaying a peculiar-looking, glittering knife. "Smell of oil, sahib," he said.

Wyatt caught the keen, sharp-pointed weapon, and raised it to his nostrils.

"By Jove!" he said hoarsely. "Dick, dear boy, you've had a narrow escape. Dropped, I suppose, in the tussle."

"And look here," said Dick eagerly; "my pyjamas are soaked with the beastly stuff."

"Better than being soaked with blood, sir," said the sergeant in a low, deep voice, and he ran to the windows.

"There's a fellow somewhere, my lads," he cried. "Yes, yes; search the roof-terrace," cried Wyatt. Then, as the men made for the staircase, he turned to Dick. "I beg your pardon, old lad," he whispered; "but are you sure you are not hurt?"

"Only wrenched about and stiff. I shall have a nice lot of bruises about me."

"Never mind the bruises; get your pistols," said Wyatt.—"Tell them to fire, Stubbs, if they see the brute and he doesn't give in."

"Yes, sir; but I don't see how he could have got here. No one could pass the gate, and it's impossible from outside without a ladder."

"Then whoever it was must have used a ladder," said Wyatt, who was busily loading the pistols. "Off with you, Stubbs, with half-a-dozen men, and go round outside. But I expect he has made his escape by now."

Lights were seen on the fortified roof, the men having started from the gate-tower in both directions, careful search being made till they met and crossed, each party searching the place in turn, while the examination was going on below; and this went on for an hour, and long after Stubbs had carefully examined all round outside.

"It's lucky for him," said Wyatt at last.—"There, dismiss the men, Stubbs; but double the guard, though there's not likely to be another attempt to-night. And I say, you might say a word or two—not coming from me— about the smart way in which the lads turned out on the alarm."

"If you wish it, sir, I will," said Stubbs, frowning.

"Well, why not?"

"Turn the lads' heads too much, sir. They're proud and vain enough as it is."

"Very well, never mind. Good-night."

"Good-night, sir."

Wyatt was left alone now with Dick, and, light in hand, the first thing he did was to close and fasten the windows, and then carefully examine the rooms and stairs, before telling the men to lie down again.

"Why, Dick," he said suddenly, "I never thought to tell Hulton and the doctor what was going on. Let's go and tell them now."

They took the light and went gently to the room shared by the two convalescents, to find that people still weak from old injuries sleep deeply. For in each case, undisturbed by the sentry's carbine, the noise of the search, and the flitting about of lights, there lay the two, sleeping as placidly as children, making their friends step back gently on tiptoe, to laugh softly together as they went back to their own quarters, where Wyatt became serious directly.

"Can you sleep after this?" he said.

"Oh, yes, I think so," replied Dick; "I feel very tired now."

"It means being half-smothered in future, old fellow," said Wyatt, "for I shall never care to rest with my window open again."

Dick laughed softly.

"I don't think I shall ever try to stop a fellow coming on such a mission as this. Better let him have what he likes. But, I say: I shall keep that knife. He will not come to fetch it, will he?"

"If he does I hope I shall be awake so as to have a shot at him. My word, Dick, you have had an escape!"

"Well, don't tell me so again; it sets a fellow thinking so."

"All right."

"I say, what time is it?" Wyatt looked at his watch.

"Half-past three. This is going to be a short night's rest."

Chapter XXVII
A Disturbed Night

Wyatt related the night's experience to Hulton and the doctor over breakfast the next morning, and then the matter dropped, for there was plenty to think about and do.

The Rajah had to be consulted about the forming of a couple of well-drilled regiments of cavalry, as suggested by the general, and for whose disciplining the two sergeants were on their way.

He took to the idea eagerly, and suggested that a beginning should be made at once; and as the days went on the officers found that they had volunteers enough for four regiments of well-mounted men; but there was a difficulty in the way, for every one wanted to ride in the front rank, and resented being called upon to ride behind his fellows.

But this was got over, and the drilling went on.

Dick was busy enough, and now he spent a good deal of spare time at the palace with the Rajah, who would have had him twice as much if his duties would have allowed it.

"I don't mean to let you go too often, Dick," said Wyatt. "The Rajah's all right, but I've noticed some rather doubtful looks being cast at his favourite."

"Meaning me?" said Dick.

"Meaning you. It's wonderful what a lot he thinks of you, poor fellow."

"Poor fellow?"

"Yes—so weak and ignorant. He doesn't know you as I do."

"No," said Dick dryly.

"I'm getting horribly jealous."

"You look it," said Dick frankly.

It was a week after the alarm, and, though there was not the slightest trace to be found outside the old palace walls, a couple of sentries were placed on duty on the roof every night, while for further safety an extra sentry was stationed at the gates.

The whole of the officers now took the precaution of having loaded pistols within reach, and a certain amount of nervousness, a feeling of insecurity, slightly marred their sleep. But after six nights without being disturbed, they began to grow more careless, and to feel that such an adventure was not likely to occur again.

Being now much better, Hulton accepted an invitation from the Rajah for him and the doctor to dine at the palace, where, for the first time, Dick had the pleasure of seeing the queen-mother—a great favour, to be duly appreciated.

The young officer was ushered into the queen's apartments by the Rajah himself, and found her a handsome, graceful, stately lady of forty, who spoke fair English and received him with grave dignity, if she felt the condescension she was showing to the youth whom her son delighted to honour, by offering him her hand to kiss, examining his countenance searchingly the while.

She was not alone, for Dick's friend, the elderly Brahmin, was standing by, ready to greet him with a smile; while a bevy of her highness's ladies stood back, closely veiled, and all in simple white silk costumes, affording a strange contrast to their mistress, who was literally ablaze with diamonds, emeralds, and rubies.

The interview was short, and the Rajah led his young English friend back to where the others were waiting.

"I want my mother to know more of what the English are, Darrell," he said. "I want her to like you, and as she comes to know you better, I feel that her bitter prejudices will soften down, and she will begin to like others."

He referred to this again and again in the course of the evening, and spoke apologetically to Hulton and the doctor about the matter.

"You see," he said, "that it is a matter of time, and it was the utmost that my mother would concede at first. After a time I hope she will often meet you, too, as her friends."

The visit was short on account of the invalids, but it was made very pleasant by the Rajah's courteous attentions; and on his return to quarters, and having a chat with Wyatt, telling him all the proceedings of the evening, and describing in particular his audience with the Ranee, Dick was in the highest of spirits, giving it as his opinion that the enmity was dying out fast.

"I believe the Brahmin councillor and the old Wazir mean to be the best of friends now."

"Do you?" said Wyatt dryly.

"Yes, and you don't. But wait a bit. The Rajah will be asking you again soon, and then you'll see how differently they'll behave."

"You seem to have been drinking of the Rajah's wine of forgetfulness, my son," said Wyatt, "and when the wine's in the wit's out."

"Oh, is it?" said Dick. "Well, I must have a very small amount of wit, then, for one little glass of that sweet sugar-and-watery stuff to have driven it out. It's all light, I tell you; and the Wazir asked me how soon the drill-officers, as he called them, would be here."

"And you couldn't tell him," said Wyatt.

"I said very soon."

"Then, now, let's go to bed."

"What a hurry you're in!"

"Yes, my son. While you were feasting your eyes on the Ranee's jewels, and kissing her hand before feasting in a more worldly way with the Rajah, I was slaving like a nigger, and I want to sleep."

"Yes, it does seem too bad to be going out like this and leaving you at work. I thought about you ever so many times."

"Did you?" said Wyatt, smiling and looking less grim.

"I did, and wished you were there."

"That's right, old fellow. There, good-night; I want a long snooze."

"Good-night," said Dick in an injured tone. "You always do want to go to sleep when I want to talk."

"Do I?" said Wyatt, laughing. "Well, perhaps so. A sleep will do you good, though."

He went to his own room, and Dick undressed and was soon lying thinking.

"Phew! how hot it is!" he said to himself. "I'd give anything for a breath of fresh air. The place is like an oven."

But the understanding was that the windows were to be kept shut, and he had no wish for such another encounter as he had gone through before; so he lay still, going over the incidents of the evening, thinking of the Ranee and the wonderful jewels she wore, and of how young she looked to be the Rajah's mother.

"I don't quite like her way," he said to himself. "It was just as if she spoke civilly to me to please her son, and twice over there seemed to be a look in her eyes as if she was jealous of his being so friendly to me. But, phew! how hot it is! I must have some fresh air."

Then, taking into consideration that he was not at all drowsy, and that it would be impossible to sleep in that torrid atmosphere, he slipped out of bed and softly opened the window, breathed in the comparatively cool air for a few minutes, and then lay down again, meaning to get up after a time and close the window when the atmosphere of his chamber had grown cooler.

The natural consequence occurred. The soft night air stole in, bringing to him a delightful state of calm and restfulness, under whose action the weary, feverish symptoms passed off, and before many minutes had gone by he was sleeping deeply, a sleep full of the keenest enjoyment, though how long he did not know: but conscience interfered and cut the repose short, making him start up guiltily in full consciousness of having done something wrong. Springing off his bed, he went to the window, stood listening for a few minutes, and gazing up at the peaceful sky, before carefully closing and fastening the casement.

"I wonder how long I've been asleep," he said to himself—"not a minute, I'll be bound;" and, stretching himself out, he sighed, closed his eyes, and went right off again, but only to start up in alarm the next moment, as he thought.

"All right, Dick, lad; don't be scared."

"Oh, it's you," he said. "You shouldn't do that, Wyatt; it's startling in the dark, and I might have snatched up a pistol and fired."

"Yes, you'd better!" said Wyatt, laughing softly. "I should like to catch you at it. Why didn't you answer, then, when I knocked?"

"Did you knock?"

"Of course—over and over again. You do sleep."

"What's the matter? Aren't you well!"

"Oh, yes, I believe so; but I woke up suddenly. Haven't heard or seen anything, have you?"

"No," said Dick; and he felt guilty again, feeling sure that his brother-officer had heard him close the window.

"Then it must have been a dream. Guilty conscience needs no accuser."

"Eh? What do you mean?"

"I'll make confession, old fellow," said Wyatt. "It was so awfully hot in my room that I couldn't bear it any longer, and I got up and opened the window, meaning to leave it for a few minutes while I lay down till the room was cooler—for I couldn't, have gone to sleep like that, tired as I was; and then I went off fast asleep."

"Oh!" ejaculated Dick.

"There, don't 'Oh!' at a fellow. It was wrong, of course, and I oughtn't to have done it, for I might have been sure that I should go to sleep. But guilty conscience set me dreaming, and I dreamed that I was seeing exactly what you saw that night."

"Wyatt!"

"Yes; it was all as real as could be, only there was no lightning. But I seemed to dimly make out a nigger's legs kicking about at the top of the window, and then getting to the side and coming down till he glided over the sill on to the floor. Then I seemed to hear the sitting-room door open, and heard him go through."

"How strange!" said Dick.

"Yes; just a repetition of your bit of experience, lad."

"But didn't you jump out of bed and follow?"

"Don't I tell you I was asleep? Of course it wasn't real. The peculiar state of mind I was in, from going off instead of keeping awake to shut the window when the room grew cool, set me dreaming it all, I suppose; and, after what seemed to be a very long time, made me wake up in a tremendous perspiration and spring off the bed to fasten the window."

"It's very queer," said Dick. "Now, do you know, I—"

"Yes, you told me," said Wyatt, interrupting him hastily; "only that isn't all. I went back and sat on the edge of the charpoy, feeling regularly puzzled. I was still half asleep, and there seemed to be no doubt about my having dreamed it all, but I couldn't settle it all in my mind, and before lying down I felt obliged to go across the room and see if the door was shut."

"Yes," said Dick eagerly; "and of course it was?"

"No," said Wyatt; "it was open."

"You left it open when you went to bed for coolness."

"I could swear I did not," said Wyatt. "It stuck a little, warped by the heat, and I remember perfectly lifting it to get it close."

Dick was silent.

"Now tell me this," continued Wyatt. "Was the sitting-room window shut when we went to bed?"

"Yes: I'm sure of that," said Dick, "because I went and looked out, and longed to leave it open."

"You shut it?"

"You saw me do it when we came to bed."

"I did. Well, I found it wide open."

"Ah!" cried Dick excitedly, "then it was not a dream. You saw it all in your sleep. He came in at your window and went out by the sitting-room, and the tulwar has gone."

"No," said Wyatt slowly: "the tulwar hangs where we put it, quite safe. I thought that, and went to see before I woke you."

"How strange! Then it must have been a dream after all. One minute. Is there any explanation of it? Could it have been the servants?"

"No; they are both fast asleep."

"Then what can it mean?" said Dick.

"I don't know, unless you've been walking in your sleep and opened the windows."

Bang!

The sentry at the gate had fired his carbine.

Bang! and then *bang!* The alarm was taken up by the sentries on the roof, and the two officers seized their weapons and, clad only, as they were, in their silken pyjamas, ran down into the yard. The guard had turned out, and all was hurry and excitement, for that soul-stirring cry which sends a thrill through the stoutest when raised in the dead of night brought Dick's heart to his mouth.

For the cry was, "Fire, fire!" and Wyatt exclaimed hoarsely, "Quick, my lads—quick! the magazine!"

Chapter XXVIII
The Work of the Enemy

A rush was made for the ground-floor of the palace opposite to the stables, where some kind of firework was hissing and spitting fiercely, and as the men ran there was a blinding flash by the door of the place used as an ammunition-store, just as if some powder had been thrown there and the sparks had set it alight.

"Forward, my lads, before it gets worse," shouted Wyatt.—"Darrell, lad, you must risk it," he cried; "we can't leave them to perish. Up with you, and bring out Hulton and the doctor."

A strange feeling of dread ran through the young officer, for the instinct was strong upon him to run for his life and escape by the gate before the native fuse, which had been placed at the bottom of the magazine door, should do its deadly work of causing an explosion and bringing that side of the old building tottering down.

But education was stronger than instinct. It was the master. Before the lad's eyes were his brother-officer and the men of the troop following; Sergeant Stubbs was carrying the keys, rushing right up to the magazine door—right, as it were, into the fire and the explosion which must occur; and nearly overhead was the room occupied by Hulton and the doctor.

Dick Darrell could not help his thoughts nor his natural instincts, whichever way they might lead. He had his duty to do as a soldier, and he neither hesitated nor shrank, but rushed forward to perform his task, meeting the two sentries, who had come hurrying down from the roof.

The next minute he was ascending the stairs leading to the officers' quarters, reaching the broad corridor and the way into their sitting-room, thinking that it was a pity for that beautiful tulwar to be destroyed, when he fell over somebody on to some one else, sending a thrill of horror through his nerves as he heard deep groans.

"Who is it?" he cried.

A bright flash which came through the open door and window showed him the two servants, with their white cotton garments deeply stained with blood; while, as he gathered himself up, he found that something wet and warm had soaked his own thin silken garments, and his hands felt sticky.

The chill of horror came again. The two servants stabbed at the door; and not many yards farther lay Hulton's room. Had he and the doctor been assassinated too?

Pity would have deterred him—duty urged him on; and the recollection of the terrible danger below, driven from his brain for the moment, came back as he dashed on, just as the door was thrown open and Hulton and the doctor hurried out.

"Who's that? You, Darrell? What is it?"

"Fire—the magazine. Quick, for your lives!"

They hurried down the corridor, momentarily expecting the floor to open with the roar and red rush of an explosion; but they paused to seize the two men lying by the sitting-room door, and among them dragged them to the head of the stairs, and then to the bottom and out into the yard, where, as soon as they were in safety, Dick left the wounded with the doctor, and ran to where, in the midst of thick smoke, axe-blows were falling upon the entrance to the magazine.

For the perpetrator of the diabolical outrage had done his work cunningly and well. Several small patches of loose powder must have been arranged about the bottom of the door, and the great keyhole plugged with it, before the fuse was rammed in and ignited, attracting the attention of the guard.

It was perilous work, for, in the effort to tear out the fuse from where it had been jammed, it broke up, and this caused the first explosion, which had destroyed the lock, others immediately following in spite of the way in which buckets of water had been dashed down.

The men worked with fierce energy to hack out the lock, in the desperate effort to get the door open before some fragment of the fuse or spark, driven in by one of the little explosions, should act upon the bags and kegs of powder and ready-filled cartridges within. Each blow, too, that was struck with the axe might, they well knew, strike off sparks, which would increase the peril. But they did not shrink, one man taking up the axe as another tired, till, just as Dick ran up, there was a loud cheer, for the door was flung open, revealing the bright sparks emitted by something smouldering within; and, even as the door was thrown wide, the puff of air finished what was going on. For, as two men rushed in together, there was a faint report, followed by another and another, and pieces of shattered, smouldering paper were thrown about the place.

The men outside involuntarily drew back as they realised that a box of carbine cartridges had been started by a spark. But the men within seized the box, and sent those which were left flying out into the yard, where another one or two exploded, as, in the midst of a dense smoke, the two brave fellows within sought for and threw out every scrap of smouldering cartridge-case, some of which were in close proximity to the flannel powder-bags of the six-pounder guns.

This work was done in momentary expectation of one of the kegs starting the general destruction; but the gallant effort saved the place, and, hot and panting, blind almost with smoke, the two men staggered out at last, to be met with a roaring cheer.

"Water—quick—water!" cried one of the pair in a hoarse voice. "I'm choking."

"Are you hurt, Wyatt?" cried Dick, catching him by the arm.

**"Are you hurt, Wyatt?" cried Dick,
catching him by the arm.**

"Fingers a bit scorched, lad, and my pyjamas ruined; but never mind—*we've* won. Here, who was working with me in the dark there?" cried Wyatt. "He saved the place, and he must be burned. Here, who are you—why don't you speak, my lad?"

The lantern was cautiously brought forward and held by Sergeant Stubbs up over the blackened face and singed hair of one of the privates.

"Why, it's Bob Hanson, sir."

"Hanson!" cried Wyatt, stepping forward to gaze wonderingly in his companion's face. "Then shake hands, my lad; you and I were never so close to death before."

A low murmur indicative of the satisfaction felt by all present rose on the night air, Dick feeling a thrill of pleasure at this public acknowledgment of Hanson's bravery. He, the man for whom the intercession had been made which saved him from the most degrading punishment that could be inflicted.

But it was a time for action, and while Stubbs was set to the duty of once more making the ammunition secure, Wyatt and Dick went to work to try and trace out everything possible regarding this horrible attempt to destroy their means of offence and defence.

"You see, we have been on the wrong tack, Dick," said Wyatt in a low voice as they stood together. "The scoundrel who did all this was not after my tulwar each time, but had planned striking a terrible blow at our prestige, for we should make a poor show without our gains."

"He must have reached the roof somehow," said Dick.

"But why come through our rooms?"

"Because it is probably the only way down into the courtyard. He could not attempt the stairs on account of the sentries."

"It must be some one who knows the place and all about our arrangements."

"Yes," said Dick; "but come and let's question the doctor's patients."

"The doctor's patient? What would Hulton know?"

"No, no; his fresh patients—the two servants."

"What! do you think they were in it?"

"They were in it, certainly," said Dick sadly. "The poor fellows were badly stabbed."

"But I saw them sleeping before I came to you."

"Yes; but I found them both lying outside the door weltering in their blood. I have an idea—but come along."

They passed together to where the men were lying freshly bandaged by the doctor, Ram Dad being sensible and able to explain what had happened.

"A dacoit, sahibs," he said firmly. "Come up by the stairs, and we tried to stop him; but he was naked and covered with oil, and, though we tried hard to hold him, he struck us both with his knife, and ran through the room, to climb up the side of the window and on to the top."

"Hah!" cried Wyatt. "Then he may still be there. Come and have the upper terrace searched."

This was carefully done by a dozen men despatched in different directions, every possible hiding-place being examined by the aid of the lanterns, without result. It was evident that the marauder could not have descended without help in the shape of a rope, for to have dropped from the parapet meant death; and, wearied out at last with searching and conjecture, the task was given up and the men dismissed.

"Dick," said Wyatt at last, "we must have a traitor in our midst."

"I have been thinking that," was the reply; "but we have not a single man with us that was not brought, or it would be an easy task to find out who is the enemy. The servants would not help."

"I would not trust them," said Wyatt bitterly. "We are their masters, and, to them, foreigners and enemies to their faith, which they know well enough we hold in contempt."

"Perhaps so," said Dick; "but it seems hard upon them to talk like this. We were ready to suspect them before, and we found two of them cruelly stabbed in our defence."

"Yes, old fellow, as you nearly were the other night. Dick, Dick, old lad, that was an escape! Well, there, I will not believe it of any one we have in quarters if you can give me a plausible suggestion for thinking otherwise."

Dick was silent, and his companion stood waiting. "Well, what are you thinking?" he said. "Have you an idea?"

"Just the shadow of one," said Dick thoughtfully; "but give me time. Let's do what there is to do, and then go and wash and change. I'm horrible with blood."

"And I with gunpowder," said Wyatt. "Well, there is nothing more to do. We shall have no further attack to-night; the sentries are doubled, and we may as well try for a bit of sleep. This is my delicious night's rest!"

Draw Swords! In The Horse Artillery | 199

"Yes, it horrible."

"We'll go and see the wounded again, and then look how Stubbs has managed, and go to our room."

The doctor said that the two servants were badly hurt, but not dangerously, and he and Hulton were going to stay and watch them till morning. Wyatt protested but Hulton was firm. "Let me have my own way," he said. "I can be of use over this, and I've been of little enough lately."

So the two officers went down to the yard, visiting posts on their way, and upon reaching the room used as a magazine, it was to find that Stubbs and a squad of gunners had moved everything to an inner chamber on the ground-floor, where it would be far more difficult for an attack to be made.

Stubbs was just locking up as Wyatt and Dick approached, and triumphantly showed them the key.

"It's just under Mr Darrell's bedchamber, gentlemen," he said; "but I suppose he won't mind."

"Oh, no; not at all," said Dick, with a queer smile, which looked to be absolutely without mirth. "Only," he added, "I should not have chosen my sleeping-place there."

"I didn't think of it, sir, till I'd got nearly everything in; but I'll see what we can do to-morrow."

"No," said Wyatt shortly, and to Dick's great discomposure; "it is a capital place for it, Stubbs, and it shall stay.—But there are two ways of looking at such things, Darrell," he continued. "I'll be hanged if I'm going to sleep over a powder-magazine that our enemies are trying to blow up, and I certainly won't let you."

"Enemies, sir!" said Stubbs. "Then you feel that it is the work of the enemy?"

"Certainly, Stubbs," replied Wyatt; "and of some one high in power."

Chapter XXIX
Hot Boiled Beans"

It was about half-an-hour later that, after a refreshing wash, the two officers sat together, partly dressed, talking in the room where the tulwar still hung, and with the pleasant knowledge that if, after all, a smouldering cartridge-cover had been accidentally taken into the fresh magazine, they might at any moment be blown up piecemeal.

"Yes, it is a nice idea," said Wyatt in reply to a remark made by Dick. "It has stopped me, too, from having a 'hubble-bubble' to smoke. But never mind; we must chance it for one night."

"Or morning," said Dick.

"Eh? Yes, it must be getting late, and I want a sleep for an hour or two, even if it is with a bag of powder for a pillow. So now to business. You have some idea of how the attacks are made?"

"I have thought of one," replied Dick, "but it sounds so silly and romantic that I don't like to tell you."

"Your commanding officer orders you to speak, sir. 'Tention! Now, Mr Darrell, what are your ideas?"

Dirk coughed to get rid of a little nervous huskiness and then he said:

"This is a very old building," —and then stopped.

"Thank you, Mr Darrell, it is," said Wyatt sarcastically; "and it is very strong."

"Thank you Mr Wyatt," said Dick, smiling, "but I have something else to say."

"Then say it, old lad, for I'm in a fever of expectation and nervous irritation. Hang it all! I never felt so disagreeable in my life."

"It was the old Rajah's palace."

"Yes, of course," cried Wyatt.

"And, foolishly or not, I have been thinking it possible that there may be a secret passage somewhere which leads to the outside."

"Known only to one of the old king's followers?" cried Wyatt excitedly.

"Yes."

"And making our place only a trap in which we may be caught at any moment."

Dick nodded, and Wyatt seized and wrung his hand.

"My dear old boy," he cried, "you'll be a general long before I get to be colonel."

"Nonsense!"

"'Tisn't. That's it, my dear boy. It's the right nail, and you've hit it bang on the head. Thank ye. Now I can go and sleep till breakfast-time with a feeling of delicious serenity, knowing that we have got hold of the end of the clue."

"Not yet," said Dick. "Where is it?"

"Somewhere in the old building. It's going to be the old nursery game of 'hot boiled beans and very good butter,' and I believe we're burning now."

"Almost," said Dick; "and we dare not open a window."

"No, we must have no more of that, old fellow. And, I say, I'm very glad you were as great an offender as I was over that business. But, look here, if we find to-morrow morning that it is as you say—"

"And find the place," put in Dick.

"Of course—and find the place—I'm going to hoist that gentleman with his own petard."

"How?"

"Don't quite know yet, but something in this style: I shall lay a trap in such a way in the passage, or whatever it is, so that he'll step on a small bag of powder and fire it off. He won't come again. Now, good-night."

"Good-night," said Dick. "But, I say, don't reckon too much upon my idea."

"I shall!" said Wyatt. "Once more, good-night; for, whatever time it is, it does not look like day."

"Good-night," said Dick; and ten minutes after, utterly worn out by their exertions, they were both of them fast asleep.

Stringent orders were given as soon as Wyatt woke that the last night's trouble should not be named outside; but the order was issued in vain. The noise and excitement had been heard and seen, and the native servants were questioned, with the result that by degrees the news, greatly exaggerated, reached the Rajah's ears, after it had passed through those of his people to the Ranee, who told him herself.

Both Wyatt and Dick were later than they had intended to be, and after a short morning parade they visited the wounded, found the men in a serious condition, but with the doctor hopeful, and then went and had a long consultation with Hulton.

"Go and search, by all means," he said, "but I would do it so as not to excite attention. It is hardly likely, to my mind. But be careful; we do not know who are friends and who are foes."

"If I had full command in the city," growled Wyatt, "I'd soon find out. But look here, we are going to have a good hunt round. Will you come? Strong enough?"

"Yes, I think so," replied Hulton; "and I'll try."

The trio quietly ascended to the roof, which was without guards in the daytime; and as if for Hulton's benefit, his companions in turn giving him an arm, the whole range of battlemented terrace was traversed again and again, till, in a hopeless way, the little party descended without a word.

"Doesn't look very cheerful, Dick," said Wyatt, "does it?"

"No," said Dick firmly; "it was all imagination."

He had hardly spoken when there was a challenge at the gate, the guard was called out, and the corporal on duty sent up word that the Rajah had arrived.

"Look here," said Dick eagerly, "he has heard of the upset last night. Let's ask him."

"Very well," said Hulton. "He is, of course, our friend, and he ought to know."

Wyatt and Dick went down to meet their visitor as he descended from his elephant; and he returned with them to their room, ready to express his great concern about the attack, and assuring them that if he could only find out who originated the affair, that man should die.

"Thank you, sir," said Wyatt quietly; "and he deserves to. But we don't know who it was, nor how he got in.—Now, Darrell, speak out and tell his highness your ideas."

These were given clearly enough, the Rajah hearing them to the end, but shaking his head.

"I never heard of anything of the kind," he said at last, "and I don't think any such passage exists. There would be no harm, though, in searching again; and I will place a guard round the place every night."

"No, sir; please don't," said Wyatt bluntly. "Don't be offended at what I say, but I don't feel that we should be so safe here with your guards about us as we should be trusting to our own men."

The Rajah frowned angrily, but his brow cleared a few minutes later.

"You are right," he said. "I cannot trust my own guards. I only hope for better things."

"Would it not be better to begin quite afresh, sir?" said Hulton. "A bold stroke would relieve you of many doubtful friends, and we would support you to the death if trouble arose."

"I thank you, Mr Hulton," said the Rajah sadly, "and I feel that you are right, but I cannot take such a step as you propose. It would mean death and destruction, and fighting against one whom I feel bound to look up to with respect. No; this is a revolution that must come slowly. I can only fight to the death against Rajah Singh. I must fight against my mother and her friends by word of mouth. I must leave you now. All this troubles me, but I will be firm as far as I can;" and he bowed and moved towards the door.

"I wish Rajah Singh would attack again, and make short work of some of the Rajah's internal enemies," said Wyatt after the visitor had gone. "He is an open enemy, and we know what to do."

"Yes," said Hulton; "and we are surrounded by secret, ones, and do not know what to do."

"Not yet," said Wyatt, "but we mean to do one thing—eh, Darrell!"

"What?" said Dick, looking at the speaker inquiringly.

"Win," said Wyatt shortly. "But come up again with me, Dick. I want to see if I can find that secret way."

The search proved to be in vain, and the occupants of the old palace, as they talked the matter over, felt more and more the awkwardness of their position, troubled, as they were, constantly by the knowledge that the place they had looked upon as a stronghold was weak to a degree in its most vital part, since their enemies could evidently elude their watchfulness and strike at them whenever they pleased.

"I don't know what's to be done," said Dick. "I felt sure that I had hit upon the way in which it was all managed."

"So you have," said Wyatt; "only you have not got quite enough. But there, I'll tell you what to do."

"What?" cried Dick eagerly.

"Nothing."

"Nothing?"

"Yes. I'm pretty good over my work as an officer, Dick, old fellow, but I'm only a big, stupid boy in other things."

"You! What nonsense!"

"It's a fact, Dicky, and I know it and have come to be a bit of a philosopher."

"I don't know what you're talking about," said Dick.

"Then I'll tell you, old fellow. When I find a thing's too big for me to think out I let it go, and I find it often comes afterwards. We can't tackle this, so let's leave it and do the best we can. By-and-by perhaps we shall find it out. Drop it now."

So it was dropped, and the days wore on without any more alarms. The two injured men improved fast, and Hulton seemed stronger, but quite unfit still for duty.

"Never mind," he said, with a smile full of resignation; "it doesn't matter. The troop couldn't be better managed, and I shall get well sooner up here in the hills than I should down in the plains."

One thing troubled the party in the old palace, though, and that was the apparent change on the part of the Rajah, who kept quite aloof from them now; while the people, after a period of comparative friendliness, began to grow aggressive.

"Seems to me," said Wyatt, "that we might as well be back at cantonments. The Rajah cuts us; nobody wants us here; there's no fighting to do, unless we set to and drive the fighting part of the population out and take possession of Soojeepur in the name of the Company. I want exercise, and I should just like that job. We could do it, too, with a bit of scheming. What do you say to a try, Dick, and being made Rajah *pro tem*?"

"Nothing," said Dick.

The very next day a larger present than usual of the produce of the country was brought for the use of the troop by the Rajah's orders, but there was no friendly advance.

"Doesn't seem as if he was tired of us yet," said Wyatt, "Look here; we shall have to send out a party to meet our reinforcements with the ammunition, for I don't like their not coming. It looks as if they had had a check somewhere."

"Do you think the Rajah of Singh could have sent a force round and captured them?"

"No, I don't," replied Wyatt. "If he had been on the move, our chief here must have heard of it. Perhaps it's all right, though, and they'll be here soon."

He was right, for the next morning a couple of horse artillery-men rode up to the gate, causing intense excitement among the Rajah's troops, who, as Dick found out later, had seemed disposed to refuse them entrance; but the news was brought in by one of the native servants, and Dick had orders to turn out with twenty men to meet the party.

In accordance, then, with his orders, he rode down to the gate, met the advance-guard, and rode off with them back along the road to bring in the little party with their heavy, slow train of ammunition-wagons and stores.

Stubbs was with the young leader, and as they were escorting the party back in a way which accounted for the length of time they had been on the road, an unpleasant thought occurred to Dick.

It was so troublous that he could not keep it to himself, and he rode up alongside of Stubbs.

"I've been thinking," he said, "that we should be awkwardly placed if the Rajah's enemies took advantage of our being outside to refuse us entrance."

"That's rum, sir," said Stubbs.

"Rum? I don't see the droll side of it, Stubbs, because it would mean taking advantage of the troop being weakened to attack them."

"I meant it was rum that you should think just the same as I did. It has been bothering me ever since I found that they stopped our two men at the gate."

"I'm afraid I ought to have halted and sent word back to Captain Wyatt."

"Would have been better, sir; but it's too late now. We must get in somehow. Bounce may do it."

"Yes; we must make a dash in if they seem to be turning queer."

"Can't turn much queerer than they have lately, sir. I've been expecting a fresh attempt to blow us up every night; and you see if they don't begin again, now that they find we have got in our fresh ammunition. There'll be no peace in Soojeepur till some there have had their bodies shortened."

"Think not?"

"That's what I think, sir. It's that party of priests at the big temple and the queen's people. They hate us, and the Rajah don't like to go against them because of his mother. But I suppose if we live long enough we shall see."

Mountains seemed to rise in front of Richard Darrell as he rode on, but they grew smaller when he confronted the difficulties. The heavily-laden wagons were slowly brought up to the bridge, and by that time Dick had come to the conclusion that his course would be to ride straight in, no matter what opposition was offered, and, if the gates were closed against them, to try the effect of a bag of powder, whose explosion would drive in the gates and bring Wyatt to their help, for he felt that there must be no hesitation. Such a party as his, encumbered with a wagon-train, would be almost helpless outside if attacked.

He rode at the head of his detachment with his lips tightened and fingers itching to draw his sword, seeing that the fortifications over and about the sides of the gateway were crowded with the Rajah's men; but the advance-guard passed in unchallenged, and a few minutes later he drew a deep breath, for the train passed in, and all rode through the crowd-lined streets, and in and out till the gate of the old palace was reached and the task was successfully accomplished.

Chapter XXX
A Dastardly Act

Wyatt set it down to the Rajah's hearing of their large accession of stores which accompanied the little reinforcement, for the very next day there came an invitation from the palace for the officers to spend an evening there.

"What's to be done?" asked Dick.

"Mustn't display doubt or hesitation," replied Wyatt, "though I trust his lordship less than ever. He's going to be civil now because we are stronger, and he feels that it is his best policy. What do you say, Hulton?"

"I quite agree with you. I'd let him see that we feel more independent, too."

"How?" asked Wyatt.

"Do not accept the offer of an elephant and party. Ride there with an escort of our own men in full review order."

"Well done, counsellor," said Wyatt. "Excellent."

"You will go this time," said Hulton.

"I? Oh, no; he must be content with you, Darrell here, and the doctor."

"No," said Hulton firmly; "you have not been there yet, and I think you ought to be present instead of me."

"Think so?" said Wyatt, hesitating.

"I do. Stubbs will be with me, and I feel strong enough to take command for the few hours you are away. Besides. I feel sure that we have been fidgeting unnecessarily. We have only to act decisively, and do as we please."

"I think you are right," said Wyatt, "and I believe if we liked we might seize the whole of the place."

"But we do not want it—only the Rajah's faithful alliance with the Company."

All was done in accordance with the little conference. The message was sent, and in due time twenty men turned out in full review order, under the command of one of the newly-arrived sergeants, and the escort dashed up to the palace in their best style, to the surprise and excitement of the people and the Rajah's followers, taking up the position of guards on either side of the entrance when their officers entered, while the Rajah's guard drew back.

The reception of the three officers was warm in the extreme, the Rajah appearing perfectly frank and gentlemanly when they met, and walking with them out into a balcony from whence he could see the escort drawn up by the entrance.

"I am glad you came like this," he said. "Your people are grand. I like the people to see your strength, and I congratulate you on the safe arrival of your fresh men."

He led the way back into the reception-room, and when they were seated he turned to Dick.

"I'm afraid you have thought me very neglectful, Mr Darrell."

"Well," said Dick, "to be frank, we began to think that there was something very wrong, as you seemed so changed towards us."

"Not changed in the least, Captain Wyatt," he said, turning now to his other guests.—"A man situated as I am, Doctor, cannot do quite as he pleases."

"I suppose not, sir. Even our King cannot at home."

"I am glad of that," said the Rajah, smiling, and he addressed Wyatt now. "You see, I could use force, but I shrink from slaughter, for I think I can achieve my ends without playing the tyrant who delights in blood. And there is my mother. After that cowardly attempt upon the old palace, I determined to try a fresh means of securing peace and the full alliance of all my leading people with the English Company, as I wish; and at last, just when I felt that there must be war and the destruction of all who oppose me, the leaders of those against me in political matters have given way. Gentlemen, you know how English I wish to be, and how hard I have fought to win my mother's old friends to my way of thinking. I have succeeded now. You will meet my mother, the Ranee, who gives up her old-world prejudices, and will act like an English lady by receiving you at dinner this evening in company with her old ministers, the Wazir and the chief Brahmin from the great temple."

The visitors murmured their satisfaction, and, at the first opportunity, Wyatt caught Dick's eye with a look which that gentleman interpreted to mean, "I wish the these people were at the bottom of the sea!"

Wyatt coloured guiltily the next moment, for the Rajah turned to him, saying:

"I am very glad to have your company at last, Captain Wyatt. It has almost seemed as if you would not come."

"Your highness praised the discipline of our men," he replied.

"Yes; it is perfect."

"It is, sir; but it is only arrived at by the officers giving up social pleasure to constant duty. I should have come before if I could have spared the time."

The Rajah smiled and turned to Dick, whom he seemed to honour above all; while Wyatt said to himself:

"And, now I am here, I hope you are not going to play any tricks with us, my Arabian knight. I shall feel more comfortable for having our lads there under the window."

There was a movement by the curtained door, and a couple of armed men marched in with drawn tulwars, to stand holding back the heavy hangings.

"The Ranee, my mother, gentlemen," said the Rajah, rising as the handsome, stately woman swept in, followed by her two elderly friends, she literally blazing with magnificent jewels, while the Wazir was in a rich uniform and the Brahmin in simple white, looking a peculiar contrast to the Rajah, who wore garments of the most sober hue.

The Ranee held out her hand to Dick, smiling in the most gracious way, and treating him as if they had been old friends. To Wyatt she was dignified and rather distant, while the doctor received a condescending bow.

The two ministers seemed to take their cue from their lady, but every now and then they were effusive to a degree, and more than once Dick noticed that downright Wyatt frowned and looked annoyed; but he strove hard all the same over the dinner, which was handsomely served in the adjoining room, the Rajah having evidently taken pains to gratify his guests by making everything as English in style as he could.

He had placed the Ranee on his right, and was about to place Richard Darrell on his left, but, at the Ranee's express desire, he had a seat on her right, Wyatt and the doctor being on the Rajah's left, while the Wazir and the Brahmin sat opposite to one another at the lower end of the table, the bottom being left vacant.

Flowers, beautiful glass, Indian china, and gold and silver plate covered the table; and, expressly for the guests, decanters of wine were placed here and there.

The two guards who had drawn aside the heavy silken hangings in the reception-room had raised them again when the party moved into the dining-room, and then followed, to remain on guard by the door, through which the servants in white and scarlet came and went noiselessly with the various choice dishes that were handed round; while, after a few minutes of stiff formality, the conversation became general.

But somehow Dick did not feel at his ease. It seemed to him, after what had passed, that there was a want of reality about the Rajah's efforts to entertain his guests; while, to his way of thinking, if ever there was treachery masked in two faces, it was plainly in the shifty, smiling countenances of the two elderly ministers who met his eyes from time to time.

Then, too, he did not like the two guards standing on duty by the door, with perhaps a score more close at hand, ready to rush in at a given signal; and consequently, choice as were the viands offered to him, he could not enjoy his dinner in the least during the early part, in spite of the ready and gracious way in which the Ranee kept talking to him and smiling pleasantly at his readiness in reply in Hindustani.

All at once there was the rattle of accoutrements below the window, as if a horse had shaken itself violently, and a loud neigh rang out, one he recognised as being uttered by his own charger, and a change came over him immediately.

"What a coward I am!" he thought. "Just as if it were likely that any treachery could be meant when we have our guards within call!"

The next minute his common-sense set to work to disillusionise him, and point out how easily any treacherous act could be perpetrated before help could come, and seemed to ask him of what use a score of mounted men would be at such a time.

But Dick would not listen to his silent mentor, for the Rajah spoke to him across his mother, the Ranee joined in the conversation, and the lad's cheeks flushed with pleasure as he found that he, as the Rajah's friend, was being made the most important of the three guests at the table.

The meal went on, and the Rajah laid himself out to introduce topics of interest to all, the last being in connection with the proceedings of Rajah

Singh, who, he told them, had been so utterly disgusted by his ill-success that, as his spies informed him, he was not likely to attempt to invade the territory again.

Wyatt shook his head at this, and took upon himself to advise his host not to be too sanguine, but to remain carefully on guard lest he should be taken unawares.

Then, as the Englishmen very moderately sipped the excellent French claret that was placed at their side, the doctor was drawn into conversation by the Rajah, who scrupulously, like his mother and the others, refrained from wine.

The doctor was asked to give his opinion about the terrible visitation of disease from which Soojeepur suffered from time to time, and, being here upon his own ground, he spoke out plainly upon the necessity for improving the sanitary arrangements of the city, assuring his host and the Ranee that if certain rules which he could set forth were observed, the mortality would cease by one-half; and he grew more emphatic as he saw the two ministers raise their eyebrows and exchange glances.

The Rajah noticed this, and spoke out at once.

"Then you shall make those laws," he said, "and they shall be carried out, for it will be to benefit all. The time has come, gentlemen, when my people must pass from the night of the old days to the bright sunshine of the new;" and he looked sternly towards the foot of the table as he spoke. "Her highness, my mother, understands my wishes now, and you, gentlemen, who have so bravely come to my assistance, shall see now that I am about to throw away as worthless all the old teachings and superstitions of the people as regards caste, and begin acting as civilised people do."

He made a sign to the chief servant in attendance: and as Dick listened and watched he heard the Ranee sigh softly, and noticed that the heavily-jewelled hand she laid upon the table close to him twitched and trembled, while the two ministers bent over the table and looked down upon their plates.

"They don't like it," thought Dick; and the next minute he was watching the chief domestic, in his white muslin and scarlet cummerbund, his dark face looking solemn and strange beneath his white turban, as he advanced silently and slowly, bearing a gold tray upon which were seven tall, old-fashioned champagne-glasses filled with the foaming wine, ready to hand first to the Ranee, who shook her head and closed her eyes; next to the Rajah, who took his glass; and then to the visitors in turn.

"No, no," said the Ranee softly as she gave Dick a troubled look. "It is not good for boys."

"Then I will not drink," he replied, smiling at her; but he saw that her brow was contracted and her eyes closed.

Then his attention was taken up by what was passing at the bottom of the table, where the Wazir and the Brahmin both drew away from the proffered glasses.

"Very well, gentlemen," said the Rajah quietly, "I will not force you; but the day will come when you will both look upon this act as innocent and right.—You, gentlemen," he said, "will have no scruples. I drink to you, even if I lose caste."

With a quick movement he tossed off his glass, and then, bending quickly to his left, he struck Wyatt's glass from his lips, and, startled by the action, the doctors fell from his hand, both glasses shivering as they fell. The two ministers started up in their places, as did the queen, who made a quick clutch at Dick's arm and then stood trembling.

"Treachery! Poison!" cried the king hoarsely, and his dark eyes flashed as he glared at the two men who had risen. "It was like fire—it means death. Ah!" he cried, turning upon the Ranee with a look of agony and grief, "this from you—from my mother!"

"No, no," shrieked the Ranee wildly, "it is not true, my son. By your dead father, I swear!"

"Ah!" he cried, with a sigh of relief, and he turned to glare at the two old ministers, who stood clutching the table without daring to move, and as if waiting for the end.

Wyatt and the doctor had in turn sprung from their seats, Dick following their example; and as the Ranee's hand dropped, the Rajah clutched at Dick's arm in turn, beckoning to Wyatt with the hand at liberty.

"It is an enemy's blow!" he gasped. "You, both of you, stop the coward stroke. Bring your soldiers here to save me, and seize the temple there. If I am to die, your people shall hold the place."

Wyatt sprang to the window, and at a word the sergeant rode close up.

"An orderly at once to Captain Hulton," he cried. "Every man to turn out and gallop here with the guns."

That was enough.

As he turned back, it was to see the doctor bending over the Rajah and the two ministers making for the door.

"Arrest those men," cried Wyatt to the two guards.

"Arrest those men," cried Wyatt to the two guards.

"They will not obey," thought Dick; but, to his surprise, they faced round, drawn sword in hand, and placed themselves before the two officials, whose dark countenances looked wild and strange.

Meanwhile the doctor had passed round behind the Rajah's chair, taken up and raised Dick's untouched glass to his lips, tasted, and spat out the wine. Then, filling a glass with water, he half forced the Rajah to drink again and again, in spite of the agony he seemed to be in.

Wyatt, returning from the other end of the room where the prisoners were, gave the doctor a questioning look, which he answered aloud:

"One of their cursed vegetable poisons, I believe," he said; and Wyatt turned upon the Ranee.

"This must be your doing, madam," he said sternly.

"No, no," she cried wildly; "he is my son—my son!"

"Prove it, then, by your help," said Wyatt.

"Yes, yes; tell me what. Oh, my son, my son!"

She fell upon her knees by the Rajah's chair and caught his hand in hers, looking up at him wildly.

Then, standing up, she looked at the doctor inquiringly.

"He must be taken to his room," said the doctor; and the servants came at the Ranee's sign to bear their Rajah away.

"You will not want us, Doctor?" said Wyatt hastily.

"No; you have your work to do, I see."

The Rajah made a sign to Dick as he was being carried out, and the lad darted to him, to have his hand seized by one that was wet with agony and like ice.

"My guards are true," whispered the Rajah; "they will obey you. Protect the Ranee—"

He could say no more, the doctor interposing, and, followed closely by the Ranee, the sufferer was borne out.

Chapter XXXI
Prompt Action

Dick's first act was to test the Rajah's words about the faithfulness of the guards, and he crossed to the two standing by the prisoners.

"Swords for myself and friends," he said sharply.

The man addressed called to one of the servants standing trembling and helpless by the door, gave him an order, and the man hurried out, to return in a few minutes with three jewelled weapons with their belts from the Rajah's armoury.

"Hah!" cried Wyatt, seizing one of them, while Dick buckled the other on, just as the heavy tramp of half the escort in their boots and spurs rang on the marble steps outside.

"I ordered half of them to come up," said Wyatt, and then, as loud shouts and cries arose, he signed to his companion to draw; but Dick rushed through the door, to find some twenty of the Rajahs guard ready to oppose the artillery-men, who were about to rush up, sabre in hand.

"Halt!" shouted Dick, and then turning to the guard, who faced fiercely round, he said in Hindustani:

"Your Rajah says you will be faithful to him. Join with our men in defending the palace against his enemies and ours."

The men looked in doubt, but Wyatt spoke out now.

"The Rajah has been poisoned," he said. "Six of you go to his door, and let no one but the doctor and servants pass. The rest of you guard the palace gates. Where is your officer?"

Their leader stepped out, tulwar in hand.

"Call out the rest of the men," he said. "You must help us to defend the palace against all who come. But these two must be kept safely;" and he pointed to the two ministers within the room.

A minute or two before, the place was all passing into a state of wild confusion, but the short, prompt words of the two officers sufficed; and when Dick, after a word or two with Wyatt, gave a fresh order, it was plain to the guard that they were working with friends, and in a very few minutes every gate was closed and held.

Dick's orders were that four of the Rajah's men should guard the Ranee.

This done, leaving Wyatt impatiently waiting for some sign of the coming troop, Dick made his way to the Rajah's room, into which he was allowed to pass at once.

"Well?" he asked.

"I can tell you nothing yet," replied the doctor. "The poor fellow is in fearful agony, but I was able to act so quickly that I have hope. It's a terrible position, though; you see. I am in total ignorance of the poison used."

Almost as they spoke, the trampling of horses and the lumbering of the gun-wheels was heard in the distance.

Dick uttered a sigh of relief.

"Thank goodness," he said. "But we shan't be many now, and it does seem such a piece of impudence for us, a mere handful of Englishmen, to take so much upon ourselves as we do."

"Knowledge is power, my dear Darrell," said the doctor. "It must always have been so since the world began, that the man who knew most took the lead. You soldiers, with your discipline and weapons, can attack and thrash twenty times your number."

"I suppose so," said Dick, smiling; "and you as a surgeon can laugh at twenty of the native doctors."

"Well, I don't want to brag, Darrell," replied the doctor, "but I think I could save twenty men's lives while they saved one. Yes, knowledge is power. I don't suppose they would own openly to my being the better man, but they'd rather trust me than one of their fellows. They can't help looking up to us. But I'm glad the troop has come, for I've felt during the last half-hour that my throat was not safe."

"Why?" said Dick. "You're a non-combatant."

"Pooh! What do they care about non-combatants? Some mad enthusiast or another might have accused me of poisoning the Rajah after seeing me give the poor fellow a dose of antidote."

"Darrell here!" said Wyatt, coming to the door hurriedly.

"Yes, I'll come," whispered Dick; but as he took a step forward he glanced towards the Rajah's couch, and he saw the victim's hand raised in a sign to him to approach.

The poor fellow's face was livid and drawn with pain as Dick bent over him and took the hand offered, feeling a pang of reproach the while at his doubts of the prince. For, in spite of the pain the sufferer was in, he smiled in Dick's face and pressed his hand.

"I heard your men come," he said. "Keep the palace and the temple. If you hold these bravely half my people will side with you, and you can set the rest at defiance."

"Captain Wyatt will fight to the last," said Dick.

"Yes, I know he will. You will too—for your friend?"

"I will," said Dick earnestly, and there was remorse in his breast as he pressed the sufferer's hand.

"One word more," whispered the Rajah faintly. "It is an enemy who did this—to poison you and your friends—but it could not be my mother. Where are the others?"

"Prisoners," said Dick, frowning.

"I ask that they may not be killed. Tell Captain Wyatt that. Now go—I cannot talk, Darrell," he whispered. "I am only a little older than you are—and I want to live; there is so much to do. Tell Doctor Robson not to let me die."

A hand was laid on Dick's shoulder, and Wyatt bent forward and pressed the Rajah's arm.

"I am very, very sorry for this, sir," he said in a low tone. "But we must go now. It is urgent."

"Yes, go," said the Rajah, clutching at Wyatt's hand as he looked wistfully in his eyes. "Fight for me and save me. I am your friend."

The doctor had come to the other side of the couch, and laid his hand upon the Rajah's forehead, with the result that the poor fellow sank back with a sigh and closed his eyes.

"Come, Dick, lad," said Wyatt. "Our work is cut out;" and they were hurrying to the door, when, to their surprise, they were confronted by the Ranee, who looked twenty years older in her horror and despair.

"Will he die?" she whispered to Wyatt.

"I hope not, madam, but we mean to live," said the captain, giving her a peculiar look of disgust which made her shrink back; while a flash of resentment swept over her handsome face, and she drew herself up as she said quickly:

"It is not true, I swear. I have always hated you and yours, but I am a queen, and I would not have done this horrible, treacherous thing. Once more, I swear I did not know of this."

"But you took pity, and warned me not to drink," said Dick sharply.

"I swear to you I did not know," said the Ranee once more. "Now, tell me what you are going to do."

"Slay all the Rajah's enemies who come and attack us," said Wyatt firmly.

"And if my son—dies?" she groaned.

"Hold Soojeepur till others decide what is best. Go to your son, madam, and help the doctor to save his life."

"Yes; but those two? You have not slain them?"

"The Rajah's orders are that you should be protected, madam, and that their lives should be spared," said Dick frankly, and the Ranee uttered a sigh of relief as he turned away.

"We're losing time," said Wyatt impatiently as he hurried out. "Dick, lad, our work's cut out to-night, and you must help me all you can. Hark! you can hear them here. The news is spreading through the place, and the people are crowding up. The enemy will have set up the report that we have poisoned the Rajah and seized the place. Heaven only knows how matters will turn out, but we are going to hold the palace and the great temple to the death, and if we have to use the guns—well, it is no fault of ours."

Dick said nothing; he merely gave his companion a firm pressure of the hand, and walked down with him into the beautiful vestibule, which was now filled with the Rajah's guards, two of whose leaders approached to meet them, looking as if in doubt whether to treat them as enemies or friends.

Wyatt stepped forward and offered his hand to both, while the fierce-looking picked men all stood blocking the way, their flashing tulwars in their hands, while both the English officers' were sheathed.

There was a momentary hesitation on the others' part, and then they passed their swords into their left hands and accepted the salutation of friendship.

"We have just left the Rajah's side," said Wyatt.

"Is he dead?"

"No. He has given us his instructions what to do," replied Wyatt.

"What are they?"

"To call upon all his brave followers to help him against his enemies."

"The English are his enemies," cried a voice from the back angrily.

"It is false!" cried Wyatt fiercely. "Your Rajah knows what is right and best for his country, and trusts us."

"Who poisoned him?" cried the same voice. "Those who meant the poison for us," said Wyatt firmly—"his enemies as well as ours.—You two are his highness's captains," he continued, turning to the two officers whose hands he had grasped. "Go up, and ask him to give you orders what to do."

"There is no need," said one of them loudly, as he turned so that all present might hear. "I was present when his highness sent despatches asking for help from the English against his foes. They came, and have worked for us bravely ever since."

There was a murmur of assent, and the chief went on. "I am captain of the Rajah's guard," he cried. "I am for the Rajah, my master, and for Soojeepur."

There was a loud shout and the clashing of weapons, but as soon as the sounds died out the chief cried: "Now, then, who is for the Ranee and the priests?" There was not a sound within, but from outside came a strange, increasing, muttering roar, as of gathering hosts hurrying through the streets and coming towards where they stood.

"It is enough, gentlemen," said Wyatt, striding forward to stand confronting the guard; and Dick's heart throbbed with admiration and pride—and perhaps slightly, too, with envy—as the big, manly, broad-chested Englishman drew himself up and spoke in his deep, sonorous tones. "The Rajah's orders are that the queen, the Wazir, and the chief Brahmin shall be protected, and the palace and the great temple with its treasurer held against all comers. You, gentlemen, will do the duty, and pass into the court here all whom you can trust to strengthen our force."

"And what will you do?" said the chief who had spoken, looking at him curiously.

"I shall guard the approach to the palace with our guns," said Wyatt. "I could sweep the streets clear, but I do not wish to fire a shot; it would mean slaying friends as well as foes. But the palace courts must be kept free, or the Ranee's followers will get the upper hand."

"Yes, that is right," said the chief. "Then get all your men in hand," said Wyatt, "and, as we drive the crowd back, station guards to hold the different entries, at the temple as well as here." The chief swung his flashing tulwar on high, and his followers imitated his action as they uttered a wild and warlike cry, all following Wyatt and Dick down into the court, where, by the light of the many lamps, the troop of artillery sat drawn up; and they cheered again in their way as the two officers sprang into their saddles.

Chapter XXXII
Mother and Son

The court in front of the palace was already filling with a menacing crowd of armed men; but as they gathered they held back from the troop and seemed to be awaiting leaders, not knowing what it would be best to do.

But there was no indecision on the part of Wyatt. He rode at once to where Hulton was seated, in uniform once more, consulted with him for a few moments, and then, in answer to an order, the six guns were unlimbered and run into position so that their muzzles were ready to pour forth a radiating discharge, and the effect was to make the gathering crowd fall back.

This done, a detachment about thirty strong was formed up, opened out, and rode slowly forward, pressing back the crowd; and as the great space was cleared, the Rajah's guards took up position to keep the people from returning.

Wyatt was right; they had their work cut out that night, and, through the apparently interminable long watches, it seemed as if again and again the moment of encounter had come.

But it did not. For it was as Wyatt said:

"It's like this, Dick, lad—we began by being ready; they were all unready. Friends and enemies were all mixed up into a confused mass, and no one trusted his neighbour. Then they seemed to have no leaders at first, or else all their loaders were in the wrong places. We've got ahead of them so far without bringing the guns to bear, but how much longer we can get on by making evolutions no one can tell. But we must keep it up."

And they did, hour after hour, thoroughly mastering the great mob which eddied and seethed round the precincts of the palace, always on the point of making a rush, but invariably driven back helter-skelter by the charges made by the horse artillery-men and their allies.

For they soon began to be strengthened through the efforts of the chiefs of the Rajah's guard, who were indefatigable. As they caught sight of friends of the cavalry they called to them, had them in past the vedettes and sentries, and then a few words sufficed to send them away again to give the word to others; and in a short time there was a constant accession of mounted men coming in from far enough away through the crowd in twos and threes and half-dozens, well-mounted and armed, and ready in the Rajah's defence to take up their positions alongside of the artillery-men, till towards morning fully a thousand troopers were in the open space before the palace, setting the mounted artillery-men free to join their comrades at the guns, and making the position more secure.

Time after time inquiries were made as to the Rajah's state, but the news Doctor Robson sent was always bad, and hope seemed to be dying out.

At last the sun rose upon the position, and by that time something like cohesion and order were asserting themselves, the two parties having gradually separated, with the supporters of the Rajah close up to the east end of the palace, those of the Ranee on the west; and the new day had come with the prospect of a pitched battle on the point as to which side was to have the supremacy—the Rajah's followers with their English allies, or the Ranee's backed up by the priests.

It had been their intention to make a bold stroke to get rid of the English invited by the Rajah—a mad and reckless blow, for retribution would have been certain to fall—but the accident to their plans had upset everything, and, just at the time appointed for their rising, they were confronted with the news that the Rajah was stricken down, and the Ranee and their chief conspirators were prisoners; while, though they had been in readiness to take advantage of the confusion that must ensue when it was found that the chief officers of the artillery were dead, their advance was completely frustrated by Wyatt's prompt action and the confusion into which they were thrown by the rush made for the palace by the Rajah's admirers, and their bold front.

The latter readily consulted with Wyatt as to what should be done, and at once accepted his counsel.

"Keep on the defensive," he said, "and in every way possible draw in all who are faithful to the Rajah. If they attack, let them find us ready; for, whatever misfortune comes in regard to the Rajah, we must hold the place. To let his enemies get the upper hand means massacre for us all."

Richard Darrell watched the faces of the cluster of officers as Wyatt spoke out clearly in their tongue, and saw them lighten up, while glances passed between them full of good omen; and as soon as his brother-officer had done speaking, they pressed round him to signify their determination to die sooner than give up, declaring that they had perfect faith in the English, and that they would carry out their gallant young Rajah's wishes to the end.

So intent were they upon the little council of war which they were holding in front of the guns, that they had noted nothing of what was going on elsewhere, and they turned as one man and stared in wonder as a hoarse shout was uttered, and even Dick imagined that a horse had suddenly turned restive on seeing Stubbs come tearing at them, sword in hand, shouting, and waving the steel.

But the next moment they saw that he was pointing, and wheeled round to defend themselves, for, from the enemies' side, a body of about fifty horsemen were charging at full gallop, in a bold dash to cut down or take prisoners the leaders of the Rajah's force.

It was so sudden that scarcely anything was done. The matchlock-men were unprepared, the irregular cavalry were away behind, and the artillery, fully ready as they were, with men at the trail and others standing linstock in hand, could not fire for fear of sweeping their own officers and their friends away.

It was a wild dash, and the first help likely to come was from the little knot of horse artillery-men mounted by the guns, who spurred forward at a word from Hulton.

The enemy came upon the group of officers like a whirlwind, taking them at a terrible disadvantage; and, for the first time in his life, Richard Darrell found himself in the midst of a fierce mêlée where discipline went for naught, and all depended upon the strength of a man's arms and his skill in the use of the sword he bore.

Wyatt shouted to him, but in the wild rush and concussion his words were inaudible. Whether it was to follow him or save himself he did not know, and he wanted no orders then, for he was nearly unseated by the shock, one of the friendly officers having his horse driven against Burnouse, making him plunge violently, bound three or four yards, and then rear up, saving his master from a savage cut delivered from the left, which passed within a few inches of his neck as a horseman swept by. Still, it was from Scylla into Charybdis. Dick kept his seat, but received a blow from a man on his right, who rose in his stirrups and struck downward at the lad's head.

There was a sharp, ringing clang as the blow fell upon the young officer's helmet, glanced off, and the man fell forward over his saddle-bow.

"Well cut, sir!" yelled a hoarse voice a short distance away; but Dick's blood was up, and he hardly realised the fact that the words were meant for him. He had the Rajah's keen tulwar in his hand, and he had long tried hard to become a master in the use of the sword, so that it was almost instinctively that he cut with all his might from his left shoulder, his blade flashing in the morning sunshine, with terrible effect upon the back of his enemy's neck, his horse bearing him on to meet another attack.

For another horseman rode at him following his fellow's tactics of rising in his stirrups to deliver a cut at his young enemy's head.

It was a fierce blow, but Dick's guard was ready, his hilt close up to his right ear, blade perpendicular, and edge outward—that thin, keen edge which seemed so slight a defence from a cut which might have meant death by an active swordsman—instant decapitation.

There was a loud, jarring ring as Dick received the blow on the forte of his sword, whose back struck against the side of his helmet with a sharp rap, and the next moment the man was by, giving the young officer's sword-arm a slight jerk before he sank backward with his arms extended, sword and reins falling from his nerveless hands.

For, like lightning, after receiving the jarring cut on his guard, Dick's keen blade dropped to the horizontal and he delivered a fierce thrust.

Another was at him as Burnouse bounded forward, and he, too, rose to cut at the English lad, who was bringing forward his blade to the recovery in a long, sweeping stroke which had, with the strength of the wielder's arm, the swift bound of his horse to give it impetus, so that the swarthy horseman received the blow full on his sword-arm, and passed on helpless.

A cut at the lad's bridle-arm missed, and the man who delivered it escaped with a sharp prick in the ribs in retaliation; and the next moment Dick was borne clear of the fierce struggle, but only to turn and gallop forward to join half-a-dozen of his own men, who were together forcing double their number back as they laid about them with their long sabres, used with the full strength of their muscular arms.

Half-blind with excitement now, Dick was riding at a dark, turbaned horseman when the trumpet rang out, and his charger followed the example of those in a line with him. The next moment there was the dull roar of a gun, so close that the horses of the enemy were thrown into a state of confusion, while the artillery-men's stood passive from the familiarity which breeds contempt.

For the opportunity had come at last, and a second gun sent forth its white puff of smoke, the sequence to the charge of grape which tore a lane through the enemy's body of horse, now coming on at a gallop to follow up the daring attack made by the first body, which had caused such dire confusion.

This second gun checked the advance, and created havoc amongst a crowd of matchlock-men coming up behind the horse; while a third discharge seemed to be the signal for a retreat to commence.

There was a pause before the fourth gun could be fired with effect. Then it and the fifth and sixth were fired in rapid succession, while the Rajah's horsemen now saw their opportunity, and dashed after the scattering enemy in a disorderly but brilliant charge, whose effect was to drive the enemy fleeing for their lives into the narrow streets of the city; and the rout was continued till fully half had poured over the bridge to make for the open country, while the rest sought shelter in the bazaars and lanes.

The little battle was only a matter of a few minutes, and as nothing more was to be done there, the artillery had limbered up ready to pursue; but Hulton saw that before he could get out into the open the enemy would be beyond his reach, and he halted his men where they stood, leaving the Rajahs horsemen to complete the rout.

"I couldn't get to you, sir—I couldn't get to you," cried a fierce voice full of reproach, and Sergeant Stubbs rode up to Dick's side. "Don't say you're hurt, sir—don't say you're hurt!"

"No, Stubbs, I won't," replied Dick. "Yes, I am," he added hastily. "My head."

He let his sword fall to the extent of the knot, and took off his helmet.

"Quiet, Burnouse!" he cried, as the horse snorted and tore up the ground with its off forefoot. "My head's all jarred and aching. My word! That's saved me from an awful cut."

The sergeant leaned forward to take the bright helmet from the lad's hand, looking down at a deep, dinted bruise, and then at its owner.

"That saved your life, sir," said Stubbs rather huskily. "Hurt anywhere else?"

"Right shoulder feels a bit dragged," replied Dick. "But where's Captain Wyatt?"

As he spoke the captain came into sight, riding back with about a dozen of the Rajah's horsemen, who came up flushed with triumph, cheering after their fashion and crowding round Dick, all eager to shake hands.

The lad wanted to cry off, for his shoulder ached violently, but he bore all without a grimace, and drew a deep breath full of relief when he was at last alone with Wyatt, walking their horses towards where Captain Hulton was seated with the guns.

"I couldn't get at you, of course, my lad," said Wyatt, "but I did my best. I'm afraid two or three poor fellows will never fight again. It was every man for himself, eh? We had no business, though, to be surprised like that."

"No," said Dick. "How was it?"

"Want of proper vedettes, my lad. These people know nothing about war. But they can fight."

"But I mean, how was it you rode away and left the troop?"

"Because I couldn't help myself, my dear boy. By the time I had whipped out my sword about twenty of the beggars were round, cutting at me and giving me all my work to guard myself; but I managed to get in a few points."

"Are you wounded?"

"It would have gone hard with me if some of our friends, seeing what a mess I was in, had not made a dash to help me."

"But are you wounded, Wyatt?"

"They charged splendidly, and took off some of the black-looking rascals' attentions, and this gave me a chance to make a few more points, for I dared not attempt to cut."

"But I asked you if you were wounded?" said Dick anxiously.

"Then there we were at it in a regular running fight, in which I was carried right away, growling savagely at being cut off from my friends. I'd have given anything to have had you and old Stubbs there with his long reach. You were better out of it."

"Are you going on like this to annoy me or to keep something back?"

"Neither," said Wyatt sharply. "It seemed such a position for the captain in command of the troop to be carried right away like that, leaving his men to take their chance, but it was impossible to cut my way out till that firing began. Did you give the order?"

"No," said Dick shortly. "Once more—and I won't ask you again—are you wounded?"

"Don't think I am, old fellow; but I got two heavy cracks on the helmet, and my uniform is horribly cut in several places."

"Oh, never mind your uniform," said Dick.

"But I do. It's my best. I didn't know we were coming in for such a scrimmage as this. If I had I'd have put on my worst things."

"But you are not hurt, Wyatt?"

"But I am, my lad. I must be bruised terribly, and my right arm feels quite numbed."

"Never mind; we've won the battle," said Dick earnestly.

"Fight or skirmish, my lad; the one out yonder was more of a battle. Well, I suppose we have got it pretty well our own way. Our friends did wonders. They'd make splendid light cavalry if they were only trained. Here's Hulton.—How are you, old fellow?"

"Glad to see you back safely," said Hulton, shaking hands warmly. "I could do nothing to help you till just now."

"And then you did wonders. But how many of our lads are hurt?"

"Three have slight cuts. But about yourself?"

"Skin not broken anywhere, thank goodness. Now, what about the Rajah?"

"I have had no news for some time. Go in, both of you, and see. You will be admitted sooner than I should."

"Come, then, Darrell," said Wyatt, signing to one of the men; and they rode up to the entrance, dismounted, handed their reins to the man, and the guards saluted them, uttering a low murmur as their officer came to them open-handed, smiling as if proud of their prowess.

"A brave fight," he said; "and we had to stay and do nothing."

"Yes," said Wyatt, smiling back; "but some of us are obliged to look on. How is the Rajah?"

"The Rajah? Ah, yes; I do not know. We were watching the fight."

"We will go up to him, then," said Wyatt; and they ascended to the sufferer's room, where the first person they encountered was the Ranee, who looked at them wildly, her lips parting to ask a question.

But she did not speak. She could read the endorsement of the defeat of her followers in the young officers' faces.

"How is he?" whispered Wyatt as the doctor joined them.

"He has just dropped asleep," was the reply. "We could pretty well tell that you drove off the enemy by the firing. Everything has gone well, has it not?"

"Yes, they are thoroughly routed. Hist! he is not asleep."

"No," said the Rajah firmly as he turned his drawn face towards the group; "I have heard all you said. I shall get better now."

"If you are very quiet, sir," said the doctor; "but you must sleep and leave everything to others."

"Yes.—You will stay here, of course, Captain Wyatt?—And you, Mr Darrell? Come to me when I have slept."

"I will, sir," said Dick quietly.

"Doctor," said the Rajah then, "the pain is less. I shall not die."

"Not now," said the doctor quietly; "the strength of the poison is passing off fast. But you must be silent, and rest."

"Yes; but you will watch over me?"

"Rest assured of that," said the doctor gravely. "Nothing shall be given to you that I have not examined. Try and rest in the full confidence that you are safe."

The Rajah shuddered, and just then he saw the Ranee approaching, and he closed his eyes.

She paused for a moment, but came on to his side to kneel down and whisper, the officers drawing back.

"Have I not sworn to you that this was not my doing?" she said reproachfully.

"Yes," he said in the same low tone; "you, my mother, could not have been guilty of such a horror. But I know—I cannot be deceived—it was the work of your friends, and it was meant for mine."

Chapter XXXIII
Wyatt Smokes the Hubble-Bubble

"What have you got there, Doctor Robson?" said Dick one morning about a month later, when the troubles of the past seemed to have given way to perfect peace, the defeat of the revolutionary party on the morning after the poisoning having resulted in the flight of most of the leaders, and the settling down of the people to the Rajah's wishes.

For during his illness, when he had more than once been at the point of death, the English troops had remained in the new palace; and, in spite of their seeming to be so much out of place there, a detachment of the horse artillery-men had their quarters in and held the huge temple, to the disgust of the chief Brahmin and his large following of priests.

Then, as under the constant care of the army doctor the Rajah began to mend, he expressed his wish that those who had saved his little kingdom for him should remain, with the result that, while the old palace was retained for the stabling and stores, the main portion of the troop, with the guns, occupied one side of the palace in conjunction with the Rajah's bodyguard, of which they now seemed to form a portion; while, to the great annoyance of the native doctors, the army surgeon completely took their place.

As the Rajah recovered his strength the time passed pleasantly enough for the English officers, for he proved to be a most grateful host, contriving plenty of expeditions for them to the mountain slopes north of Soojeepur, in a wild district swarming with game, his elephants being always at their service, with ample trains of servants and shikarees familiar with the lairs of tiger and wild boar.

At first there was a good deal of hesitation on the part of Hulton and Wyatt to engage in these pursuits, but everything had settled down so thoroughly, and peace seemed to be so well assured, that the officers of the tiny army of occupation felt themselves justified in taking a little relaxation; and many exciting hunts were the result, in all of which the Rajah and Hulton to some extent took part.

Despatches came from headquarters in answer to Wyatt's reports, and the orders received were always to the effect that the troop was to remain in occupation at Soojeepur for the present, certainly till it could be proved for certain that there was no fear of the Rajah of Singh making any further attacks upon the country.

The Rajah laughed when Hulton read portions of his despatches, and turning to Dick, who was present, said merrily:

"You may give up all hope of going south again, for you will have to stay."

"How long?" asked Dick.

"Who can say?" replied the Rajah. "Judge for yourselves. The two regiments of cavalry are a magnificent addition to my troops, and will be of more value yet when I have arranged for British officers to lead them, but even they will excite no dread amongst Singh's people—they are only natives like ourselves. Your troop is of more value to me than five thousand such men, and I know as well as can be that your leaving Soojeepur would be the signal for Singh to collect together a strong force and invade my territories. You are here, and here you will have to stay."

This was unanswerable, and, truth to tell, both officers and men were quite contented with their quarters, for the attention they all received now was everything that could be desired.

On the morning that the question which begins this chapter was asked by Dick after breakfast in the beautiful mess-room in the palace, the doctor had taken from his pocket a couple of magnificent rings, the one a perfect pearl of large size, the other a magnificent emerald.

"What have you there?" Dick asked.

"Fees, Darrell," replied the doctor, handing him the two rings. "Pass them round. The emerald is from the Rajah, and the Ranee gave me the pearl, with a mothers thanks. Sounds quite pretty and English, doesn't it?"

The officers exchanged glances.

"As for the Rajah," continued the doctor, "he sent for me last night and asked me to make up my mind to stay with him always as his mother's and his special attendant."

"Terms?" said Wyatt bluntly.

"Whatever I liked to ask," replied the doctor.

"Going to close with the offer?" said Wyatt.

"No; don't," replied Hulton. "For one thing, Doctor, we can't spare you, and some day or other we shall have to go. For another, you will never feel safe. The more I see of these people, the more I feel that it is like living on the slope of a volcano. Everything is very beautiful, but at any moment the eruption may come, and with it death and destruction."

"Hear the words of the wise man, Robson, my son," said Wyatt in a stilted, ponderous, mock-tragic way. "Some day, in spite of the Rajah's wishes, we shall be recalled, and then what am I to do with you left behind, or Dick Darrell here when he has been overeating himself, or made himself ill with one or another of his boyish follies?"

"My boyish follies, indeed!" cried Dick hotly.

"Yes," said Wyatt.—"Look here, Physic; Hulton is right. Everything is going on delightfully smoothly now. The queen worships us; the Wazir always seems as if he wanted to lick our boots; and as for the old Brahmin, I'm sure he oils his tongue as well as the rest of his body, so as to be smoother and smoother, but it is only because he is scheming to get rid of the men of the temple guard."

"And he will not," said Hulton, "for the Rajah is firmer about our holding everything than ever."

"They're a shifty, treacherous lot, doctor," continued Wyatt. "Hulton is quite right, and I'm always looking—metaphorically, of course—at the edge and point of my sword and the primings of my pistols. Some day or other the Ranee will go into a tantrum, and we shall be having a wholesale poisoning, or something worse."

"Shame!" cried Dick indignantly. "It is an insult to a noble lady. Every one must exonerate her from that piece of treachery."

"Well done, Pepper-castor!" said Wyatt, laughing. "Hark at the chivalrous young paladin."

"I should be ashamed to harbour such thoughts," said Dick indignantly.

"Good boy!" said Wyatt. "But you are no judge. The pet of the Rajah and special favourite of the Ranee is one-sided in his ideas."

"Don't shout, Wyatt," said Hulton. "Walls have ears, they say."

"All right; I take the hint," replied Wyatt.

"It would have been better if you had never spoken as you did, Wyatt," said Dick. "Her highness has always been most kind to you."

"Yes, my son, she has; but it has always seemed to me like the affection of a tigress. I keep on my guard for the moment when she may bite or scratch."

"As she has just bitten and scratched the doctor," said Dick bitterly; "and me," he added, as he took out a beautiful diamond locket he wore hanging by a chain.

"That's all right, Dicky," said Wyatt; "but that poisoning business was never cleared up."

"It was not her doing," said Dick hotly.

"She never meant to poison her son, of course."

"She never had hand in it," cried Dick fiercely.

"Don't boil over, Darrell," said Hulton. "She may have been innocent, but it was done by her party—we cannot say by whom; and she has not only remained friends with the Wazir and the old Brahmin, but prevailed upon her son to let things slide."

"She asked the Rajah to give a general what-you-may-call-it to everybody after the fight, and there has been peace and contentment ever since," said Dick.

"That's very nicely spoken, oh, brave and gallant young rider of the fiery Burnouse!" said Wyatt, "Oh, noble sticker of the unclean pig, and true-eyed slayer of the sleek and striped tail-lashing slinker of the reedy nullah!"

"I wish you were only of my age and rank, Wyatt," said Dick in a low voice.

"Why, my son?"

"Because if you were I'd punch your head."

"And so you should, brave boy; but, as I was saying, all that was beautifully spoken about the Rajah and the peace. What I object to is that a young brave seated at our council-table should mar a magnificent speech by bungling as he did for want of a proper flow of words."

"Who did?" cried Dick.

"You did, my son. I appeal to the company assembled."

"What do you mean?" cried Dick wonderingly.

"You said the Ranee asked her son to give a general what-you-may-call-it to everybody after the fight."

"Of course I did," cried Dick. "What of that?"

"A general what-you-may-call-it!" said Wyatt mockingly. "A pretty expression for the Rajah's favourite to use when he means an amnesty!"

"Pooh!" cried Dick; "I can't talk fine. You're in one of your teasing fits.—He wants some antacid medicine, Doctor."

"I'll give him a dose that will suit his complaint," said the doctor, nodding; and clapping his hands, a servant appeared.

"The Sahib Wyatt's hookah," he said, and the man went off without a sound.

"What a wonderful gift the doctor has!" said Wyatt, smiling. "That is exactly what I wanted to make me as amiable as ever. Dick, my son, forgive me if I have been too hard."

"Oh, I know you by heart," said Dick: "but it hurts me to hear the Ranee abused."

"Then we will not hurt you, my son," said Wyatt. "Ah, here is the hubble-bubble; now I shall be at rest."

The next minute he was leaning back placidly smoking invisible vapour through the long, snake-like tube, and as the attendant disappeared, he watched the doctor putting back the rings he had handed round for inspection.

"No, Doctor," he said; "you must not be coaxed away. I agree with Hulton; the Rajah's offer is tempting, and the Ranee is grateful, but we are aliens, and the people here are not to be trusted. The time might come when things went wrong, and I for one should feel troubled to think that we had left here a good, true man surrounded by enemies."

"But he surrounds himself with friends," said Dick.

"Tries to," said Hulton gravely; "but to hundreds nothing can balance the fact that he is an Englishman and an infidel. Then, too, he is a doctor, whose ideas are in direct opposition to those of the native medical men."

"Let me bring the debate to a close," said the doctor quietly. "I am very comfortable here, and thoroughly enjoy my present life, and so long as matters go smoothly I should be sorry to give it up."

"Sybarite!" said Wyatt.

"Oh, no; I'm ready for any amount of work, my dear sir. I don't want my brain nor my instruments to get rusty, but—no flattery intended—my happiness here depends on the presence of my friends. No. I am not going to be tempted away on any terms, and I have told the Rajah so."

"Bravo!" cried Wyatt.

"Then the Rajah will never let us go," said Hulton.

"Very well," said Wyatt, "I accept my fate. I only say, don't let us all be too trusting.—I'm speaking seriously now, Darrell, my dear boy. Things have happened very pleasantly for you, and the Rajah is a very good fellow, and means to be a faithful friend."

"What more could I want?" said Dick warmly.

"Nothing, my dear boy; I only say, don't trust too much. He means well, but he is not of our race, and he is still surrounded by people who wear a mask. He is very English now in all his ideas, but you know the old saying, 'Constant dropping will wear a stone.'"

Chapter XXXIV
Sergeant Stubbs is Curious

It was Dick's duty at times to visit posts and when going round the old palace, where a corporal's guard was always on duty and the gates kept shut, he often thought of their adventures in the place, and frequently took a walk round the ramparts, wondering how their nocturnal visitor had contrived to make his way into the well-guarded place and lay the train. But he made no progress.

He visited, too, the great temple, where Sergeant Stubbs had his quarters, with a small detachment of men acting as custodians of the place in the Rajah's interest. The latter had more than once talked with Dick of the treasure there, in addition to the valuables connected with the various idols and priestly ceremony, saying that it was better that the English troops should have the custody.

"We are at peace now," he said, "and I feel more secure than ever on my throne, but there is no knowing what may happen."

There were no black looks now on the part of the Brahmin and the attendant priests, and it seemed as if the officers and men were welcome, for the treatment they received and the deference paid were of a marked character; while, on the other hand, the discipline kept up by the sergeant was stringent, and the temple people saw that every object in the vast, gloomy place was treated with the greatest respect.

Oddly enough, Stubbs selected Black Bob, as he was still called, to be his right-hand man there, and once only upon one of his visits Dick made a remark about it to the sergeant.

"Well, yes, sir, it does seem comic. There was a time when I'd rather have had any other man in the troop, and I don't think I like him a bit better than then, but I'd trust him to do anything, or with anything. He don't like me either, but you know he respects me as a soldier, and I respect him. He's a gentleman still, and as a soldier—well, there, you know what he can do."

"You're not afraid of his helping himself to any of the idols' jewels, then, Stubbs?"

"No, nor to any of the gold and silver down in the vaults here, sir. Not he. It's a wonderfully rich place, sir. I don't wonder at the Rajah liking to have us here. You get him to show you what there is here some day."

"Not I," said Dick contemptuously; "it would look too small. Let's have a walk round."

"Yes, sir. You can do it now without meeting one of the priests in every dark corner. It's a wonderful place, sir; full of rum passages and dark holes. Regular dungeons, some of them. I expect they used them to put prisoners in, and there they are now, ready for any number."

"What prisoners are they likely to have in a temple?"

"I don't know, sir; but there they are, with rings in the walls, and chains, and strong doors. You might shut a man up in some of them, and he might holloa as long as he liked, and nobody would ever hear him, unless it was one of the stone gods. They might, perhaps."

"You've been having a regular rummage, then?" said Dick.

"I just have, sir. You see, I have a lot of time on my hands, and, having the care of the place, I like to know what I've got to take care of, and where to go in case of emergencies. It's the sort of place where a man might easily lose himself, and that would be awkward if one was in a hurry and wanted to get out. Regular hot out of doors to-day, sir, isn't it?"

"Yes; scorching."

"Well, up above and down below too, sir, it's as cool as cool. Just the day for a peep round, sir. Like to come?"

"Yes, if it is not likely to set the people here thinking why I've come."

"You may take my word for it, sir, that we shan't meet a soul. Besides, they talk to me here about you being such a favourite with the Rajah."

"Who does?"

"Every one, sir, from the old chief Brahmin down to the lowest priest. They think a deal here of Sahib Dah Rell, as they call you."

"Very well. I should like to see where the treasures are," said Dick.

"Then come along, sir; I'm a regular guide now."

"Only don't lose the way, Stubbs," said Dick, smiling; "I've an appointment to meet the Rajah this afternoon."

"That's all right, you trust me."

It was a change from the rather monotonous round, of barrack duties, and, after a visit to the sergeant's room, Dick followed him across the temple into the half-darkness of the great building behind the monstrous elephant-headed figure, in and out among a perfect labyrinth of grotesque carvings—illustrating, apparently, passages in the Hindu mythology—till all at once Stubbs paused opposite a flat pillar, and turned as if to speak to his companion.

"You get a good view backward from here, sir," he said in his ordinary tone of voice; and Dick looked back, to see how the pale light struck in from one side at the bottom of an irregular vista while they stood almost in darkness. "See that stone figure squatting down?"

"I can just make out the shape, but it is not worth seeing," said Dick.

"No, sir," replied Stubbs; "makes a good seat, though. Only grim darkness and mystery as these priests keep up to frighten the niggers. There isn't one of 'em as would dare to come along here among these hundreds of ugly idols after the tales the priests tell them. But it's all right; I don't want for us to be followed. Now then, give me your hand; it's a bit of a squeeze through a narrow crack, and then you have to go down twenty steps, but if you hold on to me I'll guide you."

Dick grasped the sergeant's hand, and felt himself drawn through a narrow opening just behind the flat pillar; then they turned at right angles to the left and went on a dozen feet or so, when they again turned at right angles and went sideways some forty or fifty feet between stone walls, the opening being barely sufficient to allow the sergeant to get along, while the darkness was now profound.

"Rather a tight fit for me, sir," said Stubbs; "easy enough for you. Now wait a bit while I get a light."

He passed in front of Dick, and, taking out the materials, he struck a light, blew up the match, and applied it to the wick of a curiously-shaped lamp standing upon a ledge above their heads, till the lamp burned with a clear, white flame.

"They keep it there on purpose," said the sergeant, "just at the head of some steps. They're a bit wider, but they don't give you much room to get down."

"But how in the world did you find this out?"

"Just by accident, like, sir. I was wandering about here in the dark one day, in and out among the figures, wondering where the Rajah's treasures that we were set to guard could be stored. But I didn't find anything out, for I couldn't bring a lantern and look. So I came again and again, playing at hide-and-seek, like, for it seemed so stupid to be taking care of something and not to know where it was. And so I went on for days, not making any show, like, till one day, after a bit of a hunt, I sat down in the lap of one of the small idols, to think that I must be quite on the wrong scent. And it being very quiet, and me being a bit tired, and the idol's lap making a nice, cool, comf'table arm-chair, I goes off to sleep in the darkness; and I don't know how long I was asleep, of course, but I was woke up by something, and sat listening and wondering where I was, till it came again—a queer sort of sneeze—and then I knew. 'Why, it's the old Brahmin,' I said to myself. 'What's he doing here?' Then I felt that I knew, and that he must be looking after me. But he wasn't, for he went by me and on for a few yards, me hearing big loose petticoats rustling quite loudly for a bit and then leaving off, like, all at once. The next moment he sneezed again, but it sounded smothered and stilled like, as if he was behind a door; and I just rubbed my hands together softly, for I felt sure that there must be a doorway. So, 'Success to snuff!' I says."

"What for?" said Dick, laughing, and his mirth sounded weird and strange as it seemed to go whispering away.

"Because the old chap had opened his snuff-box and let out the cat, sir."

"Then you felt that he had gone into the place you wanted to find?"

"That's it, sir; and I sat there and waited a good two hours before I heard the roosh, roosh of his clothes again, just like a woman's, and he passed me and went away. Of course I did nothing then; but a few days afterwards I came with a tinder-box and a bit of candle in case they were wanted, and, my word! what a while I did have to hunt for the way in here! It was all so simple that it humbugged me, sir. I got trying to lift idols and turn 'em round or lay 'em down, and to find trap-doors, till at last I stood leaning against that flat pillar wondering how it could be, and then I smelt it."

"Smelt it?"

"That's it, sir; I smelt it—a curious, stuffy, damp smell that seemed to come out of a cellar; and next minute I had squeezed myself through that crack, and crept cautiously a little way into the darkness before striking a light. Then I saw I had got it, and crept along, holding up my candle, which

I needn't have brought, for there was the lamp on the ledge, and just before me these steps.—Come on down, sir. I'll go first."

Dick followed down a steep flight of stone stairs, whose edges were as sharp as if newly cut, and the next minute, as the sergeant held up the lamp, Dick could see that they were in a huge, far-stretching vault, all dwarf pillars and arches.

"Rum place, sir, isn't it?" said the sergeant, holding up the light.

"Something like the crypt of a cathedral," replied Dick.

"Is it, though, sir? Never saw one. Have they got sort of cells to put people in?"

"Yes," said Dick meaningly.

"Same here, sir; reg'lar prison, like, all down one side;" and he led the way to a series of stone doors at the head of a low, square passage.

"Is this where you think the Rajah's treasures are?"

"Oh, no, sir. I think they're on the other side, through a big, square doorway with an idol sitting in front.—Look here; this place is open and ready for a prisoner—stone bed, stone stool, and a place to chain him up to. There'd be no getting out of here."

Dick shuddered as he followed the sergeant into the gloomy place, and then they examined the door—a huge slab of stone which ran in a groove, with a long stone to fall down behind it when it was closed.

"Queer places, sir," said the sergeant. "That's where they shut the wicked Brahmins up to make 'em good. Like to see where I think the treasure is put away."

"Yes; I may as well see as I am here."

The sergeant held his lamp higher so that they might be aware of the presence of stumbling-blocks, and led the way to the far side of the vast, vaulted place, where just before them sat a little, six-armed figure, armed with swords, clubs, and twining serpents.

"It's a she, sir; and she has six weapons to keep off thieves. I believe the people think that if they attempted to move the stone which closes that doorway the idol would come to life and attack them."

"Then you think that's the treasure-house, Stubbs?" said Dick.

"That's it for certain, sir."

"Well, the people believe in all these things, and it makes the treasure safe. There, we won't try to make the image come to life and show fight, for we don't want to meddle."

"Not we, sir," replied Stubbs. "Which way shall we go back?"

"Round by the other side."

"Then we'll keep a sharp lookout, sir, for I haven't been there. We don't want to tumble down any wells or flights of stairs. It's rather awkward going along a place you don't know."

Stubbs led the way with the light, once more crossing diagonally from side to side, and then leading the way along a black wall completely covered with grotesque carvings from floor to ceiling.

"Hullo!" he said, suddenly stopping.

"What is it?"

"Another opening, sir. I never saw this before."

"What does it look like?"

"Long passage, sir."

"Well, let's go down it and see where it leads to."

The sergeant turned down the dark opening, and led the way along it with his gleaming light for a good ten minutes, and then he stopped.

"Well," said Dick, "why don't you go on?"

"Don't seem to lead anywhere, sir, as I see."

"It must lead somewhere or come to an end. Go on."

Stubbs trimmed his lamp a little and went on once more, very cautiously, for fear of pitfalls; but at the end of another ten minutes the passage was precisely the same.

"Go on, sir?"

"Yes, go on. We must come to the end soon."

Stubbs sighed and examined the candle.

"Rather awk'ard, sir, if the light went out," he grumbled.

"Yes, that would be unpleasant," replied Dick. "Could you find out your way if it did?"

"No, sir, I'm sure I could not," replied the man: "and there's no end of places we haven't looked at yet. We mustn't be lost."

"Oh, we should find our way again," said Dick confidently. "Ah, look here; the path slopes upward. What does this mean?"

"Slopes up, sir, quite sudden," said Stubbs. "Look at the snakes."

"Where?" cried Dick, shrinking.

"Not live uns, sir—carved stone ones, all twisted together."

"This is very strange, Stubbs," said Dick; "the way slopes right up as if we should get out somewhere here."

"Then we ought to be out now, sir," replied the man, "for it ends quite sudden-like, and we ought to be well out of the place by now."

"It's just like the top of a well," said Dick.

"Just, sir; but I can't see how it goes next. Shall I try if I can feel the top?"

"Yes, of course."

"No trying wanted; here it is, sir," said the sergeant. "Can't stand up in it. I can't understand the place at all. Can you?"

"No," said Dick; and after a brief examination Stubbs turned sharply.

"Better look sharp, sir, or the lamp will give out."

"Back at once, then;" and they set off along the passage as fast as they could, the oil lasting exactly till they reached the ledge, when, in the jar that the sergeant gave in setting it in its old place, the wick dropped down.

"Some one'll catch it for not having trimmed that lamp," said Stubbs with a chuckle. "Whoever takes hold of it will be puzzled at finding it burnt out, for I don't mean to tell them I have had it out of its place."

Stubbs whispered to his companion not to speak now, and led the way cautiously to the entrance, and then slowly out into the gloomy back of the temple, where, as they made their way towards the entrance, Dick kept on glancing back through the gloom, where it seemed as if dark figures were following them, and creeping softly from pillar to pillar, and in and out among the many idols, startling him more than once into speaking in a whisper to his companion.

"Oh, no, sir, there's no one following us. I was scared once in the same way by seeing people, as I thought, after me; but it's only the images in the queer light."

"I am not so sure of that," said Dick. "I could be certain that I saw some one dart behind one of the big figures."

"Yes, sir; but it's all imaginary and fancy. I tell you I've often thought some one was watching me when I've been creeping about here, and gone back to find that it was only one of the idols. My sight's more used to the place than yours is."

Dick looked at his companion doubtingly, but he said no more, and contented himself with another glance round. Soon after he left the sergeant to himself, with the understanding that he was to go again and help to investigate that passage, for the young officer had an idea that he had hit upon a discovery which would make clear something that had caused him many an hour's vain thought.

Chapter XXXV
In the Labyrinth

The weird, strange labyrinths of the old temple impressed Dick deeply, and before many days he paid another visit to the place, choosing the hottest part of the day; but, to his great disappointment. Sergeant Stubbs was away.

"Do you know where he has gone?" he asked the sentry on duty by the temple gate.

"No, sir; he went out not long ago; but if you go to the guardroom, I dare say they can tell you there. Gone to the bazaar, I think."

The distance was short from his quarters at the Rajah's palace, but the heat was intense. In fact, Dick would not have come but for the knowledge that the walk through the old temple would be beautifully cool, and, in all probability, all the people in the place taking their siesta, so that they would be free from interruption.

"It's all my fault," he muttered, "for not making an appointment. Phew! it's too hot to go back."

He went into the temple, and made his way to the part of the conventual building which had been set apart for the guards, who were idling about in the coolest form of costume which they could adopt; but those of them connected with the guard of the day sprang to their feet on seeing their young officer, and stood at attention.

But no one knew where the sergeant was, save that he had gone out an hour before and had not said when he would be back.

Dick turned away disappointed, and left the men's quarters, the weapons and uniforms thereof looking strangely out of place in connection with such a building.

"I may as well stop about till Stubbs comes back," he thought; and, turning in through one of the big doorways, he strolled slowly into the great building, drawing a breath of relief, for the air within was comparatively cool, and it was like escaping from a furnace to enter the shadowy gloom.

There was not a soul visible, for, as he had rightly conjectured, the priests and attendants were fast asleep till the heat of the day was past, and for some little time the young officer stood gazing at the bright, clear-cut silhouette the sentry formed against the dazzling light outside; but after some minutes had passed he began to grow tired of waiting, and slowly strolled farther into the darkness, in and out among the numberless figures, and round by the back of the huge figure towering up towards the ceiling. Then, as it looked cooler and darker above, he went to the steps, and slowly ascended them to the great gallery which went round behind the figure.

From there he leaned against the carved stone balustrade, cut onto grotesque monkeys, Brahmin bulls, and elephants, thinking of the enormous time and labour that must have been bestowed upon the place, and what wealth must have been gathered together by the Brahmin priesthood for the purpose.

But he could tell that hundreds upon hundreds of years must have elapsed since the place was first commenced, and the priesthood would always have been able to command the services of the people in their cause.

But still Stubbs did not come; and, knowing that his heavy military stride would echo over the pavement when he did return, Dick sauntered along behind the idol, noticed the strange openings therein, and, wondering to what purposes they were put, he went dreamily on to the other side and descended by another stone staircase, which brought him down in the darkest part behind the huge figure, with its heavy ears and twining trunk, and not far from the flat pillar, nearly hidden by the crowd of smaller images.

His nearness to the opening leading down to the lower regions set him thinking, but it was too hot to think standing up, and he sought for a convenient spot where he could sit down. However, there seemed to be nothing suitable but the floor, and that was not tempting.

All at once he remembered the seat made use of by the sergeant, and after a little search he found it, and sat down in the lap of the stone figure.

It was cool and restful there, and he sat listening for the sergeant's step; but it did not come, and as he rested there, musing over what he had seen during his last visit, he asked himself why he should wait—why, as he was there, he should not go down by himself—for he felt sure that he could find his way in and out to where the lamp stood upon the stone ledge.

When he had reached as far as this his brain became more active, and in imagination he ran on down the steps, and on amongst the great dwarf pillars by the cell-like places, with their sliding doors of stone slabs; and then, after pausing for a time, shuddering at the horrors of a man being shut up in such a tomb-like place, possibly to be left to starve and die, he diverted his line of thought, and crossed to the great square doorway where the six-armed idol sat on guard over what must be the Rajah's treasure.

"I should like to see what he has there," thought Dick, "but it would be horribly mean to try and get in. I don't mind finding out where the treasure is kept, for there is common-sense in what Stubbs says about our knowing where the things are that we have to guard. Precious stones of all kinds, I'll be bound," he said to himself: "and I know what I'll do—I'll ask him to show me. He'll do anything I want. No, I'm not going to peep about like that, and I shouldn't care to be hanging about the great doorway—it would look so spy-like—but I must find out the meaning of that passage, and I feel sure it is as I suspect. Hang that sergeant! Why can't he be here when he's wanted?"

He sat for quite another half-hour waiting and thinking, and then his mind was made up.

The long, strange labyrinth below was black as pitch, and weird, strange, and echoing; but he was not going to be afraid of the dark, however weird and strange it was. Pooh! a soldier, and shrink from going down alone into a place like that! It was absurd, and the thought put him on his mettle. He would go, and surprise Stubbs afterwards. The sergeant ought to have been there, and, as he was not. Dick determined to go by himself, and rose at once to combat a slight sensation of nervousness that began to attack him.

"It will be easy enough," he said. "I have a right to be here; the Rajah considers the place as much in my charge as Wyatt's, and I will go now."

Crossing the intervening space at once, he paused for a moment or two to look back and listen, but nothing was visible from there but a faint dawn of light, and there was not a sound to be heard.

Then slipping in behind the square pillar, he made his way along the narrow passage in the darkness, feeling the side and guessing the distance, growing more and more cautious as he proceeded, lest he should step too far and go headlong down the stairs.

Ah, there was the lamp in its place; but suppose it had not been trimmed since!

He raised it and shook it, to feel that it was ready and full of oil; but he set it down in dismay, for it suddenly occurred to him that his adventure was nipped in the bud—he had no flint, steel, match, or tinder.

"How absurd!" he muttered at his folly; and he stood for a moment, thinking that there was nothing left for him to do now but to go back to see if the sergeant had returned, and if he had not, to give up the project for the day.

The thought had hardly passed across his brain when he heard steps outside—not the martial tread of the man he awaited, but a hurried pace of one wearing the native shoes.

Whoever it was must be coming there, and if he stayed where he was, Dick knew that he would be discovered.

There was no time for consideration; he must either face the fresh-comer or retreat.

To face the fresh-comer in the dark meant startling one who might reply with a knife-stroke, and, without hesitation now, Dick felt for the top of the steps with one foot, and then descended silently to the place below, where, guarding his face with outstretched hands, he cautiously advanced till his fingers came in contact with one of the great, squat pillars which supported the temple floor, and now stood ready to afford him shelter and concealment.

He did not get behind it at once, but stood resting one hand against it, as he turned back to peer through the darkness and listen for his interrupter.

He was not left long in suspense.

At first there was a dead silence, and he was beginning to hope that he had been mistaken, but not for long. All at once there was the rattle of the metal lamp on the stone ledge, showing that the fresh-comer was perfectly acquainted with the place; and then the clicking of a flint and steel was heard, evidently being used in vain, for the user uttered hasty ejaculations, full of annoyance, again and again before he succeeded in getting a spark to alight upon the tinder, and began to blow till the match was applied and a faint, fluttering sound was heard, followed by the appearance of a pale, bluish light, and then this brightened into the flame of a burning splint of wood.

This flashed out quite quickly, and Dick started, fully expecting that he must have been seen, for the face and dress of the visitor stood out quite clear in the darkness, and the young officer's hand flew to his sword as he waited for the man's angry ejaculation. But to the lad's intense relief, there was a fresh rustling sound as the lamp was taken down from the ledge, and the visitor stood in profile to his watcher, with his clearly-cut aquiline features standing out as he lit the lamp, extinguished the match, and then turned to descend.

As he put his foot upon the first step with the confidence of one evidently accustomed to descend, Dick now silently glided behind the pillar, kept it between him and the light, and softly stepped farther into the interior, making for the next pillar, so as to place that between him and the new-comer, whose presence made him hold his scabbard raised in his left hand, prepared to bring the hilt of his sword ready for his right.

By this time the man had reached the floor of the great crypt, and, as if startled by some sound, he stopped short, and, raising the lamp high above his head, leaned forward, gazing straight in Dick's direction, the lad as he peered round seeing the figure's hand, in the faint light cast by the lamp, steal slowly towards his knife.

"He has seen me and means mischief," said Dick to himself. "Well, let him come on; I have my sword."

Chapter XXXVI
Robbery

"Yes, what is it?" said Hulton as an orderly tapped at the door when he was in earnest conversation with Wyatt and the doctor, evidently upon some question of great moment to them all. "His highness the Rajah has sent a messenger, sir. He wants to see Captain Wyatt directly."

"That will do," said Hulton, and the man saluted and left.

"Now," continued Hulton, "what does this mean?"

"I don't know," said Wyatt grimly. "The plot is beginning to unfold. I believe there is some trap."

"No, no," cried Hulton. "I begin to feel that the Rajah is sincere."

Wyatt shook his head.

"Well," he said, "what shall I do? Go and see him?"

"Alone?"

"Why not?" said Wyatt. "If he is sincere there is nothing to mind."

Hulton hesitated.

"I hardly like you to go alone, Wyatt," he said. "We will go with you."

"And give them the opportunity to trap us all together if he means anything wrong. No; you stay here and quietly be getting everything ready. If I am not back in half-an-hour, come for me; and if things have gone wrong, seize him and the Ranee. It is our only chance."

"And you'll go alone?"

"Yes," said Wyatt, drawing himself up and frowning, "I'll go alone; and if I feel satisfied that he has done this, I'll cut him down even if I die for it the next minute."

Captain Hulton's lips parted to speak, but Wyatt strode out without turning, walked across the hall, and went straight to where a group of the Rajah's guards stood on duty outside the room he occupied.

One of the officers went in, and returned directly, to make way for him to enter.

He had expected to find the Rajah seated there alone, but, to his surprise, he found him surrounded by his people, principal among whom were the Wazir and the chief Brahmin; and in place of the usual smiling faces, he found himself meeting frowns and scowls.

There was a dead silence as Wyatt entered, and after a glance round he spoke.

"Your highness wished to see me?"

"Yes, Captain Wyatt," said the Rajah sternly. "You are Mr Darrell's friend?"

"Yes, sir, and brother-officer."

"I have sent for him four times this morning. I wish to speak to him on a matter vital to his honour, and I keep receiving the reply that he is not in his room."

"That was the true reason why he did not come, sir," said Wyatt sternly; "he is not in his room."

"Then why is he not in his room? Where is he?"

"That is what I want to know, sir," said Wyatt sternly. "He left his quarters about midday yesterday."

There was a keen exchange of glances between the Rajah and his officers, which Wyatt noted as he went on:

"And he has not returned since."

There was another quick look exchanged.

"Perhaps your people can give some explanation of why this is, sir?"

"I or my people? No," said the Rajah. "Can you?"

"Only this, sir—that he must have been waylaid and carried off, if he has not been assassinated by some of your people."

There was a loud exclamation at this, and several of the officers, with indignant looks, clapped their hands to their swords; but the Rajah made a sign and there was silence.

"This is an insult to us, Captain Wyatt," he said; "and if you are sincere in your declaration that you do not know where he is, you will agree to this."

"Will you explain what you mean, sir?" said Wyatt haughtily.

"Yes. The matter concerns your young officer, whom I have trusted, and to whom I have shown the greatest favour; but as the matter concerns your brother-officers as well as yourself, and the honour of all is concerned, I must ask you to send for Captain Hulton and Doctor Robson to come here."

Wyatt's eyes dilated with the suspicion he felt, and his face looked harder and sterner than ever as he replied:

"Captain Hulton is still an invalid, sir, and Doctor Robson has nothing whatever to do with the conduct of our troop. I am in command, and the matter concerns me, and the honour generally of the troop. Mr Darrell, our young officer, has suddenly disappeared; I ask you and yours for some explanation, and I am told that it is a matter concerning our honour; have the goodness to tell me what you mean."

There was again a low murmur and fierce gesticulations amongst the officers, who resented Wyatt's tone, for he was speaking to the Rajah as if he were the offender being called upon to explain.

The Rajah sat troubled and stern for a few minutes as if irresolute, while the Wazir and other officers whispered together in a way which made Wyatt feel that his life was hanging, as it were, upon a thread.

"It is most painful, and a sorrow to me," said the Rajah at last, "for I have behaved to this Mr Darrell as if he were my friend."

Wyatt nodded shortly.

"He has come and gone here as he pleased, and my mother has during the past month treated him as if he were a son."

Wyatt nodded again.

"He has been as free to go to and from her apartments as I have, and in opposition to the custom of our people, for she has often laughingly said he was but a boy."

"Well, sir," said Wyatt sternly, "what has this to do with the disappearance of my brother-officer?"

"This," said the Rajah fiercely, and with his face full of the anger and disgust he felt: "my mother came to me quite early this morning to make her complaint of the treatment she had received."

Wyatt was watching him searchingly.

"She has found that her ivory cabinet has been opened, and the whole of her diamonds, emeralds, pearls, and rubies are gone. You know the beautiful jewels she had."

"Yes," said Wyatt, "I know. They were magnificent, queenly. Well, sir?"

"Well," said the Rajah, looking at him wonderingly, "my mother, the Ranee, tells me that Mr Darrell was seen to go to her rooms yesterday, and now he has fled."

"Oh, I see," cried Wyatt scornfully; "you mean that my brother-officer, a gentleman—an English gentleman—enjoying your hospitality, trusted by you in every way, has behaved like one of the vilest budmashes of the bazaar."

"What else can I believe after my mother's words?" cried the Rajah angrily.

"Bah!" raged out Wyatt; "I'd answer for him with my life. Rajah, shame on you! How can you be such a child?"

There was a roar at this, but the Rajah held up his hand, and turned to Wyatt.

"Then where is he?" he cried. "Why is he not here to answer to this charge?"

"You have been sending for me, sir?" said a familiar voice, and Dick Darrell, who had entered in the confusion unobserved, let fall the heavy curtain he had drawn aside, and stepped forward to his brother-officer's side.

Chapter XXXVII
What Dick Saw

"Hah! Dick, lad," whispered Wyatt, grasping his hand, "never more welcome than now. Not hurt?"

"Oh, no."

"Where have you been?"

"Out. I'll tell you soon, but his highness wants me."

"Yes," cried Wyatt fiercely, "and I'll tell you why. Through her highness the Ranee's announcement to him, the Rajah, who does not know what an English gentleman is, charges you with sweeping off as loot the whole of her valuable gems. Now, then, speak out: tell his highness what you have to say to that."

"Very little," said Dick coolly; "but I am not surprised."

"What! not surprised that his highness should say that?"

"Of course he would be indignant."

"Hah!" ejaculated the Wazir.

"Well," cried Wyatt, "why do you not tell him it is an insult?"

"Because it would be too childish," said Dick contemptuously. "I take them! He cannot believe it."

"I do not want to believe it," cried the Rajah excitedly, "but it is made so clear to me that it was you."

"Absurd!" cried Dick proudly, and he laughed in the Rajah's face. "The precious stones were taken by some one in the palace."

"Yes," cried Wyatt, "and as an excuse to shift the blame on to us."

"Looks like it," said Dick sharply.

There was a roar of anger at this, and the Wazir and half the officers present drew their swords.

"It is an insult to us all, gentlemen," cried the Wazir fiercely.

"It is no insult to the gentlemen present, brave officers of the Rajah," cried Dick excitedly, "but to one man only—the man who would stand by and hear the blame laid upon another—the coward, the thief!"

"Ah!" cried the Wazir, frantic with rage. "Then who was it? Let the Christian dog speak,"—sliding forward threateningly, sword in hand.

"Christian?—yes," cried Dick excitedly. "Dog yourself, and thief!"

"Hah!" yelled the Wazir, and quick as thought he made a tremendous downward cut at the young officer. But Wyatt was even quicker, he was prepared, for, as the Wazir raised his sword, his own flashed out from its sheath as he stood on Dick's right, and in the swift upward cut it met the Wazir's.

There was a loud clang and a musical jangle as the blade of a tulwar fell quivering on the marble floor, and the Wazir stood holding the hilt only of his weapon in his hand, while Wyatt drew back his weapon to his shoulder a if about to thrust, and Dick drew and stood ready at his side.

The blade of a tulwar fell quivering on the marble floor.

"Stand back," cried Wyatt in a deep, hoarse voice. "I don't strike at unarmed men."

"I appeal to your highness," cried the Wazir. "I appeal to all who love me. An insult, an outrage!" he snarled, as his eyes seemed to blaze with the deadly hatred he felt towards the two Englishmen.

The Rajah looked at him with his own eyes flashing now, and held up his hand to quell the storm, while the chief Brahmin crept shivering to the door, to stand half behind the Rajah's guards and cling to the curtains of rich stuff hanging from the arch.

"Let no man dare to raise a sword again in my presence," cried the Rajah with dignity, and his officer drew back and imitated the action of Dick and Wyatt, who thrust their swords back into the scabbards with a clang. "Mr Darrell, you and your friends came here at my invitation, and I will defend you to the last. But you have made a terrible charge against one of the greatest noblemen of my court, the Ranee's old and trusted friend."

"No more terrible charge than has been made against me, sir—an English officer, who could not have committed such a paltry theft."

"Neither could this noble officer, my mother's trusted friend."

"Indeed?" said Dick calmly, as Wyatt stood watching his face. "I tell you, then, sir, that yesterday afternoon I saw him come down the steps beneath the great temple floor, lamp in one hand, bag in the other."

"What!" cried the Rajah wonderingly.

"And as he stepped hurriedly forward he caught his foot on something, slipped, and let fall the bag he carried. It fell with a peculiar sound, and the jerk he made in trying to save it put out the lamp."

The Wazir uttered a scornful laugh and looked round, half of those present joining in the laugh, half looking grave.

"This was beneath the temple floor?" said the Rajah.

"Yes, sir: and we were in total darkness."

"Yes," said the Rajah excitedly, "go on. But stop! What were you doing there?"

"I had gone to see the officer on guard there."

"Yes," cried the Rajah: "but how came you to know of the way down below?"

"The officer we have had there by your instructions to guard the place found the way."

"Then you were there to find the treasure-cell?" cried the Rajah excitedly.

"We were there to guard the treasure-cell, sir, by your orders," said Dick coldly. "Send and see if your place is safe."

"Yes," said the Rajah, drawing a deep breath, "I did send you there. Go on."

"I was down there yesterday," continued Dick, "for I wished to carefully inspect the place for reasons of my own, when I was surprised by the coming of the Wazir."

"Then you played spy upon him," cried the Rajah. "Why did you not speak openly to him, a gentleman you had often met here, and my friend?"

Wyatt winced a little at the question, for Dick's acts seemed underhanded. But he brightened up the next moment at his brother-officer's words.

"Because, sir, the Wazir was not my friend. I looked upon him as my enemy, and I knew that if he found me there I should have to fight for my life, perhaps against treachery."

"Go on," said the Rajah, and the Wazir repeated his scornful laugh.

"I waited in silence while I heard him go back in the darkness to the steps," continued Dick, "and then I heard him set down the lamp, and I could see him by the sparks he struck busying himself trying to relight it. But it was long before he could get it to burn."

Dick faced the Rajah, watching his face as he spoke in his simple, straightforward way, which carried truth in every tone; while Wyatt kept his eyes fixed upon the Wazir, whose eyelids were half-closed; and at any moment the English officer was prepared for treachery.

"At last," continued Dick, in the midst of the breathless interest of the listeners, "the lamp burned out brightly again, and as he came back towards where I stood looking from behind one of the pillars, I for the first time knew what the bag contained, for two or three gems had escaped from the mouth or a hole broken through, and sparkled brilliantly upon the stone floor."

Dick paused for a moment, and a pent-up sigh escaped from several present.

"He caught sight of the escaped stones," continued Dick, "and as he picked up the bag he hurriedly thrust them back into their places, and rose up to go on, bag and lamp in hand."

"Yes," said the Rajah, for Dick had halted again.

"There is very little more to tell, sir. He went on with the lamp towards the side of the great vault, and went up to one of the cells there that was lying open. I distinctly saw him go in and place the bag in a niche there, come out, and close the door."

"How did he close the door?" said the Rajah sharply. "By sliding a great slab of stone across the opening and letting fall a block behind it in the groove," said Dick quietly.

"Hah!" ejaculated the Rajah with a long expiration of the breath.

"Then he went back hastily to the steps. I saw the lamp growing less till it disappeared, leaving only a pale glow from the top; then it was extinguished, and I was in the intense darkness once more, as I crept softly after him and stood and listened till I heard a heavy, gliding noise and a dull concussion, and then all was still."

Again there was silence, and Dick drew out a handkerchief and wiped his streaming brow, looking hollow-cheeked and strange.

"I am hot and faint," he said half-apologetically, as if speaking to the Rajah and Wyatt together: "I have been twenty-four hours without food, and I am exhausted with trying to find a way out of that place."

"Hah!" cried the Rajah; "then you were shut in?"

"Yes, sir. When I had waited and then went to the top of the stairs, and then along the narrow passages, I could not find the opening out for a long time. Then I found that the narrow doorway behind the pillar had been closed and made fast, and by degrees I grasped the fact that the whole of the pillar had been thrust back against the passage wall, and was now fastened there, probably by a block being lowered, or one of the stone figures being pushed into a groove to keep it shut."

"Then you were a prisoner," said the Rajah.

"Yes, sir, till about an hour ago."

"When the door was opened," cried Wyatt excitedly. "Opened by the sergeant, who had missed you."

"The sergeant did not know I had gone down below into the great vault," said Dick quietly; "and for aught I know, it may be fastened now."

"Then how did you escape?" cried the Rajah.

"I'm devoting my attention, sir, to finding the other way out," said Dick firmly now.

"What other way out?" cried the Rajah. "There is no other way."

"There is, sir," said Dick quietly; "and but for the fact of my divining the way in which entrance was secured, I should have been there now, or till some one had come."

"Another way out?" cried the Rajah.

"Yes, sir; fastened in a similar fashion, as I found at last, by the drawing back of a square pillar, leaving just room for a man to squeeze through."

"But where was this?" asked the Rajah excitedly.

"At the extreme end of a long stone passage, hundreds and hundreds of yards from the temple walls—a strange place rising upward above my head—a place where I tried for hours till my fingers and nails were worn like this and bleeding," said the lad, holding out his hands. "But when at last I discovered the right place to touch, it yielded with the greatest ease."

"You astound me," cried the Rajah, by whom the charge was for the moment forgotten in this strange development. "And where did this other doorway bring you out?"

"In one of the rooms of the old palace, sir," cried Dick firmly. "The doorway was the one through which your highness's enemies and ours came to fire our magazine and assassinate all who came in their way."

Chapter XXXVIII
The Search for the Jewels

"Then you escaped by there back into your old quarters?" cried the Rajah as the murmur of astonishment died out.

"Yes, sir; and after coming across to my room to wash and dress, I heard that your highness had been sending for me. I came on, to find you ready to accuse me of this contemptible theft. Are you satisfied now where the jewels are?"

"Yes," said the Rajah firmly, "quite. Now, Wazir, what have you to say?"

"Say!" cried the man contemptuously; "I scorn to deny it. I, your mothers trusted friend and adviser—I steal her treasure of jewels, any one of which, if I had asked her, she would have given me at once?"

"You hear the way in which your charge rebounds on you?"

"I hear, but I scorn it all, your highness. It is a vile, cowardly invention, made to turn the light of your countenance from your faithful servants."

"You heard what was said?"

"Yes, I have heard all, your highness; but it is false. Let it be proved. If it be as the English boy says, it is true. If the jewels are not found where he says, it is false."

The Rajah bowed his head, and turned to Wyatt.

"That is fair, sir," said the latter. "Let the place be searched."

"Yes," said the Rajah; and, clapping his hands, he gave the order, and then turned to his guards, sending an officer and a dozen men to guard at the temple to see that there was no foul play.

He looked round him, to see that the chief priest was standing near the door, looking old and careworn, and he beckoned to him to draw near.

"Did you know of the long passage the young English officer has described?"

"Yes; oh, yes," he replied; "it is where those of our people who die in the temple are buried beneath the stones. They lie there from end to end."

"Hah!" said the Rajah; "but the way out into the old palace?"

"If I had known, should I have advised the Ranee and the Rajah, your father, to place their treasures there for their son? Should I not sooner have built it up with the heaviest stones that could be found?"

"Yes," said the Rajah, "of course—for them if not for me."

He sat thinking for a few moments as if turning something over in his mind, and then turned to the two Englishmen.

"Captain Wyatt," he said, "I requested in a time of emergency that a guard of your men should be placed over my treasure in the great temple."

"Yes, sir; it was done, and has been faithfully carried out," said Wyatt haughtily.

The Rajah bowed, and his face was inscrutable as he said:

"I now withdraw that request. You will give orders for your men to retire at once."

"Then your highness has ceased to confide in your English allies?"

"No," said the Rajah; "but I must have this matter made clear. Send your order to your men."

"This is hardly fair to us, your highness," said Wyatt sternly.

"I stand at the head of all justice here, sir," said the Rajah proudly, "and I go now to see to what is right or wrong. You need not fear that I shall not be just."

"As your highness pleases," said Wyatt coldly.—"Mr Darrell, you will send an orderly to Sergeant Stubbs, and bid him withdraw his men instantly, to march to the old palace, and take up quarters there till further orders."

Dick turned to go.

"Stop!" cried the Rajah. "Mr Darrell will stay with me."

"As a prisoner, sir," cried Wyatt fiercely.

"As my friend, sir," replied the Rajah, "until we have been to the temple. Have the goodness to summon your man and give him the order in my presence. I wish my people to be satisfied that there can have been no communication with your people at the temple."

"Your highness is right," said Wyatt. "I wish those gentlemen who are our friends to see the same."

He turned and spoke to one of the officers, who left the audience-room; and as soon as he had gone, a few lines were pencilled in Wyatt's book, which he read aloud to the Rajah, and as soon as one of the orderlies reached the door he said sharply:

"Take that despatch to Sergeant Stubbs at the temple, and tell him to carry out the order at once."

The man saluted and went off, just as the Rajah's elephant was brought to the front entrance. Horses followed for all whom the Rajah selected to go, and a palanquin for the old Brahmin, so that a goodly procession was formed, one which had not gone above half-way before they passed Stubbs and his men on the march to their former quarters in the old palace.

They halted, faced, and saluted as the Rajah and his brilliant party swept by, and then resumed their march; while soon after the Rajah's train drew up in front of the temple, whose guards had been so quickly changed. The dismounting followed, and by this time some twenty or thirty of the priests stood waiting to receive their ruler, who passed from the blinding sunshine into the cool gloom of the place.

Orders were given by the chief Brahmin, and in a few minutes a party of priests came forward bearing lighted lamps, and their chief led the way right on into the far part of the temple, the Rajah following next with the two English officers and the Wazir. Lastly, about twenty of the chief followers of the Rajah came, and the train was brought up by the palace guards, who formed a semicircle round the spot where the chief Brahmin had stopped short for the others to advance.

Here the first thing that struck Dick was that the opening he had described as closed was now, as shown by the light of the lamps, quite open.

Nothing was said, but the two English officers exchanged glances.

The chief Brahmin led on through the narrow way, preceded by the lamp-bearers. The Rajah requested the English officers to go next. Then he followed, and the Wazir next, followed by the guards.

As they reached the bottom of the narrow flight of steps, passing the lamp upon its ledge, the place, lit up as it was now, looked strangely different of aspect; but there were the square dwarf pillars casting their dark shadows, and dimly seen away to the left was the opening to the cells.

"Will you point out the place where you say the Wazir placed the bag of jewels, Mr Darrell?" said the Rajah gravely.

"Yes, sir; in that one where the stone has been slid across and the block keeps it shut."

"Are you sure it is there?"

"Yes, sir, I am certain that is the one."

The Wazir drew a deep breath.

"Open!" said the Rajah laconically; and two of the priests removed the stone fastening, and pushed the slab along in its grooves, when two more stepped in with lights, while Dick and Wyatt pressed forward, eager to see.

But they saw nothing. The place was empty, and no sign was shown of any one having lately been in.

"Open the others," said the Rajah; "open all."

This was done one by one till all were laid open to the glare of the lamps; but all were empty, and Dick turned to Wyatt, giving him a peculiar look.

The next moment, without a word being uttered, the Rajah gave the order for a return to be made to the palace, and Dick turned to him.

"Not now," he said; "I want to think."

The party returned to the palace, the Rajah going straight to his audience-chamber after, in a few words, giving the two officers to understand that their attendance would not be welcome; and as they turned to reach the officers' quarters, Dick said excitedly to his companion:

"Wyatt, I swear—"

"Don't, my boy, nor say another word till you've had tiffin. I'll say enough now for you and self: the old Brahmin's too many for us—we've been tricked."

Chapter XXXIX
Dismissed

Captain Hulton was waiting eagerly for the return of the two officers, fully aware that something was very wrong, but still in ignorance of its full bearing. The news of the hurried return of Sergeant Stubbs and the detachment had made the position appear more strange; and directly Wyatt and Dick entered his questioning began, and he heard everything that had occurred.

"The weak child!" he exclaimed angrily. "That is the way with these Eastern princes—they are always swayed by the one who has the last word."

"You seem to think as we do, then?" said Wyatt. "Of course. That woman is hand and glove with the other party still, and working with them. The Rajah, after all, has an intense affection for his mother, and looks upon all those ancient jewels as something sacred. It was like a blow at him for them to be stolen, and to his eyes the case looked black against Darrell here."

"You think he believes it still then?" said Dick.

"Without doubt. They are all mixed up in it—Wazir, Brahmins, and the rest of the party—I feel sure, and they have schemed so that you have not cleared yourself, Darrell."

"But I tell you I saw the Wazir, with the light shining on his face, come down those steps, pick up the bag of jewels after he had dropped it, and go into the cell I pointed out, come back, and fasten it up again."

"Yes, yes, *yes*—of course you did, Dicky," cried Wyatt impatiently; "and I wish you had gone in and got them afterwards, so as to have brought them out and shown the Rajah you spoke the truth."

"Ha, ha!" laughed Dick. "Why, that would have made the case look worse."

"Humph! so it would," said Wyatt. "I give it up. I'm better at fighting than scheming, and I feel now just as if I should like to have the guns out and a regular go-in at somebody."

"Oh, we can't fight," said Hulton. "I must see the Rajah and prove to him that it was all a trick. He'll lean to the last man."

"Send the doctor in to him to make him believe he's worse, and then he'll be ready to hang over to our side again."

"I wish Robson would give the Wazir and that sanctified old Brahmin a dose of his strongest stuff."

"To poison them?" said Dick.

"Poison! Bah! No. To make 'em both ill for six months. What shall we do, Hulton? Go and insist upon having an interview with this baby?"

"No," replied Hulton after a minute's silence. "Have everything ready for emergencies, and then wait to see how matters turn."

"Hallo! Who's this?" cried Wyatt, for there were steps outside, and an orderly announced the captain of the Rajah's guard, who was ushered in, looking very stern.

"Nice business this!" said Wyatt in his bluff way, for, since the night of the attempted poisoning, they two had been on the friendly terms that would bring two brave men into a state of mutual respect.

"I come from his highness," said the Rajah's officer. "His commands are that the English sahibs and their men leave here directly, and take up their quarters in the old palace till he has decided what steps to take; and I and my men are to see these orders executed now—at once."

"Dismissed like bad servants," cried Hulton indignantly.

"But suppose we won't go, old fellow?" said Wyatt to the officer.

"Then, sir, we must fight," said the officer, with a shrug of his shoulders. "It is sad; but I command the Rajah's guard, and I must do my duty."

"Of course," said Wyatt.—"There, Dick Darrell, you see what a mess you have got us all in by taking a fancy to the old Ranee's pretty playthings."

"It is a lie," cried the Indian officer, turning upon Wyatt fiercely. "The Dah Rel is a brave soldier. He would not do such a thing."

"Thank you," said Dick, smiling and taking the messengers hand. "But Captain Wyatt does not mean it."

"Mean it? No, old fellow," said Wyatt, clapping the officer on the shoulder. "Then you do not believe all this story about the stealing?"

"No; it is a plot—a trick," cried the messenger fiercely. "But he does—now. It is the Ranee—and the cursed dogs of her party. It was peace, and all would have been well for Soojeepur, and we should have been strong in the friendship of the English, so that we could defy all our foes; but now the Ranee will come to the front again, the Wazir will rule, the Brahmins will master him, and the poor Rajah will be a doll amongst them, if they do not poison him out of the way. But I must obey my orders. Go and tell what I have said, and my head will roll upon the pavement in the court."

"You are not afraid of that," said Dick.

"No. How soon will the sahibs be ready?"

"Now," said Hulton firmly, "as soon as our servants have put together our things."

"The escort of my men will be waiting in the court in half-an-hour's time," said the officer shortly, and he turned and left the room.

"I want to fight," said Wyatt grimly.

"So do I," said Hulton, "but with plenty of elbow-room. Oh, if we could only have the Wazir and his men out on the broad plain yonder!"

"With the two regiments of cavalry we have drilled to help him," cried Wyatt fiercely. "I begin to hate the Rajah for a coward and a fool. Fancy! we have been teaching these mounted men the quickest and surest way to cut our throats."

"The escort will be waiting in half-an-hour," said Hulton sternly. "Quick! Let them see how smartly we can turn out with all we have."

"Yes," said Wyatt. "There is one good thing to be said, though—we can hold the old palace now that Dick here has shown us how to stop the leak. I should like to use that passage for carrying a few kegs of powder to blow the temple about the old Brahmin's ears."

Within the half-hour the troop was on parade in the great opening in front of the palace, a couple of wagons holding all that the officers and men had brought in the way of extras. The escort, a hundred strong, was waiting, every man looking sullen and morose, but not unfriendly towards their charge; but at the far end there was cause for uneasiness in the gathering of a strong force of horse and foot, holding quite aloof.

All was ready, and the troop waited the order to march, when, after a few words together, Wyatt and Dick rode up to the captain of the guard, who was sitting like a statue in the front of his men.

"Send in word to the Rajah, sir," said Wyatt, "that we are ready to go, and ask him if he wishes to see us before we depart. Quick," he added in a low voice; "who commands those men yonder?"

"The Wazir. Beware. My men will not attack their friends," said the captain, making believe to calm his restive horse. Then aloud for all to hear:

"The Rajah's commands are that the English officers go at once. He has nothing to say."

"Come, Dick!" said Wyatt laconically, and the pair rode back, communicated with Hulton, and an order or two was given.

A dozen of the escort took their places in front, the trumpet was sounded, and the men with their guns began to move off; while a movement amongst the Wazir's men at the other end of the open parade-ground showed that something was intended.

But the next minute the main body of the escort had closed in behind, and Hulton saw directly after that a mounted man came galloping up to the officer of the guard to make some communication.

It was the Wazir's move on the great chess-board, but it was met by the captain of the guard obeying the orders he had received from the Rajah himself, and not giving way to the Wazir's men; while, fully aware of the peril that would await if the artillery were caught by charging horsemen in the narrow streets and lanes, the order was given by Hulton for two of the guns to go on at a gallop and take up position on either side of the street in front of the palace, to cover the rest of the troop, which was to follow at a trot.

This was brilliantly carried out, Dick being sent forward with the two guns, which were unlimbered, loaded, and stood ready as the head of the little column came up and filed rapidly in through the old palace gates.

There was barely room for the troops to pass, but ample for the two guns to block the street now as they were left free, just as the Wazir's men came on with a roar of shouting as if to charge.

The effect was magical as the front ranks crowded forward and began to check their horses at the sight of the guns and the men's smoking linstocks. A loud shouting and yelling followed, and the pursuing force turned and fled in confusion.

"Such a chance, sir," grumbled one of the sergeants reproachfully to Dick. "He could have got two rounds of grape into 'em before they were clear."

"Wait a bit," said Dick, smiling; "the game has not yet begun."

The words were spoken without thought, and their utterer wondered afterwards what he meant. Were they really likely to have a fierce encounter with the Wazir's party?

He had no more time for musing, for the orders came for the guns to be withdrawn within the great gates, which were directly after closed and manned, the troop standing ready for any emergency; while Dick played guide to show Wyatt the entrance to the temple passage, in which a mine was laid and guards set, so that an explosion might, if necessary, completely close the opening against any attack.

"For we will not blow it up yet," said Wyatt. "It might prove useful."

This done, the officers made a tour of inspection of men and quarters, but everything was ready for any emergency. Forethought had seen to that. Rations, provender, water, ammunition—all were there, without counting what might be done in the way of foraging; and at last Hulton said, with a smile:

"We can't do much in the way of attack, but their horsemen are useless against us in here; and if things go against us now, we are ready for a little siege."

Chapter XL
The Wazir at Work

Events moved fast now for the little, isolated troop. Hardly had the inspection been finished when there was a challenge from the roof over the gateway. The sentry announced the coming of horse, and Wyatt frowned.

"Oh, if we had a gun up there!" he said.

"Only a waste of fire," said Dick. "We are so out of place here."

"Yes, I know, my dear boy," replied Wyatt; "but we are surrounded by enemies now through that wretched, childish trap they laid for the Rajah, and I feel as if I must hit some one."

The next minute the head of a strong body of horse was halted in front, and all doubt as to its purpose was at an end, for the captain of the guard rode up to the gate and demanded to see Captain Hulton.

A quick movement was made in the courtyard, and then orders were given for the gate to be opened, and the captain rode in, giving a quick glance round, and there was a look of satisfaction in his eyes as he noted the state of military readiness around, as he walked his horse up to where the little group of officers sat mounted.

"I am the bearer of the Rajah's commands, sir," he said loudly to Hulton, after a quick look of recognition at the others.

"Or the Wazir's, sir?" said Hulton sarcastically.

"The Rajah's," said the captain, "given to me from his own lips, and with the Ranee standing at his right hand. He bids me say that he has no further need for the services of the English artillery troop, and he desires that it evacuates the old palace and leaves Soojeepur at once."

"Indeed!" said Hulton coldly; "and how am I to interpret the words 'at once'?"

"Directly," was the laconic reply.

"But our preparations—stores? The Rajah must give us two days for preparation."

"His highness grants no time for preparation," replied the messenger. "I and my guard, one hundred strong, have his commands to protect you and see you right out of the city, a quarter day's journey upon your road back, and to see that none of the people attack you."

"It will be awkward for the people if they do," growled Wyatt menacingly.

"Yes," said the messenger, with a smile; "but the Rajah desires that the great Company's troops shall return as they came, in haste, and you must ride out now in less than an hour."

"Then we will," cried Hulton, "and he must answer for it to our general. We will shake the dust, as you would say, of this ungrateful place from off our feet; and maybe we shall return."

"In an hour, then?" said the captain.

"Yes," said Hulton, whose pale face lit lip; and in spite of his long and wasting illness, he looked very much the man again. "In an hour, and before we have gone long he will bitterly repent his act—when he is at the mercy of this bigoted Wazir and his weak mother."

"Yes," said the officer, giving him a meaning look as he spoke in a low voice; "and would that I could surround him with his guard and the two regiments you have drilled so well to bring him away too. He cannot help himself; he is driven. You will hear soon that he is dead."

"Tell him from me," said Hulton, "that if he will give the word and come to our help, even now we will place him firmly upon his throne."

"It is too late," said the officer sadly. "He would not fight against his people and the priests."

"In spite of his brave words?"

"You do not know the hold they have," replied the officer sadly. "Even now I feel as if I am behaving like a traitor to my Rajah and the people here."

"Then—"

"I have a duty to do, sir, and it is partly done. In one hour you will ride out from here on your homeward way. If you are attacked, remember that I and my men are fighting for our brothers-in-arms, for there is not a man in my guard who would raise a sword against you. I only say, be ready and well prepared."

He rode back to the gate without another word, and Wyatt cried warmly:

"I'd trust that fellow with my life. In an hour, then?"

Draw Swords! In The Horse Artillery | 269

"Yes," said Hulton; "we must leave all our heavy stores, and go as a flying column on the march in an enemy's country."

"Yes," said Wyatt with a grim smile: "and the sooner we have got rid of our escort the better."

"Why?"

"Because there will be no friends in the way of our guns?"

The trumpet rang out, the preparations were made with wonderful celerity, and Dick looked gloomily at the quantity of ammunition and stores that was to be left behind.

"Hadn't we better blow up the powder before we go?"

"No," said Wyatt sharply. "Let it be locked up where it is. Who knows but we may come back for a fresh supply?"

Within the hour the captain of the guard was summoned from where he was busy overlooking his men, patrolling the streets and driving the people back; and when he rode into the courtyard he once more gazed round wonderingly.

"I am ready, sir," said Hulton, making a brave effort to master his weakness and retain the command of the troop, though his brother-officers and the doctor had all implored him to give up and ride in one of the wagons. But, "No," he said; "as I rode into this place I'll ride out."

Without a word the captain of the guard divided his men into two bodies for advance and rear-guard, gave the order to march, and the trampling of the hoofs began through the streets. The guns, limbers, and wagons rattled and rambled, and amidst the sharp trampling of horses the train passed on, with every man's sabre loose in the scabbard, and pistols ready for the attack they momentarily expected at the various crossings.

But, to the surprise of all, the main way was reached, and as they came in sight of the great gate opening upon the bridge, it was to see the route open, and only the ordinary number of guards stationed upon the gate-towers and about the gates.

"I don't understand this, Dick," said Wyatt, riding alongside; "surely they're never going to let us ride off without a row."

"It seems like it. The Rajah's orders."

"Then it is horribly disappointing, lad. I meant to go straight for that Wazir, and here we are riding off like a lot of mangy, whipped dogs with our tails between our legs."

"It does seem very meek and tame."

"Yes; look at our escort. Bless it! what do we want with an escort? I say, do you know what the Irishman said?"

"Which? The one who made the bull?"

"No, no; the one in a *timper*. He said he was spoiling for a fight. That's just how I feel—spoiling; and here we go riding away like this."

"Well," said Dick dryly, "it will make it easier for the doctor. I say, though, would you ever have thought that the Rajah would turn out so weak as—as—"

"To be led by the nose by the Wazir's party?" said Wyatt smartly. "Oh, yes, I could believe anything of an Eastern prince."

The conversation soon flagged, and the troop trotted steadily on after the bridge was crossed, the escort riding well in front and rear, but holding thoroughly aloof, even the officers keeping apart.

Now, for the benefit of the teams drawing the ammunition-wagons through the deep, sandy parts, the speed was eased and the horses well breathed from time to time. Then, upon their reaching some gentle slope where the ground was hard, the word was given and the horses broke into a gentle canter for a mile, but only to ease again, till at last the captain of the Rajah's guard suddenly wheeled his troop round from the front to form up in the rear of those behind, and as the evolution was in progress he turned his own horse and rode up alongside of the artillery officers.

"This is the end of my course," he said, "and I wish you safety for the rest of your way."

"Thanks; and we wish you the same," said Hulton.

"I have no right to speak," continued the captain, "but if I were in your place I would journey on the whole night through."

"Ah!" cried Dick, "you fear treachery?"

"I say nothing, only that I think the way is clear before you. May we meet again."

He turned, gave the word, and rode off at a gallop; while, after watching him and his troop till they disappeared, Hulton continued his course for a time, till a suitable spot appeared, and then called a halt in the middle of an open part of the country, where ample notice could be given by the outposts of any danger that might be approaching.

The halt was short, but several little matters needed seeing to after the hurried start. Then the word "Forward" was given once more, and the troop went on at a fair pace, the intention being to get well on with the march before dark, or till a suitable place for a bivouac could be found.

This last showed itself sooner than had been reckoned upon, about a mile on the hither side of a mountain range and a long gorge they had passed through while coming—a part so full of opportunities for an active enemy on foot to contrive an ambush, that Hulton called a halt just at sundown, keeping up the air of its being merely temporary till dark, and hurriedly making preparations for the night by unlimbering and loading the guns, which were placed at intervals with the wagons in a circle about the halting-place, the horses being picketed in the centre with their bits only removed, while the men lay down to rest, ready for action at the slightest alarm. Then vedettes rode out to keep their lonely watch, and all was still.

It was some time before sleep would come to Dick, but he slept soundly and restfully at last in the cool, fresh night air, and did not wake till the men were roused just before daybreak to partake of the simple rations they had brought, eating hurriedly in the darkness before the order was given to fall in, and the officers rode forward a short distance to reconnoitre.

All looked calm and peaceful in the soft, grey dawn, but a long reach of rugged track extended before them for miles and miles, and there was the possibility, slight though it was, of the enemy having made a détour and reached some suitable spot from whence a sudden attack might be made, this of course being chosen where the guns would be of little or no avail.

The doctor rode with them, and while they were carefully examining every rock and clump of trees, he asked Dick if he did not think they were being too cautious.

"We can't," said the young officer, "for it seems impossible that the Wazir, now he is getting back into power, could let us ride off so quietly."

"He dare not attack," said the doctor, "for fear of the punishment he would bring down upon his head when the news reached headquarters."

"I don't know," replied Dick. "These petty chiefs who have never seen England's power cannot believe that it is stronger than theirs, and—What's that?"

"Runaway horse, seemingly," replied the doctor, shading his eyes, as a swift animal came galloping out from the defile before them, straight along the track which led to where they were about to continue the march.

The officers watched the coming horse curiously, and soon made out that it was gaily caparisoned and evidently belonged to some one of note;

the question now arising—How could that horse have escaped, and be galloping towards them from out of the rugged defile ahead?

All at once it was sighted by Dick's Arab, which snorted out a challenge. This the coming steed heard, stopped short, threw up its head, answered the challenge, and then came galloping up to join the group of its kind.

"I know that horse," cried Dick eagerly, "by the one white hindleg and hoof."

"Where have you seen it?" said Wyatt.

"One of the Wazir's friends used to ride it."

"There, what did I tell you?" said Wyatt turning to Hulton. "I knew it directly. They've prepared a nice little trap for us; but we might have guessed it without this warning. Now then," he continued, as the horse cantered so closely up to Burnouse that Dick deftly caught the loose bridle and secured the steed, "how will this do? We can pretty well guess where they will be. We must draw them out."

"What! dismount men and skirmish with them?" cried Hulton warmly. "They will be too cunning for us."

"If we did that," said Wyatt quietly. "I meant something very different."

"You must bear in mind that we are being watched."

"Yes, I have taken that into consideration. Tell me what you think. The enemy know that we have just bivouacked for the night."

Hulton nodded.

"And are cautiously preparing to start."

"Yes, of course."

"Then divide the troop into two, with their three guns each; leave one with the wagons as if not yet quite ready, and send the other steadily marching to the full extent of the open manoeuvring ground, and then make believe."

"Make believe what?"

"To have caught sight of the hiding enemy; and, with a good deal of confusion, let the men face about and take flight to get back into the open."

"I see," cried Hulton eagerly. "It will be too much for the enemy, and they will pursue to a man, so as to take advantage of the panic."

"Exactly," replied Wyatt dryly. "Then the waiting troop can give them a few hints of what we can do, throw them into confusion, cut off their retreat back into the rough ground, and long before then the first troop will have begun to speak."

"But the wagons, the baggage, and guard?"

"Let the wagons take care of themselves, Hulton," cried Wyatt hotly. "You take three guns, and give me the other three; and if between us we cannot, by playing into each other's hands, astonish these irregular gentlemen, we have been drilling together all this time for nothing."

"Yes," said Hulton, whose pale face was flushed with his growing excitement; "but there is one thing."

"What?"

"Suppose they have the two regiments of horse we have been drilling for them?"

"We will not suppose anything of the kind," said Wyatt dryly. "Of course, if they had it might be bad for us. Now what do you say?"

"I am obliged to confess that the heart's good, Wyatt, but the body's weak. Take the three guns and advance; leave me with the other three. I'll do my best, but if I break down I want Darrell and Stubbs; they will carry out your plans, and we *will* do what you say. Only mind, every effort must be made to keep the enemy from getting back among the mountains. We must not have them again between us and safety."

"I see," said Wyatt, drawing himself up in his saddle. "Now for your orders."

They rode back the few dozen yards to the waiting troop, Dick taking a final glance at the lovely stretch of mountain and forest to their south, so beautiful in the morning light that it seemed impossible for it to hold a foe. Then he was listening to his orders, with his heart beginning to palpitate at the thought of what was to come.

Wyatt's proposal was carried out to the letter. The first troop rode off with three guns, and the men left stared and wondered, and then stared the more at being ordered to dismount, detach the teams from the wagons, and do over again what had already been done.

Dick sat watching the first troop, already half a mile away, till he saw that Stubbs was trying to catch his attention; and when he met the old sergeant's eye there was a question in it, and that question was, according to the young officer's interpretation: "Is the captain going off his head?" And he looked again when Hulton gave the order for the wagon teams of six to be separated from the uniting traces into three pairs, each with its well-armed driver.

But everything was of course done, and was ready for the manoeuvre long before Wyatt and his party had ridden leisurely to the end of the level ground.

Then all at once those waiting saw him call a halt, ride forward with a couple of men as if in doubt, and then wheel round, waving his hand as he galloped back, and the next minute his troop was in full flight.

Dick glanced at Hulton, who gave the order to unlimber and load, his men being already dismounted; and this was hardly executed when a faint burst of shouting was borne upon their ears, and, glittering in the first rays of the sun, a great body of horse came streaming out from different parts among the mountains, looking in the distance like living streams running together into one as they reached the open ground, and tearing on in pursuit of the flying troop.

"Hor! hor!" laughed Stubbs softly, and he looked at Hanson, who was standing at one gun; "another chance for you, my lads. Something to hit at last."

Just then Hulton gave his orders sharply to the effect that when the men ceased firing and limbered up, the drivers were to leave the wagons and fall in with the rest of the troop, thus augmenting it by the accession of so many more men and horses.

The effect was marvellous. At least a dozen white-turbaned heads were thrust out from beneath the wagon-tilts, their owners staring with horror at the thought of being left behind, but as the order to fire rang out the heads were withdrawn and seen no more.

Everything went marvellously well. Hulton waited till the pursuing enemy were gathered in their thickest mass about a quarter of a mile away before he ordered the firing to commence, and the effect was terrible; but the enemy tore on after the flying troop till two rounds had been fired from each gun, when, unable to bear the punishment longer, the whole body of horse, as if moved by one impulse, swung round to attack the battery on their flank.

This was the signal for the retreating troop to halt and unlimber; and as the enemy came on they were being raked now by grape from the fresh direction, while before they could reach Hulton's party his men were off and away, leaving the wagons looking solitary in the middle of the plain.

All happened exactly as was planned. At every turn, to punish the punishers, one or the other battery opened upon the undisciplined mob of horse, which rapidly grew more and more disintegrated, till the two troops were manoeuvred so as to join just at the right time, when the broken up brilliant force of irregular cavalry was beginning to separate into knots and retreat.

Then, as rapidly as they could be served, the six guns swept the plain, which was now covered with flying horses and men.

But the fight was not to close without its tragic incident for the victors.

Just when the final rounds were being fired and the battery was thick with the rising smoke, there was a roaring shout raised from the right, the rush of horses, the clash of steel, and, unseen till close up, a body of about thirty gaily-dressed swordsmen were upon them, leaping their horses at the guns and cutting at every man they could reach, as they tore right along the full length of the battery.

In the fierce mêlée sabres, pistols, and rammers were used for the defence, but several men went down, and with them Dick, who was conscious of a mounted man riding at him right out of the smoke to give him a terrible cut upon the helmet, and then of the flash of a sabre from somewhere by his side, a heavy concussion, and of hearing a hoarse, gurgling cry. Then noise and confusion, with darkness over all.

Chapter XLI
Friends or Enemies?

"Not dead this time, are you, Dick, old lad?" came out of the darkness just as it was beginning to get light to the sufferer, and the young officer started up, but fell back sick and giddy.

"Here," he gasped, "where's my horse—what's matter? Is—Oh, I remember now."

"Drink a drop of this water, old fellow. Robson says you're only stunned."

Dick drank with avidity, and then pushed away the metal cup.

"Where's my helmet?" he panted.

"There; but you can't get it on till it has been hammered."

"Where's Burnouse?"

"Ram Dad's got him here, eating grass."

"Then where's the enemy?"

"Where's last night's dew?" replied Wyatt. "They've scattered and got into the mountains after all. We couldn't stop them though."

"Oh," groaned Dick, who was holding his hand to his head. "But tell me who's hurt."

"The enemy—awfully."

"I mean, of our men."

"Poor Rob Hanson. The Wazir cut him down."

"Oh!" cried Dick, rising up again into a sitting position. "Poor Rob Hanson! But not dangerously?"

"Robson is afraid so."

"Where is he?"

"With half-a-dozen of the lads. Robson has them in one of the wagons, out of the sunshine."

"I must go to him."

"You can't now. If you can move you must help with the men."

"I will directly; but you said the Wazir cut Hanson down?"

"Yes—the last man he'll hurt. He had just struck you off your horse when Hanson, who was serving a gun, went at him and got the cut meant to finish you; but he ran the Wazir through first, and saved your life."

"But he ran the Wazir through first, and saved your life."

Dick got quite up on his feet now, and stood holding on by his friend, both mentally and bodily stunned.

But by degrees he came round, and, when a few minutes later Hulton rode up, he was ready to mount once more, Wyatt having managed to drive out a great dint from his friend's helmet by thrusting with his knee and delivering a few blows with the pommel of his sword.

"A good headpiece, Dick," he said. "It has saved your life twice over."

"Well, Darrell," said Hulton, who looked very white and faint, "we've scattered them, you see, and killed the arch-enemy, who made his final bite."

"Yes," said Dick faintly, "we've won."

"How is it with you, my lad? Where's it to be—one of the wagons with the wounded, or can you mount?"

"Mount," said Dick shortly. "I'm getting clearer now."

"Well, Wyatt, what now? The enemy are between us and cantonments. What's to be done? It seems to me that the fighting has only just begun."

"Yes; and it seems madness to take the poor boys through those passes. I could see that they had foot there. You look. Try this 'glass'."

Hulton stood grazing through the glass for some minutes.

"Yes," he said, "hundreds; but they are retreating."

"To where they can throw down stones upon the lads' heads. What's to be done?"

"Beg pardon, gentlemen," said Sergeant Stubbs, who had been threading his way through the resting horses and men.

"What is it, Sergeant?" asked Hulton.

"Well, sir, it's a queer thing to say, but I've got a man starving to death in my head."

The three officers stared at the powder-blackened sergeant, who stood looking strangely from one to the other, with a big pocket-handkerchief in his hand.

"Here, come along with me, Stubbs," said Wyatt quickly; "the doctor will give you something."

"I ain't going mad, sir. I haven't got a touch of the sun, sir," protested the sergeant. "I know what I say. Look here, gentlemen; I tied the bag up in this to bring it to you, but in the hurry and rush it got stuffed among my traps, and I've just got it out of the wagon and brought it. I was afraid it would be found, and I should be charged with looting."

"What is it?" said Dick excitedly.

"It's a silk bag of dymonds and pearls and all sorts, sir, as I got hold of."

"The missing jewels—the Ranee's gems!" cried Dick. "How did you get those?"

"Well, it was like this, sir," said the sergeant: "I was in the temple yonder, down by that doorway place I showed you, sir, when I hears a scuffling sort of noise, and I dropped back among the images, and out comes one of the big priests in an awful hurry with that bag in his hand. As soon as he was out of the dark hole he opens it, puts in his hand, and takes out something to look at, puts it back again, and then gives a peep round to see if any one was about, and then makes for the staircase. Then all in a minute it come to me. This bag was all precious stones, worth a lac of rupees, perhaps. 'Part of the Rajah's treasure,' I said to myself, 'that we're put here to guard.'"

"Oh!" gasped Dick.

"I followed him, of course, sir, for it was plain enough he was stealing, and I had to go gently, too, so as not to be heard. Where do you think he was going, sir?"

"How can I tell?" cried Dick, pressing a hand to his aching head.

"Up to the back of the big image, sir, where the hiding-places like cells are."

"Yes; and then?" said Dick.

"Well, sir, I arrested him for looting, took away the bag, and shut him up in the big idol, a prisoner, spite of all he could say. And there he is now, and he may shout for help till all's blue; no one could hear him call. Now do you see what I mean?"

"Yes; it's horrible," cried Dick. "The man will starve to death."

"He will, sir, as sure as I'm here. And you know it was the moment I got down to the temple floor again that one of the guard came with the order for us to evacuate the place; and from that minute, what with the hurry and confusion and one thing and another, I never remembered a word about it till just now, when the fighting and smoke seemed to clear my head."

"Then we must go back at once," cried Dick.

"Go back!" said Hulton.

"Yes; we cannot let that poor wretch die so horrible a death. And besides, we can restore the jewels to the Ranee and show her that I am innocent."

"It would be enough to show the Rajah," said Hulton dryly.

"Well, why not?" cried Wyatt. "The jewels are here, the enemy there where it would be madness to go; the Wazir is dead, and you have the priest a prisoner ready to prove the conspiracy to his highness. Last of all, you have defeated his enemies and ours."

"Yes," cried Dick, "we must go back."

"Right," cried Hulton, catching the suggestion from the others. "We can ride back in triumph and completely change the state of affairs. Sound, Wyatt! and let's ride back at once."

It was quite time to sound the trumpet for mounting once again, for the flashing of steel in the distance told of a fresh body of horse approaching from the direction of Soojeepur.

The battle seemed about to be renewed.

"Yes," said Wyatt sternly, "with fresh men; and if the Wazir's folk can see them where they are now, we shall be attacked again from front and rear."

This appearance of a fresh body of the enemy seemed to completely overset the plans just made, for the prospect of reaching the city now that the way was blocked seemed small indeed.

"I don't like it—I don't like it, Dick," growled Wyatt as he rode alongside of his brother-officer at a gentle pace, in full marching order now with all their wagons, of which, however, they were prepared to disembarrass themselves in time of need.

"Neither do I," said Dick, "for my head is dreadful."

"Poor old lad! I am sorry; but you must grin and bear it. I say, though, what about the Wazir's sword? We ought to have brought that."

"I told one of the men to take it, sheath, belt, and all, and put it in the wagon with Bob Hanson. He ought to have it."

"Humph!" growled Wyatt, and he was silent for a few moments as he rode on, watching the approaching enemy.

"How many are there of them?" said Dick.

"Seven or eight hundred, my lad. Plenty of work cut out. I say, I told you I was spoiling for a fight."

"You did."

"Well, I've had all I wanted for one day, and I'm getting stiff, but we shall have to go through the rest of it. We've only one chance."

"What's that?"

"To go at them and let them see the stuff we're made of. We shall be all right again as soon as we get warm."

They rode steadily on a little farther, with the long column of horsemen coming on in excellent order, very different from those who had followed the Wazir and his chiefs, and Wyatt's face grew darker.

"I say, little one," he said suddenly, "if you don't feel equal to this next scrimmage, you had better stop in the rear with the wagons when we go into action."

"Thank you," said Dick quietly. "Will you stop and keep me company?"

Wyatt laughed softly, and leaned over to grip his companion's arm.

"Feel giddy now?"

"No; getting clearer."

"Well, sit fast, lad, and take care of yourself. I'll tell old Stubbs to keep an eye on you. I can't stop near."

"You let Stubbs see to his men. He has enough to do. Burnouse will take care of me. I wish I knew how Bob Hanson was getting on."

"No time now. Hah! at last."

For the trumpet called a halt, the wagons were cast off again, and, with every man he could muster, Hulton gave the word and the troop went off at a canter, to reach a knoll a few hundred yards away, where the guns were unlimbered, loaded, and the horses rested while the enemy was awaited, the intention being to give them two or three rounds to throw them into confusion as they formed up, and then gallop away.

Anxious glances were directed back at the rugged elevations they had now left far behind, but not one of the Wazir's men could be seen.

"Not one, Dick," said Wyatt, closing his glass. "So I don't mind so much. We shall have time to devote ourselves to our fresh visitors," he said grimly.

"They're startled already," replied Dick. "They're halting."

"Smell powder, like the black crows they are," growled Wyatt. "Don't care for the look of the guns. Why, Dick, look at them! They're the two regiments that we have drilled. See how they are forming into squadrons. Bah! it is horrible. They'll beat us by manoeuvring."

"The two regiments and the Rajah's bodyguard," cried Dick. "I know them by their white puggrees. Look, look! A white flag."

"Same as white feather," said Wyatt as three horsemen, magnificently mounted, came sweeping across the plain, leaving the squadrons drawn up in position. One of them bore a small white flag at the end of a lance, and as the pair sat watching Hulton joined them.

"What does this mean?" he said.

"Treachery, as likely as not," replied Wyatt. "But we shall soon see."

"It's the captain of the guard leading," cried Dick excitedly; and a few minutes after their old acquaintance dashed right up to where they sat.

"I heard the guns," he cried excitedly. "What has happened?"

"If you ride on a mile, sir, you will see," said Hulton coldly.

"Where are the Wazir's men?"

"Part dead, part scattered among the mountains," replied Hulton. "Why are you here, sir? What do you propose?"

"Then I have come too late," said the officer, with a disappointed look.

"If you meant to join the Wazir—yes," said Wyatt sharply; "but we are ready for an engagement with you at once."

"Engagement? With me?" said the officer, staring. "I came to help you. As soon as the Rajah heard that the Wazir had left with a strong body to cut you off, he was in a rage. He said it was treachery to him as well as to you, when he had given orders that you should depart unmolested: and he bade me get together all the men I could trust, and fly to your help."

"And you have brought the two regiments we helped to raise."

"And my own guards, sir. They can be trusted to a man. Then we must pursue the Wazir and bring him back."

The English officers looked searchingly at the speaker.

"The Wazir is dead," said Hulton slowly.

"Dead?" cried the captain excitedly. "Then there will be peace in Soojeepur at last. His head? Where is his head?"

Wyatt smiled grimly.

"We do not take our enemies' heads, Captain," he said.

"No—no, I forgot," cried the officer; "but it must be taken back to the city that the people may see. It means peace to our troubled country, and the end of his party now. Hah!" he cried, with a smile, "it was my own head that was not safe. I feel as if I live again, and now my master may, for if the Wazir had won this fight there would have been an end of the Rajah's rule. Gentlemen, you must come back with me; the Rajah is at heart your friend. Let me escort you in triumph now."

"We were on our way back," said Hulton, smiling, for there was not a doubt of the officer's honesty of purpose; and once more the teams cantered off to bring up the wagons, while Dick sent the sergeant to fetch the sword that had been taken to the hospital-wagon.

Stubbs returned with the sheathed weapon, just as the captain of the guard had despatched his two followers back to where the three bodies of horse were drawn up, and he turned in wonder as Dick held out the beautifully jewelled tulwar.

"The dead Wazir's sword," said Dick.

"Yes," said the captain; "the Rajah's present. I know it well. But for this stroke of fate it would have been reddened with his master's blood."

"Take it," said Dick.

"No, no," replied the officer. "You won it on the field of battle, and it is yours."

He drew back with a smile, and once more the weapon was conveyed to the wagon.

In a very short time the captain's messengers came galloping back at the head of fifty horsemen, who charged down nearly to the guns, and were halted almost as well as a troop of ordinary cavalry, and then sat up in line, smiling and proud of the hearty cheer with which they were received.

It was directly after that their captain asked for a couple of artillery-men to guide his people to where the Wazir fell.

"Yes," said Hulton after a few words with his brother-officers; "but I have a word to say, sir. Your men have been drilled by English officers, and they must behave in war like Englishmen. We cannot stand by and see such a barbarous deed done as you propose. The Wazir was an enemy, but he was a great man and a brave soldier after all. I will send a gun-carriage and its team. Let the Wazir's body be brought back into the town with all respect."

The captain bowed and rode off without a word.

Chapter XLII
A Confession

It was drawing near to sundown when the head of the retiring troops filed on to the bridge and crossed the orange-tinted, flashing river. Swift messengers had preceded them at a gallop, bearing their captain's message to his master, the Rajah—the news of the safety of the artillery troop and the Wazir's defeat and death.

Consequently the bridge and streets were lined with troops and people, through whom the English and their glittering escort rode, the gun-carriage, with its dead burden, and its guard of artillery-men with drawn sabres, riveting every eye.

They were received in utter silence, not a murmur rising. Only the sound of trampling horse and rumbling gun and wagon wheels was heard.

The long line filed on right away to the front of the Rajah's palace, where the young prince stood waiting, surrounded by his people; and when the gun-carriage with its ghastly burden was drawn up at the foot of the steps, the Rajah came slowly down and stood gazing for a few minutes at his great enemy's face, before turning and bowing coldly to the English officers, who had dismounted.

"Gentlemen," he said, "it was not my will that you were attacked. I am glad that you are safe."

"And we are glad, sir," said Hulton, "that we can show you how high the honour of the English stands."

The Rajah gave him a stern look.

"Mr Darrell," continued Hulton, "you have something to give back to his highness."

Dick stepped eagerly forward to place the silken bag, bursting with jewels, in the Rajah's hands.

"Hah!" he exclaimed excitedly. "For the Ranee's sake I am glad you have brought them back. But it was a vile thing for an English *gentleman* to do," he added scornfully.

Dick smiled in his face.

"Hear all first, sir," he said; and in a few words he told him Sergeant Stubbs's tale.

The Rajah's eyes flashed with eagerness.

"Yes—yes," he cried; "I know the priest is missing. Send—send at once. No, no; we must go and see."

He waited for no elephant, but mounted the first horse that was offered, and rode with the officers and a large escort to the temple gates, from whence the chief Brahmin was about to set forth with the whole of his followers to meet the body of his dead friend, the Wazir.

The coming of the Rajah checked all this, he fiercely ordered the Brahmins to be watched.

"Where is this missing priest?" he said to the old man sternly.

"Thy servant does not know," said the old man, beginning to tremble.

"Where did you send him yesterday, when the English officer was charged with theft?"

The old Brahmin's jaw dropped, and he sank upon his knees and raised his hands for mercy.

"Bring him up," said the Rajah; and a few minutes later the whole party was standing at the back of the great idol, where one of the stones was drawn aside, and a couple of the guard entered the cell-like place, to lift out the half-demented prisoner, who crouched upon the floor.

In a few minutes he began to recover and gaze wildly round, till his eyes fell upon his kneeling superior, and he cried piteously:

"I did all you told me. I fetched the bag, and was hiding it here, but I was seized, and the jewels taken away. It has been horrible—horrible," he groaned; "worse than death."

"Stop!" cried the Rajah, speaking with fierce energy. "Brahmin or no Brahmin, I'll have the truth or you die. Was this a plot to hide those jewels and charge the English officer with stealing?"

"Yes, yes," cried the shivering creature, who had been rescued from so terrible a death; "but I did what I was told. It was he—it was he." He pointed at the kneeling Brahmin. "Is this true?" said the Rajah.

The old man murmured "Yes," as he bowed his forehead upon the stones. Then rising, he cried with wild energy, "Spare my life, O Rajah; it was the Wazir."

"Ah! and that poison?" cried the prince. The old man's head dropped again. "Was it the Wazir who prepared that draught?"

"It was at their orders I—I—"

"At whose orders?" cried the Rajah.

"Those of the Wazir and the Ra—"

"Silence!" cried the Rajah, catching the old man by the throat. "A word more, and, Brahmin though you are, you die."

Chapter XLIII
Palmam Qui—

That night the weary troop took up their quarters again in the old building. The next day the Rajah came in state to ask them to return to the new building, and it was in the officers' room that he spoke out frankly:

"Do not forsake me now," he said, "because I was weak enough to believe all I did. I was always your friend, but you cannot understand the bitter fight I had against the Ranee, the mother I loved, and her friends and supporters. Think a minute," he said; "I wanted to raise up my country and rule it as I knew the English did. I wanted to throw aside the vile old superstitions and oppression of the past, and immediately fully half of my people, headed by my mother, my dead father's old generals and counsellors, and the whole of our priests, rose against me. It would have taken a stronger man than I am to fight that fight."

"Yes," said Hulton, "we know you have had a struggle, but—"

"Don't condemn me." cried the Rajah, smiling, "for being ignorant and weak. I want to learn.—Darrell, you will not turn against me?" he continued, holding out his hand.

"No, not I," cried Dick frankly; "but it was precious hard, sir!"

"I know, I know," cried the Rajah.—"Now, Captain Hulton, Captain Wyatt, and you, my dear wise old doctor friend, who saved my life at that awful time, let the past be forgotten."

"Till there is another rising against us," said Hulton bitterly.

"There will be no other rising against you," cried the Rajah with energy. "The vile party that has fought against you is no more. It died with my bitter enemy, the Wazir, who meant to seize my throne; it died with the Brahmin power, which shall never raise its head against me now."

"There is the Ranee—strongest of all," said Hulton.

"The Ranee is dead," said the Rajah solemnly.

"What!" came in a burst of horror from all present.

"No, no; I am no savage tyrant," said the Rajah, smiling. "She is dead to power—dead to all influence here—and after what has passed she will fight no more. There, stay with me, and let this be like one of the ugly dreams from which I used to start when the doctor was saving me from that cruel poison. There is so much to do. See what you have already done. Those two regiments you raised, and my bodyguard. They were ready to fight for the English to the death, but they were doomed to slaughter for their truth. I have learned during this past night that they were to be surrounded and treacherously slain, and I suppose I was to be the next. Gentlemen, you and fate between you have crushed the Naga (cobra da capello) that was crawling up the side of my throne to sting the Rajah Maharajah of this land."

"Who told you this?"

"The Ranee—my mother—on her knees. But you will stay?"

It needs no telling, neither is there space to tell, how high the English officers rose in their position at the Court of Soojeepur, nor how Robert Hanson was recommended to the Rajah as a suitable officer to take command of one of his native regiments of irregular horse. Let it suffice to say that years after, in the dark days of Britain's peril, when the great Eastern Empire was slowly crumbling from her grasp, no native prince proved so true, nor rendered such earnest help with men and treasure, as the Maharajah of Soojeepur. His little army was in many a hard-won fight, and displayed a discipline and bravery that won praise from our greatest generals.

"It sounds like brag, Dick, old chap, but it isn't," said Wyatt one day when the Mutiny was over, while speaking to his faithful old friend, Colonel Darrell, head of the Maharajah's contingent, about to return with him to England full of honours.

"What sounds like brag?" said Dick.

"For me to say that our little troop of horse artillery was the nucleus of the Rajah's army, and that you and I made it what it is."

"Hah!" said Dick, "I'm sorry poor old Hulton was invalided home. As fine a gunner as ever stepped."

"He was," said Colonel Wyatt, "a splendid soldier, sir. But he was only with us at the beginning, not more than six months. 'Pon my word, old fellow, I think without brag it was we."

Colonel Darrell sat gazing straight before him for some moments, and then he brought his fist down hard upon the table on either side of which they sat.

"No," he said loudly. *"Palmam qui meruit ferat."*

"My dear boy!" cried Wyatt, puckering up his forehead, "don't scatter Latin all over the place. Good old English will do."

"Very well, then, we will not brag about what we did, but stick the feather in the right man's cap."

"Whose?" cried Wyatt eagerly.

"That of old Sergeant Stubbs."

"And the brave Englishmen who fought and died."